SKINNY DIPPING AT LOW TIDE

A Saga of Squeezed Shorts, Shattered Dreams, and Embarrassing Riches

written and illustrated by

M. F. HAMLIN

PERMUTED PRESS

A PERMUTED PRESS BOOK

Skinny Dipping at Low Tide:
A Saga of Squeezed Shorts, Shattered Dreams, and Embarrassing Riches

ISBN: 979-8-89565-075-2
ISBN (eBook): 979-8-89565-076-9

Cover art by M. F. Hamilin
Interior design and composition by Greg Johnson, Textbook Perfect

SDALT Lyric Permissions:

I FEEL ALRIGHT
Words and Music by STEVE EARLE
© 1996 WC MUSIC CORP. (ASCAP)
All Rights Reserved
Used by Permission of ALFRED MUSIC

I GOT A NAME
Words by NORMAN GIMBEL Music by CHARLES FOX
© 1973 (Renewed) WARNER-TAMERLANE PUBLISHING CORP.
All Rights Reserved
Used by Permission of ALFRED MUSIC

WON'T GET FOOLED AGAIN
Words and Music by PETER TOWNSHEND
© 1971 ABKO MUSIC, INC.
All Rights Reserved
Used by Permission of HAL LEONARD

IT AIN'T EASY BEING ME
Words and Music by CHRISTOPHER KNIGHT and CRAIG WISEMAN
© 1998 ALMO MUSIC CORPORATION
All Rights Reserved
Used by Permission of HAL LEONARD

PERMUTED PRESS

Permuted Press
New York • Nashville
permutedpress.com

Published in the United States of America
1 2 3 4 5 6 7 8 9 10

While this novel may have been inspired by real events, it is a fictionalized account, and liberties have been taken for the sake of narrative and artistic expression. No character or organization in this book is intended to directly represent any real person or any real organization.

To Sarah, Liza, John, and Henry.
I love you. RTF.

In memory of J. Davis Hamlin: 1932–2025

pwn /pōn/

verb

INFORMAL

past tense: **pwned**; past participle: **pwned**

1. (chiefly in video gaming) utterly defeat (an opponent or rival); completely get the better of.

"I can't wait to pwn some shorts in this squeeze play."

Table of Contents

Overture

Good things happen to bad companies. It happened. Surely, it happened. It's a tale as old as fate and as fresh as a new coat of paint. There are some razor-sharp teeth in the old saw "truth is stranger than fiction." Listen to the backmasking of the record and you'll find it's equally true that truth—the acute and profound kind—lies within the fiction.

Truth or Fiction?

You once were a Peter Pan named Haller.
In sum, a stooge, a scout, and a scholar.
You applied your candor,
Like a coarse deck sander,
"The long game's the true way to earn a dollar."

Your tale's positively Homeric,
Simpsonian that is, not the hero's epic.
And while it could've been Aesop,
That fabled up PwnShop,
This moral's more barbed and barbaric.

You were hired in twenty and fourteen,
When downloads endangered the money machine.
But there was still enough time,
To turn on a dime,
And cork the leak in the submarine.

But when the CEO got brain cancer.
The deputies raved like rain dancers.
Their chicaneries myriad,
Over a two-year period,
Your dreams met scornful answers.

The powers charted a sour concentration,
"Let's cash cow the core for diversification!"
They said with a grin,
And, whacking thy chin,
Added, "Pack your shit, you're off the reservation."

Whilst you did time at the Wearhouse of Men,
The CEO's death brought wholesale succession.
The board fired the foes,
With whom you'd come to blows,
And promoted a hapless creep from within.

But he walked the plank within mere days.
So, they tapped a knight pro tem *to enter the fray.*
A revolving door,
To you they implored,
"Please come back! We'll increase your pay!"

You're hired with their authorization,
To chase your dreams of reforestation.
"If we plant green tree sprouts,
To make the stores hangouts,
We'll proclaim olde PwnShop's salvation."

Before your plan comes to fruition,
The board and boss duel in opposition,
The knight quits, Mamma mia!
And without a better idea,
The board calls for a cost cutting mission.

With activists lurking and spanking,
And the stock price tumbling and tanking,
The directors vow to recruit,
An experienced suit,
Knowing they couldn't keep blanking.

They hire a tedious technician,
While the Big Shorter makes a prediction,
That squeezing the shorts,
(Those genital warts)
Would make the stonk ripe for ignition.

Fearing your own plank into the ocean,
You're instead handed a promotion,
To the rank of EVP,
A shield of security,
Lest control changes amidst the commotion.

Anon the chief hires his Hookian henchman,
Who removes oxygen with a boa's constriction,
Your dreams are eroded,
And not just by COVID,
But mostly by Hook's coefficient of friction.

Yonder some cat tagged Bawling Bitty,
Posts on Reddit a catchy stonk ditty,
The funds that hedge,
Swim right off the ledge,
Welcoming the jungle into Paradise City.

But your insider's hands are clasped,
Like Tantalus, peak price eludes thy grasp.
Enter the pet food purveyor,
The crocodile naysayer,
An activist and a venomous asp.

NFTs, crypto, and a new regime,
Overtake strategy, stores, and their teams,
Croc's teeth like a sword,
He devours Hook and the board,
And pilots the ship into an investment meme.

Nay, you've never sailed from Nantocket,
But the facts beget the "fock-its."
A Pan of sole season,
You resign for "good reason,"
Shaming thy soul while yet padding thy pockets.

On February 3, 2021, the stock of the dead to rights, digitally disrupted video game retailer PwnShop peaked at a closing price some 1500 percent higher than a mere two weeks prior. To put that in perspective, Michael Burry's hedge fund Scion Capital returned a comparatively paltry 489 percent to its investors after shorting the housing market in 2008. If you invested $1000 in the S&P 500 at the end of April 2020, your investment would have appreciated a commendable 27 percent to $1270 by early February 2021. Loser.

But if those limp limericks happened to you, then and only then would you see your net worth balloon by tens of millions of dollars and over 1000 percent. Easy as pie.

The story you're about to read is as true as a fable. The names and identifying details have been changed to protect the idiots—chief among them the author.

SIDE A

Vipers at the Gates of Dusk

PERSONNEL

The Band		
GamerTag	Instrument	Title
Nick Haller	Throat Singer	Chief Customer Officer née CMO
Lance Park	K-Pop Beats	Interim CEO
Tom Testa	Wax Paper Comb	Chairman of the Bored
Gerald Meade	Sousaphone	Incoming CEO
Jeff Claggart	Chainsaw	Incoming CFO
Dale Spivey	Leaf Blower	Incoming Chief Merchant
Grady Bledsoe	Hohner Melodica (a.k.a. "Hooter")	VP, Video Game Merchandising
Jack Floyd	Gong	Outgoing CFO
The Bored		
Gary Varga, Bob Blovey, David Schechter, Suprit Shetty, Kate Sloan		
The Funk Bros.		
Casey Fosbury, Helen, Jan, Shay, Terry, Tess		
The Family Stone		
Stonewall Jackson Haller, Mom, Maura Haller		
Musical Youth		
John Jewell, Eliza Bullard, Coach Coy Willard, Principal Cecil B. Holmes, John David Shiflett, Dr. Peek		
The Nashville Sounds		
Jerry Bradley, Mason, Tim DuBois, Lee Roy Parnell, Page Murphy		
Boston		
Cathy Ames, Danny O'Riordan, Julia Weeks, Elon Kohlberg		

Track 1: Slow Dancing in a Burning Room

"I think of myself as an intelligent, sensitive human being with the soul of a clown which always forces me to blow it at the most important moments."

—JIM MORRISON

Trophy Club, Texas
February 21, 2019
713 days to peak of the short squeeze (POSS)
Closing Share Price (CSP): $11.96

Call me Ishtar.

I deserve it. If ever there were a career that harpooned into the blubber of boomer memes and unfulfilled potential, it's mine. Destined for greatness? Fat chance. I'm all over the place. Songwriter. Strategist. Architect. Executive. Even recovering introvert, portraitist and professor. Ill-fitting clothes, all of them. I don't know what to call myself anymore.

Today, however, I hope to be called Superman. Not the DC Comics character, but Nietzsche's Übermensch who can rise above the thick deadlock at PwnShop and bring deliverance.

"Nice tweed," Lance says with his usual sarcasm. "Why no suit today?"

I bow my head to survey the sportcoat. A fake distressed button—as fraudulent as I—joins the wool lapels, hiding a sunken sternum and a $175 Grateful Dead needlepoint belt. Why does such a poke bother me?

I rouse, gather my defenses, dart my gaze into the brown irises beneath his creaseless eyelids, and parry.

"Thought I'd mix it up. Be the professor that takes you dipshits to school."

"Ha! After yesterday's dumpster fire, we need it." Then, with a rare vulnerable kindness, Lance continues. "You're the guy that can land the punch. Sorry we ran out of time and you weren't able to present yesterday. Sit here in the holding tank. We have exec session for about forty-five minutes, then I'll come get you. They're excited for your bit."

Great. A moment to gather my thoughts. As if stewing on it all night weren't enough.

I'm in a sterile, low ceilinged anteroom at a round eight top strewn with crumbs from this morning's breakfast. The distinguished directors of the PwnShop, Inc. board are next door in some tritely named chamber apropos of indifference. We're in Southlake or Westlake or Eastlake or any safe, corporate tax-advantaged suburb in any Wyndhilliotton Hotel.

Lance Park is a former Microsoft Xbox executive who joined the board five years ago. After the Harvey Handler mess,[1] Lance stepped in as interim CEO. His arrival was a rare glimmer of hope. But between patchy communication with the board surrounding recent holiday sales and the exorbitant pay package he demanded to offset the emotional distress of uprooting his family from Seattle, Lance has fallen out of favor. Now PwnShop is looking for a new CEO and Lance has convinced me to toss my hat in the ring.

Having never run a public company, I know I won't get it. Unless you're a founder, players' coaches never get the top spot. Resigned to this fact, I still want the intimate audience with the selection committee to describe the ideal candidate and beg them to consider investing in a growth strategy rather than continue their retreat into unimaginative

---

[1] Harvey Handler was elevated to CEO upon the death of Claude Prendas, a talented executive who held the top spot for nine years. Within weeks, Harvey resigned for "personal reasons."

cost cutting. I have the support of our 40,000 associates. This fact emboldens me to pursue the role. They need their voices to be heard.

At our annual manager's conference the previous October, I delivered a speech outlining the path forward to the audience of over five thousand hardcore gamers who moonlighted as managers—clerks reigning supreme over their twelve-hundred-square-foot strip mall domains and spreading the gospel of games to their "guests." Fed up with years of either being the cash cow to fuel a wholesale diversification strategy or the mule driver that's supposed to crack the buggy whip to push more used physical video games in a land of frictionless digital distribution, these managers were peckish, restless, and starving for a strategy. More than that, after years of empty promises, they were jaded and distrustful.

Interestingly, when I attended my first E3[2] in 2015, the year the conference reopened to the public, a sea of gamers gathered on the terrazzo entrance of the LA Convention Center. Those fans demonstrated something that isn't immediately recognizable to the non-gaming public who think most gamers are outcasts and:

- Introverts
- Predominately male
- Do-nothing
- Salad-dodging donut dunkers
- Garnished with scrimpy chin pelts
- Dwelling in dank dungeon basements lit only by their forty-nine-inch curved, high-res, higher refresh rate Odyssey G9 gaming monitors

[2] Electronic Entertainment Expo was an annual gaming conference in Los Angeles at which manufacturers, developers, and publishers introduced new consoles, games, and paraphernalia to retailers and press.

- Marching to some inane Casio-toned synth beat
- Getting off on gratuitous first-person shooter violence

What I saw, however, when the throng of five thousand voucher-holders and two-thousand interlopers surged into E3's hallowed halls for the first time in eight years, was something altogether different:

- Extroverts
- 40 percent female
- Vibrant, full of purpose
- Meat-dodging Kombucha drinkists
- Adorned with cosplay creations and artful tattoos
- Naturally lit by the eternally sunny California sky
- Marching to the beat of the moment
- Getting off on the electricity of their fellow illuminati

This was a community. A communion. Participants in the sacrament of idealized virtual worlds. Their vibrance changed my closed mind, inspiring me to craft the SAT analogy that was my presentation's attention grabber.

I continued with my speech under the slide build:

If E3 : The Vatican :: _______________?? : The Local Church

"Come on," I exhorted the store leaders, "If E3's the Vatican, what's the local church?"

It was 11 AM. The synapses don't fire for most PwnShop managers that early, especially those who just got through night three of the conference. The average manager made about $40,000 a year. They managed, on average, a $1.5 million business. Low income + super busy = "I don't get out much." So, when the conference came every year, it was a benediction for the rookie managers and an annual pagan rite for the veterans. Woe be unto you Las Vegas, Anaheim, Nashville or Indianapolis. We are PwnShop and we will sow our wild oats deeply into the soil of your city.

"I know, the sun's not yet fully warm and your collective heads hang over. But this is obvious." After a few beats, a few teetered out, "PwnShop?" More caught on. "PwnShop!" In a spontaneous crescendo, borne by years of frustration with management in divesting away from the importance of local venues, and buoyed by a cumbersome metaphor from a lanky stooped talking suit, a chant erupted. "Pw-own-Shop! Pw-own-Shop! Pw-own-Shop!"

Two slides in and this thing was taking on a life of its own. As someone who'd worked decades to hone his craft and overcome the paralyzing fear of public speaking, for the first time in my life I wasn't "making a presentation." I was orating. It was a state of flow, the "swing" in rowing terms, synchronicity between speaker, slides and audience. My plan—to create local churches where gamers can play any game on any console, gather at tables for card and board games, and have game advisor celebrants break bread and kvetch with the gaming flock—resonated.

As I stepped off the stage, the cavernous ballroom exploded. All 5000 stood, whooped, clapped and stomped wildly, many on top of their tipsy folding chairs. A joyfully lobbed Pip Boy mask from the game Fallout 76[3] landed in a jaunty tilt on the step in front of me, its face frozen in the smile of the moment.

A week later, Julie, our events manager, sent the executive team the ratings and feedback on our various presentations. The 5-point scale usually renders scores hovering around 3.5. My local church presentation, upon which I placed the handle "Starphoraflix,"[4] rated by over 3500 of the 5000 managers, garnered a 4.9! One tenth of one point from unanimous perfection. Julie confided in me that in her eighteen years

---

[3] *Fallout 76*, a role-playing video game, was Bethesda Studios' first foray into a multiplayer format, a departure from the great success they'd seen with the immersive open worlds they'd created in previous versions of the franchise. Released in November 2018, it was a commercial failure fraught with bugs and controversy. Upon the release of its expansion pack, it began to enjoy some critical accolades posthumous to its release.

[4] A clumsy portmanteau of Starbucks, Sephora, and Netflix, combining the hangout vibe of Starbucks with the intuitive customer service of Sephora wrapped in a slick, mobile-first content subscription revenue model like Netflix.

with the company, the highest aggregate score she'd ever seen was a 4.1, and that was for a speech delivered by the beloved Claude Prendas in 2011. "This group is a critical bunch," she allowed. "I've never seen a landslide like this."

The anonymous, open-ended comments were even more edifying. "Finally someone gets it." "Why the fuck isn't he CEO?" "Where has this been in the last decade?"

Given the enthusiastic response, Lance wasted no time approving the project that would transform PwnShop into "the cultural hub of gaming in every neighborhood." We were off to the races.

I was excited to present the plan to the board. After four months of work, the fruit of our collective labor, this mere PowerPoint, percolated with transformative power.

Originally, the agenda had me presenting the plan yesterday, but, in an audible, the board decided they wanted management to run through capital expense requests first and the Fiscal 2019 Budget second, before we lit the torches for the journey forward.

Casey Fosbury, head of real estate and construction, went first with our request for $30 million to replace the ramshackle shelving and paper signs with modern planogrammed fixtures and digital signage systems. It would pull our tawdry, cluttered stores—just a frog's hair nicer than any given XXX adult book store on Route 69—out of oblivion and into some semblance of organized retail merchandising. Unfortunately, Casey shit the bed. What should have been a taught presentation turned into a thread pulling exercise lasting almost two hours. Next was a $90 million IT request that didn't have a chance. Request registered. Request denied post-meeting. Then, Jack Floyd, our CFO of the past ten years, after being told that the board had read the budget plan and was ready to move on, presented the remainder of the capital requests, which lasted all of fifteen minutes with few questions.

I was set to go on next, but it was now 6:15 PM. Dinner reservations were at 6:30 PM at a soulless steakhouse. We adjourned. "Let's start fresh tomorrow."

Fresh my foot. First, I have to get through another night marinating in the grave gravy of the potential for a failed presentation. A dome of certified insomnomasochism goo, my addled and busy brain, upon being awakened by an aging bladder, can brew a pot of self-sabotage for even the most mundane meeting, much less the sermon on the mount.

This morning, on no sleep, seated in the anteroom, I'm chatting with Lance about last night's abysmal start to the two-day meeting, saying, "Yeah. That was a mess. We'll right the ship this morning."

We part, and I grab a coffee and a Nature Valley granola bar. I sit. And wait. And cogitate.

Forty-five minutes turns into two-and-a-half hours. It's now 10:30 AM. I was supposed to go on at 8 AM. My presentation is an hour-and-a-half. The board meeting is scheduled to go until 11:30 AM, and then they're supposed to go into one last executive session before adjourning at noon. Everybody's roller suitcase is in the room, perched with briefcase or backpack, ready to race to nearby DFW airport. So why the executive session at 8 AM? Was it because I was two minutes late? What the hell are they doing in there?

I flip through the deck for the tenth time, Steve Earle's "Feel Alright," which I had on repeat for my forty-five minute commute to Tarrant County, still stuck in my head.

And I'll bring you precious contraband
And ancient tales of distant lands
Of conquerors and concubines
And conjurers from darker times
Betrayal and conspiracy
Sacrilege and heresy
And I feel all right, I feel all right tonight.

At 10:55 AM or so, board members start spilling out and heading to the bathroom. Lance grabs me and asks me to come with him down the hallway. I turn to my right before I head to the left. There, I see Tom Testa, septuagenarian board chair and CEO of PwnShop in its heyday before the nuisances of digital distribution, disintermediation, and MMOs.[5] Tom grabs Jack, who was previously chatting up the universally beloved Jan and Helen, the admins who actually run the whole company. Tom takes Jack by the arm in a manner similar to Lance's grip on mine, and hauls him to the opposite end of the lengthy passage.

I speed walk, trying to keep up with Lance. Looking back over my shoulder, the aperture of the hallway has tightened, and it looks like the hotel corridor in *The Shining*. "Redrum. Redrum!" Jack and Tom are tiny shadows racing to the end of the tunnel. The laws of perspective reduce the window at the other end to a pinhole.

Are we getting fired?

Lance sucks in a big breath of sterile hotel air before sighing. "This is bullshit but it is what it is. The board has decided to hire an outside candidate. His name is..." *I immediately forget* "...and he's presently the CEO of..." *Never heard of and can't retain its name either* "...Wireless, the largest network of authorized retailers for Verizon. This is all very confidential. Since he's a sitting CEO, it will take some time for him to announce and exit. He probably can't start with us until April."

So the board, in all its wisdom, just hired a phone executive to run a gaming company? Didn't we just decide to sell Helix Wireless, the rollup of AT&T resellers, for $700 million, when it cost us over $1 billion in aggregate to acquire? Our own daft, unimaginative foray into the world of licensed stores where we don't own the brand, don't own the customer, and are subject to whatever commission rate AT&T levies?

I begin in shake voice, "So I guess this means I didn't have a chance?"

"C'mon. You know you didn't," he consoles.

[5] Massively multiplayer online. Immersive worlds with virtual economies and hordes of simultaneous players. Since gamers are on a server, human against human, every session is a unique experience. Since a player can't "win" the game, they're never finished. This is incredibly "sticky" in marketing speak. And, for PwnShop, their infrequent releases mean fewer chances to drive traffic.

"And this is how I'm told?"

"Yes."

"Do I get any feedback on my candidacy?"

"I seriously doubt anyone will offer that up."

Why the hell did I come back to work at this sinking circus? I had hoped we were going to reinvent it. Here we go again. Another role where you're always the bridesmaid and never the bride. And now, some new guy will come in, fire the whole team, and what will I have to show for myself? A PowerPoint detailing "The Cultural Hub of Gaming?" You didn't accomplish shit, you fucking washout.

"You okay?" Lance asks. "You need to make sure you have it together before you go in there. We need your advice on the way forward, particularly in how to communicate to the team as we head into this interim period."

"I'm great. Yes sir. Will be a team player, sir." Disdain drips from my acid tongue.

I've choked down bitter Kool-Aid in my past—have even swallowed—but for the first time, this batch really is laced with cyanide.

I walk down *The Shining* hall toward the meeting room. Some board members are chatting up Helen and Jan. I perceive them peering at me furtively to gauge how I've taken the news. I enter the room and take a seat between Lance and Jack. Jack apparently received his news about thirty seconds before me. We give each other knowing smirks as the board members reenter. Some of the rest of the management team that usually attends these meetings also enters—among them, the EVP of international, our in-house counsel, the chief accounting officer, and Lance's buddy from business school that he's brought in to consult on strategy and operations. An unidentified hand pats me on my right shoulder as three bodies shuffle behind me en route to their seats.

Tom, the chair, launches in. "Okay, everyone settled? Good. For those of you that have just entered the room, I would like you to know that the board has made a decision." *The board actually made a decision? Well that's a first.* "We've decided to hire an outside candidate, Gerald Meade..." *I write his name down so I don't forget.* "...as our new CEO.

Gerald is presently CEO of Victory Wireless. We're guessing it will be mid-March before we can announce and early to mid-April before he'll be able to start. We ask that you each keep this in the strictest confidence until our public announcement has taken place."

Tom eyeballs us for a reaction, looking for any kind of a tell. Stoic, deer in headlight silence. As if remembering he's forgotten to mention all the talking points the board has armed him with, he continues.

"I think you will really enjoy getting to know Gerald. He's a great guy. And he has great experience for what we need to do. A strong operator, he worked with Claude when he was at Home Stop and ran their services business. You know, carpet and tile installations, rentals, and so on. Then, he went on to run the Nerd Squad for Better Buy. And, as I stated earlier, he's an existing CEO, something that was very important to the board." No public thanks to me and Jack for having gone through the emotional gauntlet and time commitment to interview for the role. Instead, he adds, "As we move into this next phase for PwnShop, and because we have a few months before Gerald gets here, the board has decided not to approve the fiscal budget and the capex requests so that Gerald, uh, rightly, has a chance, uhm, to allocate capital according to his vision. Is there anything else the board needs to consider as we start to think about a communication plan?"

Again, resigned quiet. Really? Nobody's going to say anything? They're going to let Mikey Ishtar do it? He'll do anything. Here we go. Get your popcorn ready.

"Uh, Tom?" I begin. "There is something. You are aware, I think, that every district and regional leader in our company is arriving on Sunday for our annual district leaders conference in Fort Worth. Today is Friday. Presentations, uhm, start first thing Monday. What, uh, do you want us to, y'know, say to that team?"

Eye darts of blame shoot about the room, each board member shifting in their seats. It's clear nobody was aware. I guess Lance forgot to mention this in their three-hour executive session. Probably wasn't enough time to squeeze that tidbit in.

The lead independent director, Gary Varga, weighs in with a half-statement, half-question. "Why don't you just tell them the search is completed? We have a candidate, and until he/she works through his/her internal announcement and the appropriate public disclosures, we can't disclose who it is. Doesn't that make sense?"

"Makes total sense," I stroke, knowing damn well their heaven-sent decision—hiring a CEO—means they can kick the can down the road on all of the tough decisions until the new guy is onboarded. In for a penny in for a pound, I continue, "I have one other question. Jack was planning on presenting the decisions from this meeting as it relates to the fiscal 2019 budget. The sales budget, after all, is how we waterfall the sales targets and bonus criteria for every region, district and store. I was hoping, perhaps foolishly, that we'll have clarity on the store improvements and whether or not we'll be able to make a dent in the technical debt. The stores would love to hear about those potential improvements. Additionally, I was planning on presenting the innovation plan—overhauling all the stores in Oklahoma City—to that audience. Do we have any decisions on those fronts that we can relate?"

A different director, and in an ironic twist also an ex-phone executive named Bob Blovey, bristles, "Nick, I think it shows complete disrespect of this board for management to assume that they can build presentations to present things that haven't yet been approved."

Lance immediately counters, "C'mon Bob. That's unfair. What are they supposed to do?"

At least there's one human in the room. Well, Bob, you 'ignorant slut', I presume you'd have us not build our decks until the Saturday before the conference? If we waited on the board for every decision, we'd never present jack shit to the store leaders. Somebody's got to do something. I should probably step outside and count to ten before I do something I'm going to regret. Fuck!

"Build a presentation of materials that doesn't require board approval!" Bob tongue-lashes.

My wits and nerves fraying, I dig a deeper hole, knowing the answer before I even ask. "So I presume this means I can't present Oklahoma City on Monday?"

Gary, the lead director who apparently has some semblance of a heart, and is clearly a peacemaker, says, "Nick, in fairness to Gerald, we don't think it's appropriate to green light that project until his perspective can be incorporated. You understand that, don't you?"

Where's the fairness to this sumbitch and the other sumbitches who envisioned this, and put our blood, sweat and tears and burned all our internal political capital to make it an executable plan?

"Yes sir. I understand. But what I don't understand is we haven't even had a chance to present our plan. It's only $3 million, one-tenth of the fixture request. Five basis points of our annual sales. One-half of one-tenth of one percent. Even if it fails, there's little risk."

I'd already memorized that salient point for the formal presentation to hammer home the mere rounding error that the expense represented.

"Nick, just because you didn't present the deck, doesn't mean we didn't read it. We're all excited about the potential. But, we can't say it's approved until Gerald weighs in. He's a great guy. I'm sure he'll love it."

"Sir, with all due respect," I say as I pause, weighing whether I should proceed past the point of rescue, "saying you read the presentation without seeing the presentation would be like, uh, let's see, oh I know, like handing *The Lion King* screenplay to my eight-year-old—y'know, all words and no pictures—for him to read on his own and, uh, I guess, this board presumes that's the same experience as going to the theater with our figurative eight-year-old to watch it and discuss what we liked and didn't like over ice cream on the way home."

Oh god. That was a convoluted run-on sentence. Did I really just blurt that out? In the boardroom? What the fuck am I doing? Is it lack of sleep?

Unable to contain myself, I take a deep breath, rotate my shoulders to the posture God intended but I've never been able to maintain, and elocute, in as calm a manner as I can muster, with just a hint of shake in my voice, "I would like the minutes to reflect," my eyes darting to the general counsel and board secretary, "that management has spent months, engaged numerous internal and external resources and a fair amount of capital to come forth with the way forward for this troubled company. Further, I would like the record to state, uhm, that management believes the board didn't give us the time..." I turn my head clockwise around the room to meet the eyes of every director "...or the courtesy..." I reverse course and do the same stare down in a counter-clockwise fashion, "...to hear management out."

Lance puts his forehead to his palm and sighs, then looks at me like an ashamed father out of the corner of his eyes.

Oh my. Did I really just say all that? What a dumbass I am.

Like *Ishtar*, the 1987 film Warren Beatty produced and co-starred in opposite Dustin Hoffman, I had promise. The production had blown budgets. I just blew it. I was a smartass antagonist, tossing unprofessional barbed flies into the professional ointment. Like the movie, an epic symbol of stank, my tarnish can be described as delusions of grandeur scraped with a lack of grit and rubbed with attention deficit disorder. Hypocritical critics, like their widely polarized opinions on licorice, The Grateful Dead, *Fallout* 76 and *Ishtar*, can't decide if my shit was brilliant or brainless.

I'm a box of Wheaties adorned with the athlete of the moment—sort of handsome and sort of a flake. When you pitch the script, set it up as follows: Make him a ham-fisted songwriter. Place him in the Moroccan desert with a raconteur's dilettante ideals. Have him stumble into a Cold War Mexican standoff amongst the CIA, left wing guerrillas and the government of the fictional emirate, Ishtar. Better yet, place him and his half-assed songs in the Bored Room of PwnShop amongst ex-military officers, demented directors, and shameless shareholder activists. Has some potential, but instead turns out to be a notorious, cataclysmic, white whale of a comedic failure at the box office. Fuck. You can call me Nick Haller. But you'd be a lot better off calling me Ishtar.

Track 2: It Ain't Easy Being Me

"Meet the new boss. Just the same as the old boss."

—PETE TOWNSEND

PwnShop Corporate Offices
Vineland, TX
February 22, 2019
712 days to POSS
CSP: $12.04

My ego, a leaky boat, hung up in the sand. I'd made my bed with the boardroom blowup. On the way to my car, my adrenaline mostly ebbed, I embrace my ego's undress and await the turn of the tide.

I get in the car, and begin the ten-minute drive back to the office. When I connect my phone to CarPlay, Steve Earle's "Feel Alright" returns, but I don't feel all right. I feel like spewing vinegar into the ether. What to play? Jerry Jeff's "Pissin' In The Wind?" Nah, I'm old now. I'll just be drippin' in the wind. I'm petulant. Maybe I'll play the scornpocalypse that is Iggy and the Stooges' "Search And Destroy." Grow the fuck up. "Loser?" I'm a pitiful excuse of a chimpanzee with butane in my veins. But, Beck's a foppish Fauntleroy. I stop in the middle of the lot and opt instead for Chris Knight's "It Ain't Easy Being Me." Knight's tale of bridge burning and self-sabotage soothes the pus-filled boil that is my mood.

Track 2: It Ain't Easy Being Me

There ought to a bridge somewhere they could dedicate to me
I'd probably come to the ceremony with a can of gasoline
Walk on over to the other side where I'd light a match
Sit and stare through the smoke and flames and wonder how
I'm gonna get back
Why do I do the things I do?...
...It ain't easy being me

Jack's office is on the way to mine. I see him sitting at the table with key members of the finance team.

"Well that was a disastrophe," I interrupt. "Ladies and gents, can you excuse us?"

His folks gather their notebooks and laptops. One says, "Door closed, I presume?"

"Completely, literally and figuratively," I eye roll.

Once the door clicks, I sit down at the conference table so I can face him.

"What the fuck are we going to do?"

"I have no idea," he says, slumping in his overly expensive desk chair. "There's no winning with that board. But I will say, in my twelve years here, your antics were as brazen as I've seen."

I retort, piling on, "Wheels off, more like, and no filter. It's a fine line between courage and self-destruction. It was nice knowing you."

"Yeah, well, me too," Jack agrees. "New guy will come in and blow us all out anyways."

"So, what are we going to do about the meetings on Monday?"

"I was just posing that very question before you walked in. I guess we need to work over the weekend to pull out everything that was awaiting approval. As far as the budget is concerned, we decided we'd cascade the first quarter numbers from the budget so the store teams can build their region, district and store sales targets and labor plans for Q1, and once the new guy comes in, we rewrite the rest."

"That makes sense for you," I allow. "What am I going to present, the fucking marketing calendar? 'Look, team, here are all the games we thought were going to release in Q1, and, as you can see in this next slide, they're all pushed indefinitely. Not to worry. We don't have a strategic problem. You guys just aren't selling enough ice to Eskimos, I mean, uh, Inuit tribe members. So, guess what? We're going to run a buy two, get one used games and collectibles sale. People will come in droves to pick up a three-year old copy of *Madden 16* with the fine patina of its previous owner's scratches. Sound good? Are. You. Ready? We. Will. Win!'" I vent.

Jack chuckles. "Bitter I see. Pissed you didn't get the job?"

"My Peter Pan ass as CEO? Never had a chance. I just couldn't believe how we were told."

"What'd you expect? A dinner at Nobu? Tom told me I was being considered two months ago, and I never heard from a soul. Did you ever get interviewed?"

"Wow!" My anger subsides somewhat, realizing his relative injustice is worse than mine. "Yeah, I traveled to DC, Atlanta, and the Admiral's Club at DFW to meet with the search committee."

"Really?" His eyes lower, a bit of shame apparent. "I never even got a call, just a side conversation with the committee chair at the end of a call on another matter. When I asked Tom why I didn't need to do anything formal, he said my body of work spoke for itself."

"Aw, c'mon man. You've served this company faithfully. They appreciate that."

"Doubtful. Ever since Claude's death and the game of thrones that ensued, I think they were pissed off that I didn't expose the financial weakness of the diversification plan. Even though they ended up firing those clowns, I think I'm still in the penalty box for not being a whistle-blower. As if whistle-blowing is ever a good career strategy."

"No doubt."

"So, what did they ask you?"

"Mainly about my plan for the way forward."

"The local church of gaming presentation?"

"Basically. But we also got deep into investor relations—the principal area of my candidacy that was, frankly, their biggest fear with my unfiltered ass. Seeing that you have much more experience with IR than I, you'll probably think what I told them was crazy too."

"What'd you tell them?"

"That we should tell the Street we're going to tank it and spank it."

"You're a piece of work. And what does tank it and spank it mean, Beavis?"

"Heh. Heh. Spank it. Heh. Heh." I can't help but let my Gen-X nostalgia rear its ugly head at least once a conversation. At least I'm mimicking Beavis and not Butt-Head. "We're like Apollo 13. PwnShop is breathing its death rattle and we have one last chance for reentry. We have to fashion random parts into a repaired craft that can make it through the atmosphere one last time. If I were in charge, I'd go visit with our 'long' investors and show them that we have to transform or die. We have to invest and embrace a lot more risk. In the face of Amazon, around 2013, Walmart, Target and Best Buy all announced transformations. Their stock prices plummeted, but they're all much stronger for having done so. It takes leadership. Tank it and spank it."

"What about cost cutting? That's clearly what the board wants, and we have a bunch of new investors chirping about how bloated our administrative expenses are."

"No doubt about it. The only way off the beach is through the guns. We have to cut costs. But blanket, across-the-board cost cutting without a notion of the way forward is idiocy. It's just hunkering down in the boat and either drowning or eventually being shot when the bullets pierce the hull. We have to attempt to take a new beach."

"Did you use that many bad analogies in the meeting?" Jack winks. "And how did they react?"

"I might have gotten an 'interesting' out of one of them. Wait, I take that back. One told me that I had to present my plan to the board."

That's why the subliminal came to the surface, the real reason I'm so pissed. David Schechter, board member and president of an NHL franchise, told me I *had* to present my plan to the board, which included getting rid of Jack just because it was time, as well as moving on from the rest of the old guard. When I asked him, "How can I present that part of the plan with half of those guys sitting in the room?" he simply said, "If you want to be CEO, you'll figure it out."

"That's right. He told me the board needed to hear me out. Those motherfuckers. I guess that's why I lost my shit and dug my 'let the minutes reflect' hole."

"Well, it did make for good theater," Jack chuckles.

"So do you think I'll get fired for that?"

"Be real. We're both going to get fired. You're smart enough to know that. By not promoting someone from within, the board is signaling they want a fresh start. It's obvious. I guarantee you that's the charter for the new guy. Clean house."

"Yep. You're right. Incidentally, I was thinking about this in the car, why, when we just sold off the phone business, do you think they hired this guy Gerald Meade?"

"It is ironic," Jack nods.

"I just can't wait to read the headline in the *Journal*—'PwnShop Jettisons Phone Business; Hires Phone Executive.' Do you think they hired him because of his phone experience?"

"I doubt it. Even though it is a weird coincidence. You heard Tom say this guy worked with Claude at Home Stop?"

"I blew that off. My blood might have still been boiling at that point."

"Tom is just grasping in the dark for another Claude. That's my guess."

"You're probably right." I sit up. "I know what I'm doing on Monday. Fuck 'em running. I'm going to present exactly as planned to the regional store leaders."

"Nick, if what you did in the boardroom was a cry for help, that's suicide. Talk about self-sabotage."

"More like seppuku, but so what. You correctly said we're both gonna get fired anyway. I'm not going to stand up there with my scuffed up disc in my hand. I'm going to at least let them know I'm attempting to do my job."

"You go, Beavis."

"Seriously. You should do the same. Present the budget. Present the capital asks. We can truthfully say, 'The board is hiring a new CEO. In fairness to him, they've postponed decision-making on all of our proposals so that he, rightly and fairly, has a chance to weigh in on them. You folks, as the leaders of our store organization, have the right to know what we're proposing. We don't know what will get approved, but we'd love your thoughts.' That'll work, dammit. What's the downside? Otherwise, it's going to be the most boring and meatless conference in history."

Jack leans forward. "You know what? You're right. Let's do it. Saves my team a shit ton of work this weekend."

And that's what we did. I laid out the plan for the cultural hub of gaming in every neighborhood. I showed the various formats of stores we were envisioning, the math on why Oklahoma City, Oklahoma, as odd as it might sound, was the perfect microcosm for all 3000-plus PwnShops in terms of store sizes, mall vs. strip mall mix, and customer composition. I showed them the technology we'd been working on to distribute video game play on any platform to any gaming station in the store. I showed them the couch with all four platforms in the media center that would be in the front of every store. I showed them the community table at which customers could host birthday parties or participate in pickup games of *Dungeons & Dragons*, *Catan* or *Magic: The Gathering*. And I showed them the touch screen technology we had dubbed "the endless aisle" and the drawer fixtures that would enable us to reduce the number of item facings in the store by 50 percent, making room for the entertainment experience that could become the future of our dilapidated boutiques. "And all of this could be yours," I told them, "assuming our new CEO approves this plan."

Another standing ovation. Another 4.9 rating on a 5-point scale. How can the new guy deny me?

PwnShop Northern Europe HQ
Dublin, Ireland
April 30, 2019
645 days to POSS
CSP: $9.88

"Nick. I've arranged fahr you to use de executive cahnference room fair yooehr call with Gerald. It 'as de best video cahnferencin' equipment," lilts Shay, swallowing the "h" on "has." She's the matronly executive assistant for the vice president and general manager of PwnShop Northern Europe, and her almost too true to type working class Dublin brogue is just a hair shy of landing her a voice-over gig as a Lucky Charms spokeswoman.

I'm in Dublin with the international corporate marketing leaders for the annual PwnShop marketing summit to share best practices across the territories. After Gerald's public announcement, it occurred to me that his first week at the office was the week I was scheduled to be here. I considered canceling so I could meet Gerald in person, but thought better of it as I'm probably getting fired anyway. And if I decide I want to work with this guy, won't I make a better impression by signaling that my daily job is more important than his heralded arrival?

"Thank you, Shay. How are you today?"

"Oh grand."

"Grand indeed. You're the absolute best."

"Ah, Nick, it's a wee trifle. Helen'll be dialin' in at tree o'clahck. You set yoehr arse down 'ere." (We're on a first arse basis.) "When you see de green light blenkin, press dis boehtton dat looks like a micrahphone, and den Bob's yooehr uncle."

"Again, the best!"

She begins to leave, then pauses. "I'm prahbably oohed o' line, but you never sugar coat it eider. Dahn't foehck it oehp, Nick, ya eejit!" she smirks. "Ahr, maybe do. You know we all 'ave bets on who's goin' to get fired and who isn't. 'Eard abooeht yooehr board room blow oehp. In my mind, you're at de tap o' de lest."

"That's already made it across the pond? I guess I shouldn't be surprised. Thanks for the vote of confidence. Who the hell told you about that?"

"I'll never tell. Anyway, I'm joehst takin' de piss. I dink you're de only one who soehrvives. You're de ahnly Yank wid any bollix. De rest o' dem dryshites deserve de axe. At least dat's me 'oehmble ahpinion."

"Why are you taking the piss?"

"Ahh you Yanks. I dink you wooehld say, 'I'm keddin.' We say, 'I'm takin de piss.'"

"Learn something new every day. Sorry to be such a, what was it, dryshite? And I'm not kidding. Nor taking the piss for that matter," I say with eyebrows raised.

What I didn't tell her was that I went on a call by call apology tour to the board about my shit(e) fit. Interestingly, with ample opportunity to dress me down, I mostly got the opposite. In fact, Gary Varga, who told me that just because I didn't make the presentation didn't mean they hadn't read it, showed as much contrition toward me as I did toward him. He said it was nice to see someone in the building had a passion for the business, that we've all been there, and that he wanted to spend the bulk of the call hearing more about OKC. It took everything in my being not to say, "If you'd just heard me out back in February, I wouldn't have to tell you about it now."

I gather my things into a neat stack while I attempt to gather my thoughts. The green light blinks and I press the *boehtton* that looks like a *micrahphone*. Bob is indeed my uncle. There on the massive 85-inch Samsung screen is the beloved Helen. If Shay is matronly, Helen is the matriarch who has seen and heard it all. Twenty years at PwnShop. Not a mean bone in her sixty-two-year-old body. In both my tours of duty, I've been lucky enough to share her as my executive assistant. On the screen, her selfless face is five times its natural size, which is good. Normally, a pretty low maintenance DIY executive, today I need five times the TLC I normally require.

"Nick! How are you? How's Dublin?"

"It's great. Or *grand*, I should say. Always fun to see the team here."

"Please tell Shay I said hello. I'd love to meet her in person someday."

"That'd be something. If the walls could talk, it might knock an executive or two down to size. If you and Shay talked, it could bring the company to its knees."

"Oh, please," Helen says humbly. "I'm lucky if I can remember to turn off my computer at the end of the day. Anyway, I'll get Gerald."

"Before you go," I lean in and whisper a bit. "What's he like?"

"Oh, Nick. Don't ask me that. Particularly over the video conference system. He's nice enough. Doesn't talk very much."

"Yeah, you're right. Go get him. I'll let you know how it goes."

She leans into the camera, her face growing another two exponents, and whispers, "Good luck! We're pulling for you."

A pregnant moment gestates. Finally, I hear shuffling. At the left edge of the screen, I can make out the hinged edge of the doorway to the main conference room back in Texas. In strides a man somewhere in his late fifties to early sixties, of average build, spectacled with frameless lenses. His hair, thinning on top, has eroded its former dirty blond into a mostly grey cul de sac, with a few wisps combed neatly to the left. He looks nothing like his LinkedIn picture, and more like Ian McDiarmid, who portrayed Emperor Palpatine in the *Star Wars* franchise.

"Nick. Gerald Meade. Nice to meet you," he intones matter-of-factly. He raises the right corner of his mouth in a faux smile and then looks down to his notebook.

"Nice to meet you too, sir."

"How are things in Ireland? I'm going to have to make it out that way at some point."

"I imagine you have plenty of drinking to do from the headquarters firehose for the next few weeks."

He chuckles politely. "Indeed I do."

"Well, listen," I continue. "I'm sorry I'm not there to meet you in person on your first week. Bad form on my part, I'm sure. We're having our annual international marketing meetings, and since it's my department, I felt like I needed to be here. I hope you understand."

"Of course. The business can't stop just because I'm arriving," his voice still lacking emotion of any form.

Is he bullshitting me? Is this some passive-aggressive jab because I didn't stick around to kiss his ass? Ah, shut up Nick. Don't overthink it. He's just probably not wired like you.

"Regardless, I'm sorry."

"You shouldn't be." He moves his eyes back up to the camera, a penetrating two-dimensional brief stare, magnified. "Listen, I've heard a lot about you. I'd like to hear it from the horse's mouth. Tell me what I need to know."

"I'm sure my reputation precedes me. I used to think I needed to work on my filter. After I turned fifty, I quit trying. Y'know, old dog, new tricks. Can't learn 'em. Or maybe old body, adolescent brain. Either way." I look for a sign of life on the screen. His eyes look up for a half second, and then set again to the notebook. "I guess the best thing for me to do is give you a brief history of PwnShop from my perspective, along with my own journey within the company. Does that sound okay?"

"It's your hour. Whatever you think is best."

Another mindfuck? My hour? It ain't my hour. What do you want to know? You want me to dig my own grave? Gladly.

"Uhm, first of all, I guess I should say congratulations are in order. But, I'm sure by now you realize this ain't gonna be a walk in the park."

"Indeed. Agreed," he says with just a hair more animation.

"I'm sure you're aware I was a candidate, albeit a token let's-just-check-off-the-new-slash-old-flaky-marketing-guy-so-we-as-a-board-have-done-our-obligatory-promote-from-within-diligence candidate."

"Yes. Thank you for your participation in the process."

Not going to comment on the cynicism, eh?

"It was interesting to say the least." I clear my throat and take a sip of water. "So, I guess I'll just give you my summation and, uh, definition of the problem state we find ourselves in and what my plan is for potentially solving that problem. Sound good?"

"Again, your hour."

Thanks for the warm fuzzies.

"Before I start, how well-versed are you in the video game industry?"

"Well, I did a stint running the services business at Best Buy, so tangential experience from being an executive there. But admittedly, most of my work was in home installation of home theater, home automation, computers and appliances. Other than that, in all my preparation for the interviews and in my downtime, I've done a huge amount of reading on the topic. That said, assume I know nothing."

Wow. That's what I would say. Maybe he's actually got a head on his shoulders and knows enough to know what he doesn't know.

"Are you a gamer," I ask.

"I play *Madden* occasionally with my son. If I have any free time for games, I prefer to play golf, but come on, none of us in retail ever has time to play Wii golf much less real golf."

"True that. I'm not really a gamer either. Whenever I get a rare spare moment, writing and playing music is my thing. From that journey, I think I get the passion of these consumers, but I don't fully connect with their desire to spend hours upon hours staring at a monitor. Plus, I grew up on an Atari 2600. Give me a joystick and a button."

He smiles.

"Anyway, as far as the industry, I'm still learning it too. But, with this being my second tour of duty, I do think some themes are beginning to ring true. Prior to here, I cut my teeth mostly in the record business at Sony and Arista Records and then four years at Guitar Mart in MI—the largest retailer in the musical instrument industry. When I switched over to PwnShop in 2014, I thought I knew everything, as I thought both categories were comprised predominantly of male introverts. Wait until you go to your first PwnShop store manager's conference. The only difference between a Guitar Mart and PwnShop conference was a marginal difference in incidence. Both had droves of store managers and associates that were tatted up, pierced, and in need of a smoke or vape break every forty-five minutes. Neither company would have any field employees if you did regular drug testing."

He smiles again. I figured he might bite on that one—fucker's a grizzled Navy vet. He's gonna respond to jokes about lack of human discipline.

"Anyway, I had an old colleague at Guitar Mart that used to say about the musical instrument industry, 'build your hypotheses out of ice, because they frequently melt.' I'd say the same applies to the video game industry."

"I like that."

"So, where to start? First off, I guess I need to apologize up front for the use of metaphor. Oops. Melting hypotheses. Just used one didn't I?" I pause. Stare at the screen thinking my comedic timing is solid. Deadpan big brother face in 2D stares back at me. No response. Humor, apparently, doesn't travel well over IP. "I was a music major with a minor in history, who only went off to business 'trade school…'"—I make air quotes with both hands to the screen—"…to cover my backside during the implosion of the record business back in the late '90s."

"Harvard Business School, correct?"

"Yes sir. The super impressive stigma. We used to make bets on how much time could go by before we dropped the 'H-bomb' in introductory conversations. It's not something I'm super proud of. In fact, I mostly hated my experience there. Always said, 'HBS: two-thirds BS.' But, I did in fact go to the hallowed Harvard Business School."

"Mmm hmm."

"Anyway. Where was I? Oh yes, metaphors. What I was trying to say is I appreciate my liberal arts training more than my business training. Have always felt like it's helped me to think more spatially. As such, metaphors help explain complicated concepts more simply."

"Only if it's a good metaphor."

"Touché. All my metaphors are bad ones. That's why I'm apologizing up front," I smile. He doesn't. "Well, try this one on for size. PwnShop 1.0 is basically a movie theater business. New video game releases drive traffic to our stores in the same way Hollywood blockbusters drive traffic to local movie theaters. *Star Wars* or *Guardians of the Galaxy* drives traffic to AMC and Cinemark. *Call of Duty*, *Grand Theft Auto* and *Madden* drive traffic to PwnShop. Agreed?"

"Got it."

I detect a hint of "no shit Sherlock" in those two crisp, monosyllabic words. "The problem is, movie theaters don't really make money selling tickets. The margins are thin. But, those releases are the lifeblood of traffic that gets people to the theaters to buy ridiculously profitable popcorn. You following?"

"Following."

"So, in the retail video game business, new releases get people to the store so we can sell our more profitable categories like used video games, accessories, and so on. The release is the movie. Used games and accessories are our popcorn. A few years ago, we added pop culture collectibles to the list of these metaphorical concessions. It's super profitable as well. So now we sell popcorn *and* soda. Metaphorically, of course."

"Understood." He might as well have added, "Ya feckin' eejit."

"But that's the problem," I continue. "Hollywood's releasing fewer movies, and the ones they do release are going to home exhibition sooner, and the consumer is happy to watch the same movie over and over."

"I get the fewer releases and the digital releases concurrent with street date. I don't get the 'watch the same movie over and over' bit." He perks up and leans in a bit.

"I guess that's really not happening in the movie business. Or maybe it is now that you can stream it. But it is happening in the video game business. I can argue that multiplayer gaming is a bigger nail in our coffin than digital distribution."

"How do you mean?"

"Look at *Fortnite*. Or, uh, how about a case study with more data, more time in market—*Grand Theft Auto*. In both of those games, the programming the developers do is more about creating a virtual world for communal and competitive human interaction than simply *beating the game*. These environments are incredibly immersive and provide little reason for the gamer to switch games, much less get off the couch. Ever. In both examples, Epic and Rockstar continue to string the gamer along with new content drops of maps—battlefields basically—and weapons, vehicles, costumes, dances, and all sorts of cool engaging tools to create stickier environments. Hell, for young folks, *Fortnite* has probably built a better Facebook than Facebook. It's a completely virtual metaverse."

"I see what you mean."

"Look, you've read all the stuff from analysts saying we're the next Blockbuster. Digital disintermediation leaves retailers hanging in the wind. Simply put, we have one, and only one, problem—a traffic problem. The only reason this business has lasted so much longer than record stores and movie rental outlets is bandwidth."

"Really not following."

"I'm sorry if I'm all over the place. It's an illness. I'll try to be more linear. In the mid to late '90s, with the advent of e-books, MP3 song files, and then in the late '90s and early aughts, with the advent of video on demand and streaming services, the retailers in each of those industries were no longer needed. Consumers could download directly items that they used to have to consume physically."

"Look, I get that," again verbally, but not expressively omitting, "you fucking idiot." "I don't get your comment about bandwidth. Actually, maybe I do. I now see where you're going."

"I guess I should have said file sizes. The reason the video game retail business is still somewhat viable is file sizes. Think about it. E-books are just words. They don't take up a lot of memory. In the early days of the web, even on dial-up modems, it didn't take much bandwidth to download a book."

"Ahh, now I see where you're going."

"Music was next—there's a lot more information in an MP3 file than a book—file sizes move from kilobytes to megabytes. And then a bit later, it took the movie industry a bit longer to figure out the best method of digital distribution—whether to stream or download—as the file sizes were geometrically bigger. An HD movie is a gigabyte or three."

"Right."

"Well, the file sizes for these modern games are huge. The latest *Call of Duty* was something like 150 gigabytes. That's fifty to one hundred times larger than a movie. Even on a fiber U-verse connection like we have at home, it took my son over nine hours to download the damn thing."

"Yes. I understand. Interesting."

"That's why we still exist, for now. But as bandwidth increases, the advent of 5G networks, edge computing, and so on, the need for a physical copy is going the way of the buggy whip."

"All crystal clear. It's been widely covered. Digital disintermediation. It would be sad if I took this job without understanding that." For the first time in our conversation, Gerald utters four sentences in a row. "I tend to believe, however, we're still a few years out before the consumer no longer finds utility in physical discs."

"I agree, but we need to be thinking about that now," I nod. "The interesting thing about all this, and we've done tons of consumer research on attitudes toward physical versus digital, is the reason the laggards still buy discs. Do you know why?"

"I presume residual value. A gamer can trade in an old game to get a discount on a new game."

"That is indeed a reason. And that's the reason we, by far the biggest seller of pre-owned video games in the world, wish were the most important. But, it's a distant fourth or fifth."

"Well then, what's the number one reason?"

"It's what we call the 'trophy on the shelf' driver. These core gamers, even after they've finished a more traditional campaign game—where you level up and figure out how to beat the artificial intelligence—want to hold on to the memory. It's a photograph, a trophy on a shelf. Y'know, 'I beat this damn game.'"

"Uh huh. And we know this?"

"Yes sir. Have done loads of qualitative and quantitative research on it. And, then, the second most common reason people still buy physical is bandwidth. If you have bad bandwidth, downloading a game is a horrible experience. Lack of residual value and the fact that a digital file is simply a nontransferable license hardly weigh into the decision. Business people like us, especially with our retail bias, logically think those would be the most important reasons. But the reasons are much more emotional than rational."

"Yeah. I can't believe consumers don't understand how much more monetary value for them is in the physical disc than in a digital file."

"Well, they don't. You should go talk to them."

"Maybe we should do an advertising campaign on why physical discs are more valuable," he says, his eyebrows rising above his glasses.

And maybe your tired old boomer mug can be the face of this Luddite movement. "With all due respect, Gerald, the train has left the station."

He gives me the look I've gotten from every CEO I've ever worked for, the look that says, "You fucking marketing know-it-all. You don't think CEOs can be creative." I sigh. I'm pretty sure audibly.

"Sorry. Thinking out loud. I guess what I'm saying is that collecting physical games is more like keeping books. How many times do you reread a book?"

"Almost never."

"Exactly. And how many times do you take your books to Half Price books to sell them?"

"Almost never. It's a lot of work and a lot of books for five or six ragged dollars," he admits.

"Indeed it is. And, by the way, we've earned that reputation as well over the last few years—getting greedy and expanding the margin for used, since there's really no place else anymore to sell your used games. Our reputation for the price we pay is at an all-time low." I continue, "And back to the utility question, here's some interesting data. Books have leveled off at about 60 percent physical. Digital's encroachment has stopped. Held pretty steadily for the last three years. Turns out, a physical book is easier to read in the sun, its batteries never need charging and you don't have to be connected to download the words to the page. You just pick up a paperback and you're good to go. As a result, while not the thriving business it once was, Barnes & Noble is still sorta viable. Even more interestingly, independent bookstores are making a resurgence. Turns out readers like to hang out, and more importantly, discover great reads from other like-minded, well-read literati."

"Interesting."

"On the other side of the coin, for music, and even worse, for movies, home consumption patterns are trending toward 100 percent digital. Both categories have out of home exhibition possibilities, live concerts and theater screenings, but virtually nobody's buying DVDs, much less VHS tapes. And nobody's buying CDs or cassettes. So the question is, where will video games go? This past year, we were still about 60 percent physical. But the *Call of Duty* that came out in November went 70 percent digital—I'm sure you heard that from the board during your interviews. It was ill-advised, to say the least, that we, mainly Lance and Jack..." *I'm not really tossing them under the bus am I? It is the CEO and CFO's job to relay financial news to the board, isn't it?* "...didn't relay that vital information to the board until the meeting. It's the thing that caused us to miss the quarter, and it's the thing that's creating a bit of a panic."

"So where do you think video games will land."

"Wide speculation on that one. It's a race, in my opinion, between the creativity of the game developer and bandwidth infrastructure to the most socioeconomically challenged. My belief is the most pessimistic. Physical games other than limited edition collectibles—much like LPs today—will also go the way of the buggy whip. Basically 100 percent digital in the next five to ten years. A lot hinges on whether this next generation of consoles comes with disc drives."

"Pessimistic indeed. I disagree. I think it will level off around 30 to 40 percent of gamers still wanting physical."

"Regardless, if it's 60 percent physical now, that means our new software business shrinks by at least 50 percent. That means 50 percent fewer footfalls and 50 percent fewer copies of discs in the universe for us to buy and resell at extortive margins. It's just arithmetic."

"You're not only a pessimist—I see that you're a cynic. So, Chicken Little, how do we solve the problem?"

"Do you mind if I share the presentation I had planned to present to the board back in February?"

"Go right ahead. But before you do, I'd like to get your perspective. I heard there was a bit of commotion in the board meeting over this presentation," Gerald says, raising his voice inquisitively at the end of his sentence.

"I figured you'd heard. As I mentioned earlier, no filter. Not much emotional intelligence, I guess. It's my tragic flaw. But, cynical pessimist that I am, I am passionate about the way forward. I'm still pissed they never sat through the presentation. I'm not sure they fully understand the situation, much less have a notion for a way out of it."

"I can assure you they do."

"Then why aren't they doing anything about it?" I blurt. I immediately backstroke, "Did I say that? My apologies. I guess they hired you. Again, sometimes my passion blinds me."

"It's okay. The presentation. Back to the traffic problem."

"Yes. At the end of the day, I believe the only problem we need to solve is the traffic problem. Except for hardware, however, which only comes out every seven years or so, every other category we sell is an add-on category. They're not the types of purchases that get you to the store. They're not 'destination' categories. And, for hardware, it's speculation, as we don't know when the next consoles will release, but it's widely thought this may be the last generation of consoles. New consoles might drive traffic, but their margins are even thinner than new video games."

"They're like what, 15 to 20 percent?"

"Hardly. More like 3 to 4 percent. We take more dollars to the bank selling a game than we do a $400 console. Completely empty calories. It's insane."

"We need to negotiate stronger with Sony and Microsoft."

"If wishes were horses. Good luck with that. They have *all* the power. Anyway, to the presentation. Have I told you my bad church analogy?"

"I don't think so."

I turn to the intro slide. I've found higher res images, but otherwise the slide is remarkably unchanged from the uproariously received intro now almost six months ago.

"Gerald, have you heard about E3?"

"Yep, that's the big expo for gaming like CES."

"Exactly. And these days, on the last two days, they've allowed the general public into the convention center. It's a benediction. A communion of throngs of gaming acolytes."

"You like the religious metaphors don't you? Probably not very politically correct."

"Probably not. But it's the right metaphor. We have 3500 stores that are a mere skateboard ride away from 85 percent of the US gaming population. We have clerks and store managers that barely exist at the fifth percentile of retail wages because they love to proselytize video games. They're ascetic monks, doing what they consider to be the Lord's work. And over the last seven to ten years, we, as a corporation, have done everything in our power to marginalize and minimize the experience that exists in our stores. We've coerced our teams to hard sell our customers shit they don't want. We've deinvested in our stores. Look at them."

I hold my iPhone up to show him the dog's breakfast that has become our stores—eight-year old carpet, paper signs galore, dilapidated fixtures, shit shoved in every nook and cranny.

"It's amazing anybody comes in at all. But they do. So, my plan is to completely overhaul this experience. Modernize it. Digitize it. Create an inviting hangout rather than a stinking shithouse. Allow gamers to sit next to each other and talk trash while playing *Fortnite*..."

I walk through about five slides outlining the plan to test the concept by overhauling all twelve stores in Oklahoma City, Oklahoma. Just as I'm hitting my stride, Helen walks in.

"Guys, sorry to interrupt. Ya'll have run over. Gerald, do you want me to reschedule your meeting with Jack?" As she points over her shoulder, I see what looks to be Jack's left elbow and foot protruding from the edge of the doorway.

"No, I need to talk to Jack. But, we're finishing up. Thanks, Helen," he says, his head turned to the doorway. Turning his head back to the camera, he says, "Nick, I'm going to have to move on, but one last question. Don't you think we'll get a much better return investing in state of the art e-commerce? I mean, the world's gone digital."

"Well, in short, no. We're woefully underinvested in that area too, sir, but that's another meaty topic. Probably for our next meeting. I'll leave you with this question to ponder. If e-commerce is so important in this category, why, when they enjoy number one or two market share in books, music and movies, and just about every other stinking category, is Amazon number seven in video game market share?"

"I presume because they haven't really tried. Thanks for your time. Nice to meet you." He raises his eyebrows as he gathers his things.

"Nice to meet you too, Gerald."

As he greets Jack, I faintly overhear the following.

"So he got fired the first time. And you and Lance and Tom brought him back?"

"Uhm, yes sir," a note of anticipatory hesitancy in Jack's response as he's not yet sure what the new boss thinks of me.

"Good call."

Intermezzo Primo

*"If you think about stuff that happened when you were young,
it stays with you forever."*

—ICE CUBE

The first thing you'll probably want to know is how did a Holden Caulfield like me even have a chance to present "a way forward" to PwnShop. You might also want to know what my resume was like, and how my wife has stayed with me these twenty-nine years. Don't care. Don't feel like going into all that crap.

Instead, I feel like slaydreaming in the TikTok of my mind.

Stone Haller Household
Sunday, April 11, 1976

"Hey Ni-uck, come heah and read this ahticle in the pay-puh," mom blurted out excitedly as her face emerged from the newspaper.

I was on the floor with Sam Cobra, the black hatted villain in Marx toys' Johnny West action figure adventure series, placing his derringer in the fake plastic doctor's bag that schlepped his contraband.

"I'm playing, Mom."

"Ni-uck, come on," she continued in her singular southern accent, a puree of Tidewater Virginia and the sultry cadence of her recent decade in Georgia and South Carolina, topped with seven years in Texas. "Ah think you'll enjoy this."

I stood beside her and read the article. I was in second grade. Mom, the smartest and most well-educated of my parents (she graduated Phi Beta Kappa and holds a master's degree in English from Johns Hopkins) insisted reading was fundamental. And, while I was probably reading at a fourth grade level, I didn't fully grasp the intention of the promotional piece.

"All you young artists? Paint your mother? I don't get it."

"The ceety along with Olla Podrida is sponsoring an awt cawntest," mom explained. "Fo Mutha's Day. You uh supposed to paint a pictcha of me showing what ah do evry day."

"Okay. So draw a picture of you doing what you do?"

"Yeah-us. Exackly."

Never one to shy away from a creative challenge, I returned to the den floor and bulldozed Sam Cobra, Johnny West's horse Thunderbolt, and other accessories into a hillock of polyethylene western paraphernalia. I went to the closet and grabbed the art board Dad had made me out of three-quarter inch, cabinet-grade plywood, a big sheet of newsprint, and the dog's breakfast that is the box of crayons and oil pastels. Lying prone, the board in front of me, my legs in the air, kick crossing in little ellipses perpendicular to the floor, I began to draw. Generous sweeps of color outlined mom's profile. I had a hard time with her left hand holding a phone to her ear. I was enraptured with the phone cord, going over the spiral cable in heavier and heavier strokes, each in different bright colors. When satisfied, I gazed upon the creation. Large blocks of brown, peach, blue, magenta and orange form a primitive looking hominid, but the color "goes all the way to the edge" as my art teacher had drilled into us. In the hand of the asexual cretin I'd drawn is what appeared to be a bone, narrow in the middle and bulbous at each end, in 1970s harvest yellow, held to the alien's ear, with a tight spiral of harvest yellow and orange cable shooting from the bone and down into the left corner of the 16" x 20" piece of paper, composing a nice rule of thirds division. Howard Finster would have been proud.

I turned it over, and, in large irregular block letters of black pastel graffiti, wrote "MY MOM ALWAYS TALKS ON THE TELEPHONE."

Three weeks later, amongst five-to-nine-year-olds in the entire DFW metroplex, I learned my drawing had been awarded second place. Mom got a gold-plated necklace with what looked like a Red Hot as a heart pendant. I got a seventy-five dollar check.

"Ni-uck, Ah've always told you you can do anything you put yo mahnd to. You uh so smaht."

December 12, 1980

"All right guys. Scrimmage time. Coach Nobles is using the pennies, so we're going to have to go shirts and skins. Jewell, Shifflett, Haller, Callahan and Gosling, y'all are skins," shouted the seventh and eighth grade head football coach, not excited to be running basketball practice.

My tweenage self's worst nightmare. The cheerleaders were practicing on the sidelines, and I had to take off my shirt to reveal my starveling frame and the hole in my chest.

I sheepishly removed the white and gold McCulloch Middle School practice jersey, my head, as ever, nodding downward. I drew my shoulders inward, thinking they'd hide the indention, but they only created a larger vortex, casting a foreboding shadow, deepening the cavity. I was twelve, but looked eight. Next to me stood John Jewell, a swarthy primate who was thirteen going on twenty, his arms and ankles sprouting wild hairs like the North Texas grasslands. Though a bit of a bully, he liked me for some reason—irreverent thoughts, I imagine. I watched him cross his arms below his waist and grab the bottom of the jersey, and like a B-list actor in a bad beach movie, pull his arms in a smooth deliberate motion over his head to reveal a brick house chest with a full pelt of hair spread in a smut of thicker and more virile sod. If this were a Rorschach test, the axis of his torso would be the crease in the paper, and his chest hair a blot of bilateral symmetry, broader at the upper reaches of the axis across his bulbous pectoral muscles, narrowing to the navel, and then spreading out slightly to make private inroads into the elastic waistband of his too short gym shorts. A healthy individual might have perceived in this pattern of chest hair a butterfly, the Winged Victory, or the Vitruvian Man. I saw the head of Wile E. Coyote.

By the bleachers, the seventh grade cheerleader squad with their taut tanned legs, their tittering gossip, and their ribboned pony and pigtails, mustered for their stunts and drills. As I peeked through the veil of my lowered brow, I was convinced they were whispering about me, wimpy white male that I was. Then I realized these Lolitas couldn't give a shit about my scrawny ass; they were focused solely on Jewell's studied striptease.

Eliza Bullard, the tautest and tannest alpha female, gushed in a loud, breathy whisper, "Oh. My. Gawd. John. Jewell. IS A MAN!"

December 15, 1980

"Coach, do I have to shower? I didn't even break a sweat."

Coach Coy Willard, stationed in the locker room, shook his head and said, "Ev'ry day. Rain or shine. Sweat or no sweat."

I rolled my eyes and moved to the bench, took off my gym clothes and shoved them into my locker. My bony birthday suit wandered over to the table where the towels were usually folded. Typically, you'd grab one before heading into the shower room—a yawning expanse of bleached tile with two posts of six shower heads each blasting water out in every direction. Therein, a conspiracy of adolescent lemurs played grab-ass, splashing and popping each other with wet tipped rattails made from their diagonally rolled towels.

But not today. Just Coach Willard guarding the shower entrance like Cerberus, the folded towels stacked on a chair beside him.

"Can I have a towel, coach?"

"MAY I have a towel, Haller."

"May I have a towel, coach?" I eyerolled and fig leafed my hands over my nether regions for a modicum of privacy.

He giggled. "You may. But you gotta jump for your towel, boy."

He raised his arm to its uppermost reach, probably some seven and a half to eight feet, holding the two ends so that a festooned "U" dangled down from his hand. The towel being not much larger than a hand towel, the target was still more than seven feet over head. I was a mere forty-six to forty-eight inches tall.

I removed my hands from my crotch and jumped. He flipped the towel higher just as I reached the zenith of my jump, eluding my grasp.

"Jump, boy, jump!"

I kept jumping, like Sisyphus, never completing the task. The boys in the shower started chanting, "Jump, boy, jump! Jump, boy, jump!"

Finally, on about the eighth jump, Coach let me grab the towel. I slunk into the lukewarm showers, a sheaf of stalks and shame.

April 7, 1981

"Mr. Jewell. Mr. Shifflett. And, uh, you, Mr. Haller. I gather y'all do know why you're here?" Principal Cecil B. Holmes, a dumpy, egg-shaped Weeble of a man who looked just like Mayor Teddy Burnside in the threadbare sitcom *Carter Country*, interrogated.

We nodded in synchronous unease.

"That's right. I have it on good authority that you three gutless wonders thought it was a good idea to toss Paul Gosling into the dumpster."

Paul was a nice enough kid. Didn't mean any harm. But my socially anxious mind convinced itself he was making fun of me out in the parking lot behind the cafeteria where we gathered every day after lunch. In a mischievous moment, trying to suck up to the cool kids, I enlisted my bully buddy, the aforementioned John Jewell, who enlisted John David Shifflett, who'd bully me as soon as anyone else, and convinced these louts to help me gather up Paul and toss his would-be turncoat ass into the dumpster. A flight of Valkyries meting justice for a crime he didn't know he committed, we surrounded him. Jewell put him in a half nelson while Shifflett grabbed his left arm and left leg. I flopped around holding on for dear life to his flailing right leg. We jerked along like a murder of crows toward the receptacle, hoisted him through the side door and dumped him in yesterday's chalupas. Then we ran.

"Mr. Shifflett," Principal Holmes continued. "We meet again. This is your third infraction. Not only am I going to have to call your parents, you're to report here for the next four Saturdays for detention. Ah yes. Mr. Jewell. This being the second time I've seen you this year, I'm also going to call your parents and need you here Saturday."

The principal gave me a once over, and shook his head in disbelief. "Mr. Haller. What on God's green earth are you doing in here? This seems very uncharacteristic."

"Uhm, yessir," I muttered. Not experienced in playing any kind of poker in this situation, I unbosomed myself immediately. "I'm a bad kid. And, uh, you shouldn't be mad at them. It was my idea."

"Mr. Haller. You're the worst kind of person. You surround yourself with bigger, stronger guys to protect you, and use your ways, your wicked ways, to tempt them, to coerce them to act out, to perform dastardly deeds. You should be ashamed. Utterly."

"Uhm, yessir. I am."

"I can't believe I have to call your fine mother. She serves faithfully on our PTA for crying out loud. And you honor her in this way? Shame, shame. You'll be joining Mr. Shifflett for the next four Saturdays. You will write Mr. Gosling and his poor working single mother an apology letter. You will go through the cafeteria line on his behalf and deliver him his lunch every day for the next week before you are able to feed yourself. Do you understand?"

"Uhm, yessir."

February 17, 1984

"Mom, who is this doctor we're going to see?"

"Don't you remembuh this discussion with Doctuh Roach during yaw physical? Weuh goin to see Dr. Peek. He's an endocrinologist."

"I don't remember. What does an encronologist do?"

"En-DOE-cronologist. They ah expuhts in ho-uh—mones."

"Why do I need a hormone expert?"

"Hopefully you don't."

I sat in the waiting room, flipping through a *Sports Illustrated* while Mom filled out the requisite paperwork with the receptionist. It was the January issue. The cover—Joe Theismann and his single bar facemask leading the Redskins back to the Super Bowl. The February Swimsuit issue with Paulina Porizkova on the cover was nowhere to be found. Not to worry. My buddies had already shown it to me. My mom canceled my subscription the year before. Soft porn in her estimation.

"Haller? Nick Haller," the nurse honked from the door next to the reception glass.

"Yes," I muttered, flapped the *SI* closed, and stood.

"Come on back."

"Mom, aren't you coming?" I entreated.

"Naw, son. I'll tawk to the doctuh aftuhwahds."

The nurse led me to the examination room. On the wall was an anatomical illustration of the endocrine system, its essence the exploded anatomical view of a nondescript Caucasian asexual human torso—gender neutral but racist, as it was the color of what used to be called a 'flesh' crayon. Only the main glands sat atop the skeleton. All organs and musculature removed. Callout lines extended from each gland to an inset view sitting in one of two columns on either side of the central drawing. On the left were detailed drawings of the pineal gland, the thyroid, the thymus gland, the pancreas, and the testes, in vertical order. On the right, in a similar columnar layout, respectively, were images of the pituitary gland, the hypothalamus, the parathyroid glands, the adrenal gland, and an ovary.

The nurse entered, took my blood and sent me to the bathroom to pee in the inescapable cup. To this day, I've never learned how to pee in one of these without some collateral damage. Upon delivering the sample, washing my hands and sopping the urine spittle from the edges of the now sealed cup, I returned to the exam room.

I stared again at the chart. I was in tenth grade. I'd had health and biology. I was pretty sure, although I must admit I was questioning myself, that the average human didn't have both a testes and an ovary. A timid knock on the door interrupted my troubled thoughts.

"May I come in?" asked a deep voice that belied the faint rap.

"Of course," I replied.

In walked a tall man in his mid-forties with jet black hair and a pronounced five o'clock shadow wearing a white examination coat. Embroidered in navy blue above a breast pocket protector holding various medical looking utensils and a gold Cross pen with the doctor's full name: Howard M. Peek, M.D.

"I take it you're Nick?"

"Uhm. Yessir."

"I'm Dr. Peek. Do you know why you're here?

"No, sir."

"Your mother and your pediatrician want me to make sure you're on a normal growth curve. Since you're now almost sixteen, you might have noticed you're still considerably smaller in height and weight than most of your peers."

No shit Sherlock. I wasn't wrestling at ninety-eight pounds because I chose to.

From the larger cargo pocket of his jacket he pulled out what looked like a cheap costume bead necklace. But, instead of spherical beads that decreased in size on each side symmetrically to the largest bead in the middle, these beads were ovular, little pinkish-yellow colored eggs, and only went one way, asymmetrically, from small to large.

"This is an orchidometer," he said. "It's kind of like a stethoscope for pediatric endocrinologists like myself. We use it to measure the size and volume of the testicles."

And you chose this as your profession? You sick fuck. I had no idea what I wanted to be when I grew up, but it's safe to say that was the day I removed endocrinologist from the possible list.

"You see, the first physical sign of puberty we see is testicle growth. If your 'nuts' are growing..." *Did this pederast just use air quotes? As if I didn't know what nuts were? You're the nut, you vile shaman.* "...You'll be growing soon too," he chuckled. Not even awkwardly. He'd obviously given this speech before. "Do you understand?"

"Uhm, yessir."

"Okay then. I'm sorry to ask you to do this, but I'm going to need you to remove your shoes and jeans, dressing down to your underwear. And when you're ready, I'm going to need you to stand and pull your underwear down to your knees."

I scoffed. Shook my head. *Need or want? And I needed you, Doc, to self-administer an enema, because your shit was impacted.* I thought about walking out. Instead, just like I did with Principal Holmes, I folded. I kicked off my Stan Smiths, pulled my Wranglers down, wriggled my socked feet out from the legs, and stepped out. A pair of Fruit of the Loom briefs sagged around my bird legs, and my left testicle sagged along with them.

"Okay, if you could pull your underwear down to your knees, I promise this won't take long."

I did as he said. I stared down at my boyhood. In modern terms, one might've thought I'd manscaped for the occasion. If you looked, as I had, you'd see the stirrings of two sideburns of faint hair framing my radish. Beneath it was a disproportionately long turkey wattle, carrying two duck eggs, the left one dangling about a centimeter lower than the right one.

"Oh, I see we're going to be just fine," Dr. Peek exclaimed, passing through the smaller eggs, like a nun casting prayers of ever-growing importance from increasingly larger rosary beads. He picked the egg that was about two thirds of the way along the chain of bollocks and held it next to my right boy, weighing it in this primitive methodology like Indiana Jones judging if his sack of sand corresponded to the weight of the effigy he'd raided from the tomb.

"I think this is it. Fifteen cc of volume." He pulled the brass pen from his pocket protector and then twisted it in a single motion with his right hand, exposing the point, and memorialized my measurement right then and there in indelible ink. "Not to worry, Nick. You're going to be just fine. You can get dressed now."

Track 3: Won't Get Fooled Again

"You ain't gonna learn what you don't wanna know."

—JERRY GARCIA

PwnShop Corporate Offices
Vineland, TX
May 17, 2019
628 days to POSS
CSP: $9.52

I'm an indivisible man. Not a conjoined twin. Nor am I one of your Hollywood movie Tyler Durden[1] dissociative identities. I'm paradoxical, of art and science, bile and phlegm. I might even be said to resemble a fussy quilt. I'm indivisible, understand, because most people refuse to see me binocularly and hear me in stereo—with two eyes and two ears.

"How was your Ireland trip?" Gerald queries from behind his desk.

"Fantastic. Have you been to Ireland?" I counter from the far side of the large rectangular conference table dominating the south quadrant of his corner office.

"Yes. A couple of times."

"Well, it was my first time. Nicest people in the world. There's now a direct flight from Dallas, so my wife Maura and my son George flew in

---

[1] Tyler Durden is the split-off dissociative personality state of The Narrator, the protagonist in the 1996 Chuck Palahniuk novel and its more widely known 1999 film adaptation, *Fight Club*. The film casts Edward Norton as The Narrator and Brad Pitt as his imagined übermensch Tyler Durden, a symbolically pure embodiment of machismo that satirically represents triumphant, Darwinian capitalism.

for the long weekend. We spent Friday in Dublin then went west to the Cliffs of Moher and Galway. Went deep on the Easter rebellion and the War of Independence—y'know, the General Post Office, Kilmainham Gaol, Bloody Sunday, and so on. Fascinating. Plus, music guy that I am, I went to see the studio where Thin Lizzy recorded. I'm a bass player. Big Phil Lynott fan."

I show him the picture on my iPhone of me standing next to the Phil Lynott statue on Grafton Street, and then swipe right to the picture of me sitting at the big Neve console where Thin Lizzy recorded such gems as "The Boys Are Back in Town," "Whiskey in the Jar," and, my favorite, "Cowboy Song."

"Anyway, back to the revolution stuff," I continue. "It's baffling to me how Michael Collins, after finally getting the British to agree to the Irish Free State, the guy who created the IRA, is killed by IRA extremists because the treaty that fundamentally allowed Ireland to self-govern required a symbolic oath of allegiance to the crown. Nobody is ever satisfied with a compromise. Emotions over common sense. But I digress."

"I've noticed that's an habitual imperfection of yours."

God forbid we do anything but talk shop, General Meade.

"Which? Inability to compromise or non sequiturs?"

"Yes," he smiles at his own indivisible deflection.

"Pobody's nerfect." Polite chuckles all around. "So, Gerald, how's the firehose drinking?"

He darts his eyes upward. "We're making progress. Opinions galore around here."

"I'll bet. Between the board, investors, old guard management, consultants, and wisecracks like me, I'm sure your head's spinning."

"On the contrary. I think it's pretty clear what needs to happen."

"Care to elaborate?"

"I don't think that's appropriate. Yet." He loosens the top of an Ozarka water bottle, tilts up a quick swig, swallows and says, "But, I would like to continue where we left off last week."

"About that. Apologies for not being here on your first week."

"No apology necessary."

Man, I wouldn't want to play poker against this guy. "Well, uhm, okay," I continue haphazardly. "What else do you want to talk about? I've brought along the strategy deck I prepared for the board, as well as my org chart, so, I'm happy to take this wherever you want."

"I think I get OKC. I'd like to discuss digital and some organizational changes I'm contemplating. I recall you saying you didn't think digital should be part of our go forward strategy," he goads.

"In fairness, sir, I think that's putting words in my mouth. If by digital you mean e-tail, I think I was saying we won't win on e-tail alone. Amazon has already out e-commerced everyone and their dog. We can't compete with their front-end search and UX, their supply chain, and their cloud infrastructure. Plus, if memory serves, I think I was saying if e-tail alone were the way forward, Amazon would dominate market share in video games. They don't. Not even by a country mile. We're number one. Walmart is a distant second. Best Buy and Target are always hashing it out for third and fourth. Sony and Microsoft and sometimes Steam and sometimes Nintendo have higher market share than Amazon. In most other categories, Amazon is number one or two. You have to ask why are they so far behind in this category."

"So again, your plan would ignore an investment in digital?

"Absolutely not. We have to invest heavily in digital/e- tail. I'm just saying that digital alone is not a winning strategy IMHO. We need to zag if everyone else is zigging."

"(A) If I had a nickel for every marketing exec who told me to zag when everyone else is zigging, I'd be a rich man, and (B) I think you can eliminate the letter 'H' when describing your opinions."

"Perhaps. And my apologies if I'm being too, ah, y'know, expressive. I guess it's another one of my 'nicks.' I'm just passionate about this business, the way forward, and the importance of the store and the store associates in that strategy." *Why the fuck am I pandering to this guy? Are you trying to kiss his ass because you think you might actually want to work for him?*

"Look," I tack on. "At least I think we can agree that we need to invest in this business, yes?"

"Yes and no. This place is completely over-staffed, over-stored and under-managed. Significant austerity needs to take place before we can truly invest in a transformation."

"Agree. But don't you agree that a transformation has to happen?"

"I don't know. The new consoles are coming out in twelve to eighteen months. Our collectibles business is doing well—it just needs better inventory management—and our SG&A is bloated beyond belief. I think there's significant money to be made in the next three to five years just by managing this thing more efficiently, building a better digital experience, and growing a few product categories like proprietarily branded goods and financial services."

"So you don't think the stores matter?"

"Now you are putting words in my mouth. I think we have way too many stores for the current state of our business. And you seem like a smart guy, don't you believe that channel shift is manifest destiny? After all, clicks have been replacing bricks over the last ten years."

"I believe strategy is as much if not more about being steadfast in what you aren't as in deciding what you are. Southwest Airlines built a business on NOT having first class, NOT allowing reserved seats, and NOT having multiple types of planes. All of those things allowed them to convert flights much more quickly, allowing them to keep costs much lower than their competitors. No they weren't as fancy as the other guys, but they knew where they could win and they built their culture around that winning strategy."

"And what does this have to do with PwnShop?"

"Everything. You could argue that PwnShop used to *be* the local church of gaming—the religious metaphor you don't like. We had huge new release parties when big titles came out. We bought pizzas. We worked with our vendors to create gameplay experiences. Customers would line up around the block on Monday to pick up the game at midnight Tuesday. It was a happening."

"We don't do that anymore?"

"(A) We half-ass it. (B) With many titles going digital, those releases are fewer and farther between. It used to be the most hardcore gamers would come to PwnShop because it was the fastest way to get to play the new experience. The experience in store was an artifact of that desire, not the driver to the store. Just like Southwest had to embrace a friendly culture because they were a cattle car. The customer's motivation was to get the title, and beat the game, before their lame friends picked it up with their moms five days later at Target and Walmart. It was a badge of badassness. These days, for core gamers, the fastest way to get the game is a digital download, particularly with publishers allowing gamers to prepurchase the download. The game downloads in the background on their consoles in advance. When you log into the game at 12:01 AM on street date, if you've prepurchased, you can begin playing immediately."

"Why don't we just ignore the publishers and release the physical game before street date?"

"Well, that's a great strategy. Once. After that, they'll cut us off. Or, they'll give preferential treatment to a partner who obeys their rules. Part of the reason Amazon's share is so piss-poor is that they've tried, on multiple occasions, to use their weight to strong-arm their vendors, like they do in every other category. The publishers and hardware guys kneecapped them, quit selling to them for a period of time. These titles are unique IP,[2] the consoles one of a kind. They aren't commodities. They aren't widgets. Amazon's power isn't as palpable when they can't copy the IP. They can't knock off a cheaper version like they can with most physical categories. It's an ecosystem, and the retailer's role in that ecosystem, with publishers and consoles now allowing direct downloads at home, if you're pessimistic, is going away completely. If

[2] Intellectual Property. Not Internet Protocol. Nor Idiot Proof. IP has become shorthand for just about any game and all of its in-game microeconomies—*Call of Duty* is IP. *Fortnite* is IP. *Farming Simulator*, the only game I can play because it doesn't require twitch and perfect usage of the modern controller, is the most intellectual of properties. I can plow a field all day long. But I can't catch catfish from dusk til dawn.

you're optimistic, like I am, that role is still needed, it just needs to be completely reenvisioned."

"Okay, smart guy, then what is our role in a digital world?" he asks while removing the comb from his back pocket.

"To use a buzzword from the dot-com boom—to be an infomediary. To create discovery for new releases and to become the distributed salesforce for the industry."

"Not sure I'm following," he says, brow slightly furrowed either at my outpouring of blubbering B-school jargon or at the lack of resistance his thinning hair is giving his comb.

"Look. The wet dream of any marketer is to have perfect market share data down to the individual customer level. My old boss, the loyalty guru Hal Brierley, drilled into my head that the principal strategic role of any loyalty program should be to understand who your category heavy splitters are."

"Heavy splitters? Please elaborate." He slips the comb back into his back pocket.

"Frequent fliers who are flying on multiple airlines, not just one. Luxury shoppers who spend loads of money at Barneys and Neiman Marcus and, I don't know, Fred Segal. And then there are, y'know, hard core gamers, those with a PlayStation, an Xbox, a Switch and a souped-up gaming PC. The ones playing anything and everything. As a marketer, if you can identify those folks and separate them from your brand loyalists, you know precisely where to invest your dollars to shift market share."

"Okay, I'm following."

"We have some customers in our database that spend well over $2000 a year with us. What we sort of know that Sony and Microsoft and Nintendo and Steam don't is how much money these whale customers may or may not be splitting amongst the platforms. One $2000 customer could be spending all their money within the Sony ecosystem, for instance. Another could be spending, through PwnShop, $1500 on

Sony, $500 on Switch and $500 on Steam POSA cards. If you're Sony or Nintendo, which customer would you rather talk to?"

"Leading the witness. The category heavy splitter."

"Exactly. For Sony to know that a customer is cheating half their wallet on competitors is valuable information. Same for Nintendo. We have that data; they don't."

"Elaborate."

"Imagine if your son plays *Madden* and *Halo* and *GTA V*. Imagine he plays *Madden* and *GTA* on his PlayStation, and *Halo*, by definition, on his Xbox. Sony can see how long and how many micropayments he's making within *Madden* and *GTA*, and if his gamer ID shows up with the same or different gamer IDs between those two games. Microsoft can only see the activity for *Halo*. EA can only see the activity and monetization on *Madden*. Same for Activision and *Call of Duty*. And PwnShop, if we sold all of those games, can see that your son is playing all three, and because of the format in which they were sold, we know he has both consoles. Of course, if we sold him both consoles, we know that as well."

"Understood."

"Here's the problem. Nobody has the complete 360 degree view of your son. We all know from consumer research that splitting happens in droves. We can use expensive customer data platforms and data warehouses to cookie all of your son's activity and make inferences as to what he's up to, but we don't have perfect data. Nobody does. But I believe that's our north star."

"I thought you said Oklahoma City was our north star?"

"OKC is a means to an end. The stores become our traffic and data collection device. Right now, the magnetism to our stores weakens by the day. The OKC bet is that building fun, environmental, community rich experiential stores is how we become the best collector of every social gamer's cross-platform activity. OKC enables gameplay on every platform. It links to our customer's PowerUp Rewards loyalty accounts. We can see, for the first time, what they're playing—even free-to-play games to which we're completely blind, like *Fortnite*. We can see who they're playing with, at least locally. We can match that in-store gameplay data with their purchase data. We will be the best at identifying category heavy splitters. Armed with that data, and our army of associates that know and love the gamer, and our technology forward video-enabled stores, we will become the most immersive media company and best salesforce for the video game industry."

"Sounds pretty big brother and like an enormous privacy invasion."

"Now who's being cynical? It's a fine line between being creepy and being relevant to both our customers and our vendors. If you talk to a video game developer or publisher, especially with new IP, the hardest problem they have to solve is discovery. There are so many good games that most gamers, even the most hardcore, have no idea exist. With OKC, we have an environment within which we can not only recommend trial gameplay, we can create gameplay and esports competition events around it. In short, instead of thinking of ourselves as a retailer, we should think of ourselves as an out of home experiential media company. In a small-box distributed sense, our stores can be ad revenue machines just like football stadiums or airports. We just need foot traffic. Then it's a closed loop system. We aren't selling customer data outside our four walls. Media buyers are harnessing our data inside our walls."

"Don't we already sell co-op advertising to our vendors?"

"You mean shitty paper posters that get lost in the mail, that have no digital tracking, and use two dimensions to describe an immersive, tactile, audiovisual EXPERIENCE? Yes, but it's like peddling a newspaper in the world of Instagram. We sell video games. VIDEO. Our stores are merchandised with game spines and posters. Nowhere other than our shitty little PwnShopTV screens in the uppermost corner of the store, can a customer see moving images, much less experience gameplay. OKC fixes all of that. Video advertising pushed to every corner of the store. A couch to try before you buy whatever game you want to play. Gaming stations where you can immerse yourself away from the Eye of Sauron of your mother or wife, where you can hang out with your buddies and talk trash and knock elbows against shoulders when your buddy does something stupid in game, and a place where you can high five when you defeat the Kraken. Gaming stations where you can hold a full-on esports competition."

"How much does it cost?"

"Our initial estimate is about $200 to $250K per store, but that's buying everything, assuming no vendor partnerships."

"Whew. Five thousand stores globally? That's about $1 billion."

"No, it's about a $3 million investment to understand what works and what doesn't. Twelve stores in Oklahoma City. And I'm almost positive, after the proof of concept, between vendor partnerships and value engineering—y'know, scale efficiencies—I think we can get the cost to about $100K per store, a $350 million investment, assuming we keep the entire store footprint. And if it works, the investment pays for itself. We wouldn't roll it out otherwise."

"How long to get it up and running?

"Timing is a whole other question. I worry it's too little too late to begin with."

"How do you mean?"

"Short story—we need it up and running before the holiday. With the board pushing the decision in February until your arrival, we don't have a lot of time to get them ready. Part of the reason I was so pissed off. For these stores to outperform the chain, they have to be able to pull their weight when the fish are running. The only time the fish run anymore is fourth quarter. Theoretically, these stores should crush the rest of the chain in the first three quarters of the year. But the number of SKU facings is half of a regular store, because of all the experiential equipment. The only worry I have is whether these things can do the same sales volume in the critical holiday period."

"A good point. And what's the long story?"

"Now the cynical ball's back in my court. In 2015—during my first tour of duty with this stinking company—I floated the idea of building the local church in every market. I was told by the then president, 'Why would I invest a single dollar in these shitty stores?' I tend to believe the old Chinese proverb. The best time to plant a tree was twenty years ago. The second-best time is today. And every day we wait, is another day, or potentially another year before we see if that tree bears fruit."

"Got it."

"So, can I move ahead with Oklahoma City?"

"Before I answer that, give me your opinion of the existing executive team."

"Well, that's a change of gears." I take a gulp of water. Audibly. "But before I answer that, you need to know I agree that this place is bloated with SG&A. Claude was a mensch. His motto was 'protect the family.' He prided himself on never having to do an across-the-board layoff. It was noble. It's no longer practical. Our sales base continues to shrink. We must get our costs back in line with our sales volume. And, yes, I'm a marketing guy saying that."

"Heh. I don't think I've ever had a marketing executive recommend cost cutting."

"It's not my nature. But it needs to be strategic. We have to jettison waste, but we have to keep and even invest heavily in the new way forward."

"Okay, so back to the people."

"Jack is a super nice guy. Has loyally served this company for the last twelve years. I'm sure the board wants him gone based on the fallout from the poor return on the Spring Wireless investment. The finance, tax and accounting teams are bloated in my opinion. I would let him retire gracefully, and then take the axe massively to the one main department here that doesn't generate any sales."

"And what about you? Should I keep you?"

Wow. Pretty fucking direct.

"Well, uhm, that's your decision."

"You have a choice of places to work. It's your decision too."

"Fair enough. It takes two to tango. Permission to speak freely?"

"As if you haven't already?"

"Touché. Okay, so here's my deal. I've thought a lot about it. First, I cannot and will not work with assholes. I was initially worried that you might be an asshole, but so far I think you're asking the right questions and going about things in a perfectly logical and methodical manner. In fact, I applaud your thoroughness. If I'm being completely honest, I thought the board was going to hire a hatchet man. My early conversations with you give me reason to believe you're more than that. Which leads me to my second consideration. I need to be all in. And for me to be all in, I need to know that no matter what happens, you are steadfast on two things. One, you kill guidance and tell the Street this is a fundamental turnaround. We have to embrace risk. We have to invest in the way forward in addition to cutting costs. And that notion feeds number two—that you promise me you will hold innovation dollars sacrosanct. That no matter how poorly we're doing in a quarter, you don't come to me and pull back dollars that are an investment in our future just to hit the quarter."

"Thank you for your time."

May 28, 2019
Palace Arts Theatre
Vineland, Texas
617 days to POSS
CSP: $8.08

Some of my direct reports and I are milling about between the front row seats and stage of the Palace Arts Theatre we've rented for Gerald's coming out party, his first town hall. While the corporate staff isn't as feisty as the store managers, they have a huge amount of skepticism and cynicism. The prevailing sentiment—fear. Gerald is the would-be angel of death about to swing his reaper in ever deepening cuts through the hundreds of folks who have given their professional lives to this disrupted company. Their tragic flaw: blind loyalty, an idealistic notion that if I'm loyal to the Company, the Company will be loyal to Me. Yes, there have been executives who "decided to pursue other opportunities" or "spend more time with their families," and there are folks who have been fired for fraudulent expense reports, engaging in insider trading, or not kissing their boss's ass enough. And there have been multiple reorganizations and realignments of the field staff. But never has this company seen a systemic massive layoff, the proverbial downsizing that just about every major corporation in America has implemented at some point to show the Street that management means business and shareholders will be rewarded with the celebrated spilling of blood.

Terry, our director of corporate communications and PR, a nine-year loyalist himself, along with Tess, the director for PwnShop TV—our closed network channel that runs in all stores during business hours and is our most consistent form of communication to field associates after hours—are tasked with pulling off this town hall. Terry helped Gerald with his presentation, and Tess did everything else.

I've just waltzed in from my forty-five minute commute from Dallas. After the boardroom blowup, I've turned over a new leaf. In a half-assed attempt at self-help and emotional intelligence, I've switched to podcasts over protest and self-pity songs.

"So, is he ready?" I ask my two lieutenants.

"Who knows," Terry plows in. "I made him a bunch of slides, and explained that everyone thinks he's been hired to clean house. He barely nodded. I'm not sure what he's going to say."

"The guy's got ice in his veins," Tess says. "He wouldn't let me touch him when I tried to put his lavalier on."

"Tess, you're such an invader of personal space," I kid. "Seriously, though, I think the guy's just trying to figure it out. This is not an easy problem to solve."

"So do you know what he's going to say, Nick?" Terry asks.

"No idea," I respond. "I'm just saying in the few meetings I've had, he's asked very thoughtful, fair questions. Granted, he hasn't shown his hand but, by the nature of his questions, my hunch is he's more than just some grimnocerous Witcher."

Terry volleys, "Since when did our chief pessimist entertain optimism?"

At that moment, Jack heads to the podium. The restless natives quiet almost immediately, as if they know their medicine is coming and they may as well choke it down.

"Ladies and gentlemen," Jack begins. "It is my pleasure to introduce you to Gerald Meade." He recites the bio I've now heard ad nauseam. "So, PwnShop family, welcome our newest edition and next CEO, Gerald Meade!"

Polite, non-uproarious golf clapping applause as Gerald takes the stage, cool as a powder blue cummerbund. And equally as stylish, dressed in his black and red two-tone polyester PwnShop polo, Lucky Brand jeans with a braided brown belt, and what appear to be brand new navy blue mesh Cole Haan zero gravity wingtips with white soles. Boomer to the core. After a parental lecture on the lack of discipline that has existed in the company over the last two years, Gerald warns the crowd that winter is coming, before hinting that spring can arise from the tundra. And then, like a Zamboni driver he smooths the ice in ever decreasing circles. I've always been mesmerized by a good Zamboni driver.

"But cost cutting is a means to an end. We must transform ourselves. To do that correctly, we must invest our savings into a way forward that embraces our position as the largest retailer of video games in the world. Let it be known, I am going to establish a pool of innovation dollars that we will hold sacred. We will invest these dollars in promising ideas, product categories and channels that will shore up our future. Thank you for your time. Let's get to work."

Seated applause. Stronger than polite. Weaker than an ovation.

Mom raised me to handwrite thank you notes. As an eight-year-old ingrate kid, I thought it was a waste of time. My handwriting was crappy and my sentiments were sterile. As a fifty-one-year-old adolescent, I still think they're mostly a waste of time, as typing is so much more efficient and my sentiments are cynical. But, I need to decide if I want to work with Gerald. Based on his speech today, I can't believe he'd say what he said in front of 300 plus corporate employees without having some level of integrity in his declarations. I pull out the Crane note cards engraved with my name in Copperplate, pull out the black Flair pen (finer points betray my ever-present hand tremors, which are frequently amplified by caffeine), and jot down the following:

> Gerald—
>
> Nice job today. Thank you for sharing your belief that cost cutting alone won't fix the problem and that we, a) have to admit to the world this is a fundamental transformation, and b) we must hold innovation dollars sacrosanct come hell or high water.
>
> As you might remember, those two notions are my emotional price of entry. Since you announced them publicly to the company, I'll take this as a sign of conviction.
>
> I am therefore,
>
> All in,
>
> Nick

Track 4: Riding Shotgun Down the Avalanche

"Never wear your necktie while you're operating a lathe."

—JOHN PRINE

PwnShop Corporate Offices
Vineland, TX
June 5, 2019
609 days to POSS
CSP: $8.56

It's a scorching day for late May, and the Apple Watches are striking thirteen. The Texas wine country withers. Not that it's really wine country. No microclimates here. Just weather. Vineland has a "Vinefest," and there's a plot of land on Highway 360 between a Jiffy Lube and a CVS that has grapevines, grows some grapes, and has built a faux chateau of Texas hill country limestone. Other than that, it's all a ruse.

Gerald asked me a month or so ago about my thoughts on why the company never had a chief merchant whose span of control covers both used and new products. It was a good question. The historical reason, I observed, was that putting the chief buyer of new video games in charge of the used business created a conflict of interest, at least in the eyes of our vendors. But since the pre-owned (as if the consumer can't see right through the maquillage) business was cratering, it might make sense to put the whole offering under one chief. And, I offered that having one leader adjudicate and break ties between the new and used merchants made good decision-making sense. One throat to choke on the overall presentation of our stores.

Apparently, the decision to hire a chief merchandising officer had already been made. He asked me to talk by phone with his preferred candidate, Dale Spivey. I was relieved Gerald thought enough of me that he would at least let me talk to the folks he was going to hire in advance of their onboarding. Gerald and Dale had crossed paths briefly at Best Buy where Dale was SVP of the entertainment business group, overseeing, among other things, new and used video games.

Dale seemed like an independent thinker. Not sure that he'd fully thought through the problem, but he seemed like he mostly knew what he was getting into. His manner of speech was a bit broken, and filled with "uhms" and "y'knows." But, I was impressed he asked my opinion on the problem at hand. I shared that I thought the circus needed complete reinvention.

He asked me my thoughts on Gerald. "Jury is still out," I remarked. "I was impressed by his town hall speech where he emphasized what I believe to be the two lynchpins to the transformation."

"And those are?" Dale inquired.

"One, that he go to the Street and state publicly that we're killing guidance and this is a fundamental transformation that will take two to three years. My opinion—a fundamental transformation like we need and dependable quarterly earnings are, in almost all cases, mutually exclusive."

"Totally agree. But don't you think it's possible to hit earnings and transform."

I thought you said you totally agree? Are you going to be one of those leaders that talks about the possibility of "AND"? We can walk AND chew gum? We can grow customers AND gross margins? We can hit earnings every quarter AND fundamentally transform? Yes it's fucking possible. But likely? Not at all. Prioritize and stick with the decision.

"Possible?" I answered. "Yes, if our vendors release big hits. But, that wouldn't have been the guidance we gave anyway. We'd get dinged for guiding too low. It's a trap attempting both. A fool's errand."

"Totally agree," Dale rejoined. *Really? Can I trust you?* "And what's the second thing?" he asked.

"Well, it stems right from the first. No matter how bad it gets, we don't sell our future to hit short-term numbers. We hold investment, particularly in transformation and innovation—y'know, potential ways forward, new revenue streams—sacrosanct above short-term earnings."

"Totally agree."

Despite his noncommittal "total agreements," I told Gerald I liked Dale and thought he'd be a good addition. I'd already read the tea leaves. They'd all but hired the guy—he'd spoken to five board members before he ever talked to me. It wasn't like they were going to have me interview multiple candidates. No point in rocking the boat unnecessarily at this moment. And, most importantly, I told Gerald how much I appreciated him including me in the process.

"Goes without saying," he said.

Last week, Gerald brought me into his office to tell me he was promoting me to EVP and chief customer officer, and giving me a 30 percent salary increase.

Not looking a gift horse in the mouth, but why the big bump for doing the same job?

I thanked him. He relayed that HR was working with our general counsel to finalize my contract, that I should be pleased, but to feel free to run it by my attorney. It included two years of severance, forward vesting of any granted stock awards, and eighteen months of health-care coverage through COBRA in the event of termination "without cause" or if I left for "good reason." It was largely the same terms I had negotiated with Lance upon my return. I wouldn't have come back without it. It's sad to acknowledge that no corporation in America is loyal to their employees. Oh, they all say they are, but earnings trump people in just about all cases. Add in changing leaders who always want to bring in their own people, activist investors, private equity LBOs, and the like, and the only hope you have as an executive is to negotiate how they treat you when they let you go. I learned the hard way, particularly after my first tour of duty—ask at the point of hiring and get it in writing.

"Oh, one other thing, Nick," Gerald added after shaking hands on the promotion and handing me the new contract. "We're going to be moving on from Jack as CFO. I'm bringing in someone who's much more up to the task. I think you'll enjoy getting to know him. A West Point graduate, he was most recently interim CEO for a large restaurant group. His name is Jeff Claggart. He invested in a microbrew with some buddies of his in Idaho. Creative guy."

Nice of you to let me meet him in advance. I thought you said "goes without saying" when I thanked you for giving me the chance to talk to Dale? Where I come from, that implies it would be routine, that you would extend that courtesy repeatedly. Must not have liked what I said to Dale. And, a microbrew? Who gives a shit? Are you just trying to be down with my inner dilettante? He's a CFO. They all hate marketing guys.

I returned to my desk and looked up this Claggart character on LinkedIn. A finance guy through and through. His picture made him out to look like a nice enough guy. A super fit all-American war hero type. We had one mutual connection—the current CFO at Guitar Mart—Andy Raven. We overlapped my last year there. Turns out Jeff worked for Andy at a mall retailer, and when Andy took the job as CFO at Guitar Mart, Jeff became CFO at Andy's former company.

Initially, when Andy came to Guitar Mart, he had the makings of a prick. But, he was disciplined and balanced. Definitely never met a nickel he didn't like saving, but would at least embrace risk for good ideas. And, we left on good terms. Bridge burning is bad business. I ping Andy on LinkedIn's messenger function.

> "Hey Andy. Long time no talk. Confidentially, it looks like we're hiring a former colleague of yours as CFO at PwnShop. Jeff Claggart. Good guy?"

A few hours later I get a notification on my phone that Andy has responded. I swipe the screen open to read the following:

"Yeah. Taught him everything he knows. He's tough. Ask him what his nickname was at West Point. It'll tell you everything."

"Will do."

I think about double-clicking on "He's tough," but think better of it. Andy's a busy guy and what the hell difference is it going to make? Sounds like the guy is hired. At least I'll have some common ground when we meet.

Today, Gerald's new direct reports are meeting together for the first time. I walk into his office. Seated at the head of Gerald's conference table, his chair pivoted to face Gerald's desk, is a lean slab of a man. A man who believes that prematurely pulling back from the dinner table is the purest of virtues. The type of guy that wants you to know he could hold his own in a tussle. But to me he looks like Joe Piscopo during his juiced phase. Or one of those older guys in a Cenegenics ad. Ridiculous lean muscle mass. He's wearing a white tattersall pinpoint Oxford with a spread collar—so tight that the tank top straps of his Stanley Kowalski tee appear embossed into the over shirt, navy blue five pocket pants with a brown leather belt, and, curiously, expensive trainers—polished dark brown leather running shoe looking things. Probably made by To Boot New York or Magnanni. The kind of shoes that try to say, "I'm down with sneaker culture even though I'm an old white guy who's desperately in need of hip replacement surgery from squatting weights heavier than your average small car."

He rises with valor, holding sway. His sleek fuselage consumes a refrigerator's worth of air space. He turns to me, pausing to look me in the eye and ensure I catch the power emanating from his unceremonious glacier blue eyes, narrowed by years of squinting, with hints of freckles strewn about. He then extends his hand, announcing, "Jeff Claggart."

No "pleased to meet you" or "I've heard a lot about you, Nick," just an upturn at the right corner of his lip. Military training has a lot to say in the nature vs. nurture argument. Training codified his martial instincts. And they still persist even though he left the service over twenty-five years ago.

I smile, extend my hand to shake. I have trouble getting my hand positioned in his, and he makes it known by squeezing the blood out of mine.

"Nick Haller. Chief marketing, er, uh, chief customer officer now, I guess. Very nice to meet you."

He pivots with precision and pulls the chair back under him. I sidestep shuffle around his DMZ perimeter.

At the back corner of the table, a tall middle-aged man is in the process of standing. Balding, with spiky wisps of sawdust hair neatly trimmed over his ears and wrapping around the back shadow of his skull, he extends his hand. Since his hand doesn't have the same amount of flesh as Jeff's, I'm able to get mine situated properly and we share a mutually firm shake. His eyes are larger, but still the usual blue. He must be 6'4". *Geez Gerald, got a thing for the big men, dontcha?* His dark indigo 7 for All Mankind jeans have at least a 36-inch inseam, with a slight boot cut flare that covers a pair of black bit loafers. Not Gucci or Ferragamo or anything pretentious like that, but also not Cole Haan or Johnston & Murphy or anything ubiquitous. More pedestrian with a nod to comfort. Based on the horsebit that looks like a bad tie clip, they're probably Florsheim or French Shriner. *Why is it that peas from the lifelong corporate pod have such a hard time with business casual?*

"Nick! Nice to put a face with a voice."

"Great to meet you in person, Dale." I sit beside him, facing Gerald's desk.

"All right," Gerald says, rising and taking a seat across the conference table from me and Dale, with Jeff on his left. "Seems like everybody has met. And, I'm sure you've all read up on each other. No need in prolonging introductions. We have a lot to do and not much time to do it. First off, Nick, I know you, Lance and Jack were talking to Austin Consulting Group about cost cutting. I've met with the lead partner and like his plan."

"Yes, I think they'll be good. But we need a strategy before deciding which costs to cut," I interject.

Gerald retorts, "We're the biggest retailer in the video game business. We need a bigger digital footprint. That's strategy enough. Rationalization of our operating costs and getting SG&A in line with our revenue, those are the number one, two, three, four and five through ten priorities."

Jeff nods vigorously.

What? I thought Gerald agreed that a go forward strategy and innovation were top priority? For the love of Pete, don't just be a hatchet man!

"I've been studying the P&L and org charts, Gerald. It's absurd. Whoever was running this company was asleep at the wheel." Jeff tilts the right side of his head to his flexing right shoulder, continuing, "We're over-stored, over-staffed, and over-inventoried. Lots of work to do, but we can make significant headway in just a few months," he declaims.

"Totally agree," Dale adds.

"Good," Gerald says. "ACG and I have talked about creating a transformation office. I think a substantial portion of their fees need to be at risk—the bigger the reduction in SG&A, the more money they make."

"What about revenue/gross margin positive activities? Will those be part of this transformation office?" I enquire, brow furrowed.

"Of course. They're just much harder to prove. Our primary method needs to be a commission on every dollar saved. The more costs they cut, the more money they make."

"But if the fees are at risk, don't they have a perverse incentive to only cut costs? Why don't we start with a work for hire fee structure and decide on a go forward strategy? Then, within those confines, we can decide what to prune and what to invest in."

"Because their fees are ridiculously high, and I don't want the hit to earnings without the commensurate lift. Jeff, when we're finished here, I'll email you the contact info for the head guy at ACG. Do you mind working through the business arrangement and making sure they're not taking advantage of us?"

"Mind? It's what I live to do," Jeff bootlicks.

"Once that's settled, I think we use the transformation office to talk about organizational structure, which functions report up through each of you. I don't think the way we're functionally organized is correct, but I imagine there will be some debate. That's why we hire management consultants. Let's use ACG's impartiality to help with decision-making on that front."

"Makes sense," Dale adds.

Gerald pauses and pushes back from his desk. "Now, I need to fill you guys in on the activist[1] development. As you may have seen in the SEC filings, we've reached an agreement with Pestia and Hermit that avoids a costly proxy fight. The agreement requires us to add two independent directors, mutually agreeable to the board and the activists. I think we've landed on those candidates."

"Sorry to interrupt, but may I ask another potentially stupid question," I chime in.

"Of course," Gerald allows, with a hint of condescension in his voice.

"I'm not super experienced in investor relations, but didn't these guys only aggregate like 5 percent of the company? Why humor them? Do they have the money for a proxy battle, and would they have a snowball's chance of winning it?"

"Actually not a stupid question. Here's the problem. In reaching out to all of our long, institutional investors, almost all of them are renting their shares to the shorts. If your shares are rented to someone holding a short position, SEC rules disallow you to vote your shares in a proxy battle. We have very few investors other than employees and a few small

---

[1] Financial industry code for a corporate busy body, someone who invests in what they believe to be an undervalued business due to either the board or management or both being asleep at the wheel. They take a significant enough percentage of the company to threaten a proxy fight, basically calling a vote of common shareholders to decide on keeping the existing board or tossing them for a slate of directors recommended by the activist. Like most litigation, concessions and compromises are usually made to the activist before it reaches a vote, as proxy fights are expensive for both parties. Often, if the activist has a feasible chance to disrupt the structure, they get a board seat or two.

holders that could vote. We're pretty sure we'd lose the proxy. And, as I'm sure you're aware, our short interest is well over 100 percent."

"I'm aware. It's ridiculous. Super interesting that none of those guys can vote their shares. That's a little tidbit I bet most of the market has missed. And, then, wait, that level of short interest? Isn't that mathematically impossible. How can more than 100 percent of your shares be rented?" I scoff.

"Another good question," Gerald responds. "Not really sure."

"It's simple." Jeff chimes in, exasperated. "Borrowers of shares are free to lend their shares to more shorts. If 90 percent of our shares are shorted, and 50 percent of that 90 percent are relending their shares, we'd have 135 percent short interest. It's simple arithmetic."

"Well, it's positively un-American," I editorialize. "It's hard enough to turn around one of these companies. But to have a whole host of traders rooting for your demise, and seeding the news with negative press to bolster their trade, just seems unfair."

"It's the problem we're in. Naivete and silly conspiracy theories aside. Enough on the financial lesson. This will be my problem to deal with, not yours. Gerald, I'd like to hear more about your developments with the activists," Jeff swats.

Wow. This guy might be a real Dick, and not just a good-natured nickname.

"Thank you, Jeff," Gerald continues. "Here's the skinny. This actually gives us a chance to remake the complexion of the board. There are some folks that have been on the board well over a decade, long in the tooth and not equipped to help us work through the digital disruption. I think we've landed on two candidates—Suprit Shetty and Kate Sloan. Kate is an investment banking analyst, put up by Pestia. Suprit is a recommendation. Very entrepreneurial guy. Made his money in a web startup. Now works at a sports holding company. And Nick, you might find this interesting. The holdings include an *NBA 2K* esports team. So, very interesting experience as it relates to what you're working on."

"Interesting indeed. It'll be refreshing to get some new thinking and ideas on the board," I reply in my best eager business speak.

After a few more words exchanged around various workaday items, we adjourn. As we're gathering our things, Gerald says to Jeff and Dale, "I have reservations tonight at Perry's. You guys in for another dinner?" Then, as an afterthought, he adds, "Nick, you're welcome to join us geographical bachelors if you're available."

"I can't, unfortunately. I've got my son's strings recital."

As we're walking out, I nudge Jeff, saying, "I think we have a buddy in common—Andy Raven. He said he taught you everything you know."

"Hah. If only. I can swim circles around him. And I'd say that to his big face."

"I'm sure you would. Anyway, my dad was a naval officer too. I've always had tremendous guilt for not serving, Gen-X Beavis that I am. Thank you for your service."

"You're welcome. It was my duty."

"Andy told me to ask you what your West Point plebe nickname was?"

"Oh, *that* Andy." He tilts the right side of his head to his rising right shoulder again. Is this a nervous tic or a windup for a fight? This gesture has goon written all over it, as if his inner Luca Brasi is about to subdue me with his bare hands.

"'Taps' was my nickname." He winks in warning and walks away, his massive glutes staring back at me.

I text Andy. "He said his nickname was 'Taps'?"

He texts back almost instantaneously, "Tight Ass Pants ;)"

Grady Bledsoe, veteran VP of video game merchandising, enters my office. He's also the chief gossip officer who now finds himself reporting to Dale Spivey. A gay African American with previous stints at behemoths Blockbuster and Walmart, he's slurped a casserole's worth of straight white male dominated corporate crapellini. No wonder he's now a Cordon-Bleu-trained chef in the art of corporate polytricks. Grady's stocks in trade: globes of gossip from the grapevine, mad knife skills, and his signature finishing touch—a healthy smothering of thickly grated guilt. “I have the scars on my back to prove it” is a favorite exploitation.

“Did you read today’s *8K*,” he blurts while rubbing the tidy goatee on his chin.

“No, but I just met the two new EVPs. Why?” I enquire.

“Those guys are making $700K and each got $50K signing bonuses. I thought Gerald said we needed to cut costs, not inflate them?”

“Never mind the bollocks.”

“No, it’s the truth,” he retorts. “And I saw what they’re now paying you. The new guys are worth $150K more than you?”

“Well, if I hadn’t gotten the raise, it would have been a $350K gap. I guess Gerald didn’t want me to get pissed off that I was at the same level making almost 50 percent less than the new mercenaries. Gotta love public filings. Gotta hate being promoted from within,” I submit.

Somewhere between Vineland and Frisco, TX
June 12, 2019
595 days to POSS
CSP: $5.52

“Welcome to the Texas wine country. Be-you-tee-ful, ain’t it?” I emote.

In the passenger seat of my SUV is Suprit Shetty, one of the two new board members Gerald mentioned we’d be onboarding a few weeks ago. Not short per se, but less than average in height, with an oxymoronically well-groomed salt-and-pepper four-day beard growth thingy beneath his jet black, slick-backed hair.His jacket is a little too big across the shoulders. In the back is Kate Sloan. About the same height as Suprit, she wears a sensible suit and blue leather pumps, looking a bit like she’s dressed for a campus interview, even though she’s about twenty years older than the typical coed. I’m driving them to the Star in Frisco to see the fruit of our new sponsorship with Complexity Gaming, a professional esports training center for which we have naming, usage and content creation rights—The PwnShop Performance Center.

"So, Nick, tell me everything I need to know. How did we get into this mess, what are the key considerations, and what's your perspective on how we get out of it? I hear you've done some thinking on a potential plan," Suprit goads.

"Really? You're asking me that open-ended of a question? You do know candor is my greatest strength and my tragic weakness?"

"So I've heard. But yes, I want all the gory details."

Is this a trap? Enough rope to hang myself? Probably. Fuck it.

"If you really want to know the whole story, do you mind if we start back when I was hired for my first tour of duty in 2014?"

Firmly setting the hook in my waggling jaw, he says, "Be my guest."

I proceed to take him through the vision summoned by my first trip to E3, Claude Prendas's brain cancer diagnosis, Joe Engels' and Stephen Gossamer's diversification diversion, my departure, Claude's death, the board's crack 360 degree review of the executive team, Joe and Stephen's firing, Harvey Handler's anointment, Handler's call to me, Handler's "resignation," my rehiring, Lance's endorsement of my store transformation plan, Lance's desire for a location-based entertainment concept and his hiring of Eli Geller, the young guy from Topgolf, my boardroom meltdown, Lance's recalcitrance on not moving and not having any pay at risk, my initial fears about Gerald, my change of opinion and hope for the future, and the current state of the Oklahoma City project. Whew. All in the amount of time it takes to drive from Vineland to Frisco.

It wasn't a state of flow, but it flowed in a spew of cathartic consciousness. As I turned on my blinker to exit the Dallas North Tollway with Jerry Jones's Dallas Cowboys Star complex—the mixed use development laid out around the Cowboys' headquarters, the cultural hub of Football with a capitalism F—shining to the west like a chrome and glass St. Peter's Square, the Indian American Hindu on my right says, "You realize you spoke that entire ride and didn't ask me or Kate a single question."

"I thought that's what you wanted—everything you needed to know?" I ask defensively.

"I just thought you'd have the sense to take a breath."

The Cowboys Club at The Star

"Gerald, that PwnShop Performance Center is super cool. I'd like to talk to the designer. We're working through building a similar center for our *NBA 2K* team in Milwaukee."

The five us are seated for an early dinner at three two tops pushed together in front of a banquette. Gerald is in the middle of the three low backed leather chairs. Flanking him are the two new board members, Suprit to Gerald's right and Kate to Gerald's left.

"Don't ask me, Suprit. Ask Nick. He and his team put the whole thing together long before my arrival."

The guy hasn't said a word to me since my SUV soliloquy. In my paranoid mind, it's clear I've already been judged and sentenced.

"Sure thing, Suprit. Happy to put you in touch with the guys at Complexity. Since they don't have an *NBA 2K* team, I'm sure they'd be happy to exchange ideas. I'll get your email from Gerald and broker an intro."

"Please do," he commands.

Through our salads, we exchange small talk. Most of it is Suprit chest beating about his exploits in the world of internet startups and professional sports, both e and e-less. Whether Kate has anything to offer is unclear, as she can barely get a word in.

After the entrées arrive, Suprit says, "Nick, I hear you guys decided to hire Ciao World for your loyalty redesign. Why didn't you choose B Session? They're the better vendor."

"Well, most of the search happened before my arrival. Kevin, the director in charge of loyalty, performed a very thorough search process.

I reviewed his thinking, both on price and capability, and decided he had done solid, detailed work. I let him make the decision."

"You let a kid make a decision like that on PwnShop's crown jewel?"

"Like I said, I reviewed his process, realized we'll be okay with any of the three finalists, and since he's a smart thirty-six-year-old *kid*," (I stab air quotes to point out Suprit's potential ageism), "I want him to stay motivated and accountable for his work. Yes, I *let*," (more air quotes) "him make the decision."

Thinking I've whacked the mole, Suprit won't let it go.

"Well, it's the wrong decision. I'd suggest you take another look and fix the error of your ways."

I look to the corporate secretary on my left and then across to Gerald for air cover. Both are chewing intently, engrossed in the heightening drama, waiting to see how the plot unfolds. Once again, I can't help myself.

"Mr. Shetty, is this your first public board?" I spur his flanks.

"Of course not. What a disrespectful question."

"I don't mean to be disrespectful, sir. But I also sit on a public board. My rule of thumb has always been 'nose in, fingers out.' It's management's job to make decisions to run the company. The board helps set strategy and makes sure the right management team is in place. The board can question the process, but it's bad pool if the board starts making ordinary management decisions. You can't remain independent."

"I so appreciate your lesson in governance. All I'm saying is this clearly is a topic about which I know much more than you. Management would be well served to listen to the wisdom of its board members."

"I appreciate that. I think I have. But when the board, in all its wisdom, wants to micromanage, I think I owe it to the board to let them know when they're treading into nonindependent territory." I look to Gerald again for an intervention. Nothing. In for a penny, in for a pound, I dive deeper, "Anyway, you may not be aware that I served for three years as the SVP of strategy for Brierley+Partners, one of the leading loyalty design firms in its day, working on programs like United MileagePlus,

Hilton Honors, Hertz #1 Club Gold, the My Sony program and the Sony Credit Card, Vail Resorts Epic Pass and Blockbuster Rewards, among many others."

"Well, clearly you didn't help Blockbuster."

"I left well before Netflix was even a figment of a notion." I can't believe I'm defending myself. "Regardless, if I'm making a grave error, I'd like to know why."

"Look, I'm an investor in B Session, and I…"

"Whoa, sir. Stop right there. That's an interesting tidbit, innit? You're an investor? You could make money if we announce a big contract with them? Conflict of interest much? Have you disclosed this? Van?"

Finally, Van, the corporate secretary, jumps in, "Nick, technically, he's not yet a board member. Suprit, before we continue on this topic, I'd suggest you and Kate go through the orientation material and disclosure requirements for new board members."

Intermezzo Secondo

"I really had rambling on my mind. I wanted to go.
One of the prettiest sights in the world was a big Cadillac rolling
down the road with a big doghouse bass tied to the top of it.
That looked like the car I wanted to be in."

—LEVON HELM

Charlottesville, VA
April 10, 1988

All this happened, more or less. The melodramatic parts, anyway, were pretty much true.

"Hey mom. It's Nick"

"So good to heuh yo voice, sun. How ah thangs?"

"Things are good. But I'm on the dorm phone, so I don't have a lot of time. Kinda need to talk to dad. Is he there?"

"Lemme git him. I luv you," she said, a tug of sadness in her voice.

"Love you too, Mom." Somehow I always felt guilty when I asked to talk to Dad over her.

I heard the obligatory shuffling and Mom's muffled shout, "Stone! Nick says he needs to tawk to you." Stone is short for Stonewall, which is the root note in the preposterously maudlin triad, Stonewall Jackson Haller. Then I faintly heard her whisper to him, "Hurry up. He's on the do-uhm phone and doesn't have a lot of tie-uhm."

More receiver shuffling.

"Hey sonny boy," Dad answered, catching his breath. "Whatcha been up to?"

"Ya know, college."

"Heh, heh, heh," he chuckled. "Ah'll bet. Dese ah yo salad days. Enjoy it. It goes fast."

"Not to worry. Not to worry."

"What can I hep ya with, sun?"

"Uhm, well, y'know how I applied to the architecture school when I applied to UVA, and then changed my mind when I worked for Shepherd & Associates the summer before college?"

"Yep, I remembuh."

Dad grew up in the small depression era textile town, Danville, Virginia. While Mom's accent has a certain aristocratic lilt, presumably from Tidewater Virginia being the crucible of the English monarchy's manifest destiny (or so it's been drilled into my head, because after all, Jamestown was founded thirteen years before Plymouth), Dad's is a bit less refined. Importantly, his best friend in his elementary years was the son of the sharecropper that managed the family tobacco farm. Dad's drawl, inflection, and idioms, much to my genteel grandmother's chagrin, my educated mother's annoyance, and my brothers' and friends' amusement, sprout from fields irrigated with a decidedly African American watershed. Only in the South can a white man carry the name Stonewall Jackson Haller, talk like a black man, and be universally and rightfully beloved by blacks and whites as a fine man. Everywhere else, he's written off immediately as either a Klansman, a Kaveman, or a Karikature.

"And you know how I told you when I started school I was going to do business or economics, and, for the last two years, have been taking all the prerequisites like Statistics, Accounting, Micro and Macro?"

"Yes son. Sumpin tells me this ain't goin' anywha-uh gud."

"Aw c'mon dad. It just depends on how you view it."

"Well, the way I view it is I'm payin' fo yo education."

Fuck. Always the guilt trip. Yes, I was a spoiled privileged pissant.

"Yessir. And I can't tell you how much I appreciate that. But you know how you also taught me to appreciate music?"

"Uh huh," he drawled, dripping with misgiving. "You betta be goin someway-uh bettah than South widdis."

"I am. Don't worry. So, when I got into the architecture school, part of the curriculum was a class called Introduction to the Arts. That was the one class I kept from that path. It was taught by the heads of the Studio Art, Drama and Music departments."

"Get to da pint, sun."

"Well, dad, the guy who's the head of the music department is a genius composer named Walter Ross. You'd love him and his quirky, sometimes dark, sense of humor. Like, uh, he knows how every composer and most famous authors died. For instance, did you know that Tennessee Williams choked on the cap to his nasal spray bottle? They think he put the cap in his mouth for whatever reason, and then tilted his head back to get the spray down his nostrils. The cap slipped down his throat and choked him."

"Well, dat's no way to go. Can't say dat I knew dat, sun."

"I looked it up because I thought Dr. Ross had made it up. It's fact. The guy is for real. He's nerdy, but smart as a whip. And strange in a good way. Like, uh, he named his dog Peeve. Get it? His pet Peeve?"

"Heh, heh, heh. Dat's purdy gud. Sounds a bit queeah, but funny."

"Yeah, he's a super smart old guy. And no, he's not queer. He's married with kids."

"I didn't say he was left-handed. I said he was queeah. Funny. Quirky."

"Right. Anyway, he's become a bit of a mentor for me. Has gotten me hooked on *New York Times* crossword puzzles."

"Yo mutha would luv dat."

"Well, anyway, Dad, he says I have a good ear. I took his advanced music theory class, a prerequisite for music composition majors, and got an A. I'm really thinking I want to pursue music instead of business. I didn't realize there was so much math in music. It's fascinating. The physics of harmonics, the algebra of intervals, the geometry of scales and patterns. But along with all that logic, it's also very creative and nonlinear. It's like architecture, but for the ears instead of the eyes. I just want you to know I think I'm going to declare music as my major instead of economics or applying to the comm, uh commerce, uh, you know, undergraduate business school," my voice trailing into a mumble at the end of the soliloquy. Then I added tentatively, "Whaddya think?"

"Well well, sun." He cleared his throat. "He-uh's whut Ah think. Ah think you ain't goin' to have a pot to piss in if you declare a music majuh."

"Yeah, I know. I guess that's a risk. But I think I've found my passion."

"Sun, you have a passion 'bout ev'ry t'ree weeks. You been drawin' since befo you cud tawk. You bilt some int'restin' thangs in science classes. You played piano as a boy, and den bass guitar in that devil worshippin' rock 'n' roll combo in middle school. Let's see. You drew cartoons for the school newspapuh, you was photographuh and illustratuh fo da ye-uhbook. You played tennis and den quit. Wrassled and den got injured. I still think you enjoy watuh skiin'. You just need to decide on sumpin and go be it."

"Yes sir. You're right. But that's what I'm telling you. I think music is my calling."

"Look sun. I luv you mo than anything in the whole wide world, 'cept fo equal luv fo yo mutha and yo older bruthas."

I interrupt, "Dad, I'm not my brothers. I'm the youngest. I can't help it that I want different things than they do."

"Dat ain't at all whut Ah'm sayin'. Lemme finish. I'm just sayin' Ah luv dem as much as you. Ah don't give a rat's ass if you want to shovel shit fo a livin'. Ah'm just sayin' you yo' own damn fault. And you just need to decide what to be and go be it. And you need to live wit' da consequences of yo' decision. You'll be sleepin' in da bed you make."

"I know. I guess I'm saying I have decided."

"Well gud, den. Look, Ah thank it's wundahfuhl dat you sowin' yo wild oats. Ah rilly do. Awl Ah'm sayin' is, you been sucklin' on the fammuhly tit yo' whole life. No mattuh what you do, you need to know dat the fammuhly tit runs dry the day you graduate."

"Dad, I must say, they broke the mold. I got it. Thank you for the opportunity." I hung up the phone. Chuckled a sobbing snort reflecting on the conversation. Then, I declared a music major. And wondered, *What in the hell am I going to do when the family tit runs dry?*

Track 5: Give It Away

"I'll play it first and tell you what it is later."

—MILES DAVIS

PwnShop Offices
Vineland, TX
July 15, 2019
569 days to POSS
CSP: $6.44

Strategies, at a distance, have every company's wish on board. For a rare few, they get implemented. For others they sail forever on the horizon, never mooring until the strategist turns his eyes away in submissive defeat, his conceptions mocked to death by myopic operators and niggardly bean counters.

"I still don't get it. Tell me about Oklahoma City again," Jeff , CFO, prods, from the chair at the end of the conference table in the "Bored" Room.

"Let me try it this way," I grasp. "Do you agree we have a massive traffic problem? Fewer and fewer customers are coming through our doors."

"I don't. Every bricks and mortar retailer has the same problem. We may have fewer store visits, but our web traffic is growing and I bet our conversion rate at the store is growing."

"Sadly, we don't have traffic counters in the stores. Nobody ever thought it was worth the investment. So, technically, we don't know for sure, but we do know about transactions. They're down each year double digits. I think it's a fair assumption the decline is coming from fewer door turns. And as you stated, mathematically, if the conversion rate is higher, then traffic is dropping at a rate faster than the drop in transactions. Agreed?"

"No. Assumptions. You said it yourself," Jeff asserts forcefully.

"Okay, can we just for the sake of argument assume I'm right?" I plead.

"No. I'm not sure. We have to be precise. We have to know what the problem is."

"Okay, then are we willing to invest in traffic counters? The problem there is we won't know trend data for a year, until we lap the same seasonality and can compare traffic year over year."

"I think you answered your own question. We don't have time. We need to act now."

"Jesus. I'm trying to act now. You're acting like the innovation prevention committee. Uhm...how about this? You said yourself every bricks and mortar retailer is experiencing traffic declines, yes?"

"That's not what I said."

"Throw me a bone, man."

"I'm looking at a business that is completely digitally disrupted, whose margins are being compressed, and the only positive number I see is web traffic. I need to know why it's even remotely a good idea to invest in these stores."

"Because that's where the magic happens. It's our only point of difference. Our locations are hangouts. Our store associates are gaming gurus. They're the Sherpa that gets the average gamer to level up in whatever game they're climbing."

"Sherpas? What the hell does that have to do with anything."

"It's a metaphor. Our store associates are helpers. Enablers. Assistants. Samwise Gamgees. They help Frodo on his quest."

"Enough with the metaphors. Particularly fantasy metaphors. They're not helpful."

My eyes roll to the ceiling. I look around the table to Gerald and Dale, neither of whom want to offer any bailouts or olive branches.

"Regardless, we're half pregnant on Oklahoma City," I continue. "Gerald greenlit the project before you got here. We're into construction docs, we've ordered the gaming equipment, and we've got our first prototype of the gaming distribution software. The board is on board."

"Is there a budget? A pro forma? What's the return on investment?"

"We have that, and I'm happy to share it with you. But frankly, we won't really know until we try it, live in it, and course correct it. I can give you a piece of paper that's rife with assumptions, that...uh...clearly... uh, based on this conversation, you'll happily just shit all over. Or, you can give me a modicum of latitude to at least explain what we're trying to accomplish."

"That's not how this works. I don't ratify any investment unless it has an ironclad business case."

"I can't give you an ironclad business case unless you take the risk of building a prototype and putting it in market. We don't know what it's going to do until we do it. It's a catch-22. I'd love to Babe Ruth it and call it a home run, but it's not a home run unless we swing the bat, connect with the ball, and hit it out of the park. Sorry, I'm not a bullshitter. I'm not one of those guys that will hand you a sheet of paper and guarantee it will come true like a used car salesman. I can tell you what I think it will do, but we need to hold hands on the risk."

"You should at least be able to predict the metrics, the KPIs that you expect to drive."

"I think if you were listening, that's where I started. We have one and only one metric that matters. And it starts with T and it ends with C, it rhymes with graphic, and it doesn't stand for the nervous TIC I'm going to develop if we can't get through this conversation."

"Look, I have a call with the activists. I've been sitting here for twenty minutes and I still have no idea what you're trying to accomplish in Oklahoma City."

"That's because I can't even get a sentence out without you henpecking the syntax."

"I don't have time for this. OKC is on hold until I fully understand it and give it my approval. IF I give it my approval." He swats his iPad closed, places the Apple pencil on its magnetic perch, and ceremoniously parades out of the conference room.

I look at Gerald and Dale. "Is it just me? Doesn't it feel like the guy is just stonewalling me on purpose? I mean, aren't we all trying to achieve the same goal—transform this beast?"

"He has a lot on his plate," Gerald lectures. "I think he's asking the appropriate questions. His role is to make sure we're allocating capital in the right places. It's your job to convince him that OKC is worth our time and money."

"But you already approved it. Does this mean it's on hold until I have him on board? We don't have time for this level of bureaucracy. We have to get it in market before the holidays, otherwise we're waiting a whole year until we have the appropriate sales data to understand if it's working. The whole thing is a rounding error regardless."

"Just communicate the plan with him. We'll make this one of the projects as part of the transformation office, and we'll monitor its progress accordingly. Part of it depends on how much savings we can add to the P&L from cost cutting activities."

PwnShop Corporate Offices
Vineland, TX
July 17, 2019

ACG, the Austin Consulting Group, has shown up in all their glory. It is a cast of well-bred minions, male and female, representing a much too perfect cross section of diversity, as if their diversity, equity, and inclusion initiative was spit out from an algorithm housed on each of their souped-up PCs, as no legitimate quant would ever carry an Apple. Oddly, there's not much diversity in their age, education or attire. But on race and gender terms, they look like an '80s Benneton ad. And, their given names are perfectly curated by parents who can't fathom their child to be anything but completely special. Their age—late twenty-something to early thirty-something. MBAs from Harvard, Stanford, Wharton, or Kellogg. The collected, combined wisdom of this crowd's experience can't be more than fifteen years, less than any of the single executives sitting at the table. Not one of them has ever worked in a company that sells to the general public. They cloak their taut frames, chiseled from their ninety-minute cardio back at the Four Seasons, with a crisp pinpoint oxford or blouse enwrapped in a forest green fleece vest emblazoned with the ACG logo on the panel opposite the Patagonia logo. In July. In Texas. They say the air conditioning chills them. Now Asher, now Addison, now Nobu and Nixon. On Muhammad, on Yasmine, on Pablo and Tristan. We have earth to scorch and projects to maul. Now slash away, slash away, slash away all!

"Okay, it looks like we're all here. Let's get started," says Tristan, the junior partner from ACG who's on point for today's kickoff meeting. I awake from my daydream.

We sit through a thirty-minute PowerPoint that describes the engagement, "PwnShop Reboot," that will be run by the newly created Transformation Office. Gerald penned the inelegant handle, PwnShop Reboot. He asked me, surprisingly, for suggestions for the name a week ago. For some reason that I can't remember, the initiative had to start with the letter R. I tossed out Renaissance, Rebirth and Rising. All three were dismissed. The first because it was "too hard to spell," the second because its overtones were too religious, and the third reserved potentially for the next phase. Not being able to keep my trap shut, I did offer that Reboot sounds like a Hail Mary—what one does when they've lost all hope recovering a document because the computer has frozen up and you don't know what else to do. Gerald defended it as being well within videogame culture.

The Transformation Office, or TO, its immediate corporate jargon reductionist acronym...*Time Out? Terrell Owens? Why do companies obfuscate understanding with mindless abbreviations?*...will manage ten separate workstreams, each with a designated executive sponsor. Chief merchant Dale gets "Gross Margin Enhancements" and "Category Expansion," neither of which has anything to do with erectile dysfunction. Casey Fosbury is in charge of "Store Dedensification." I get "Loyalty Optimization" and "Innovation," which is mainly The Oklahoma City innovation project. The head of supply chain gets "Procurement Efficiencies" and the head of HR, Naomi Koller, gets "Organizational Optimization." Translation—slash away all.

The meeting is a pile on session—a bunch of sycophants trying to keep their jobs, offering up every major amputation their fallow minds can muster. ACG creates a fundraising thermometer tote board in the form of a PowerPoint slide. The goal—$200 million. Gerald, ACG, and mainly Jeff, go around the table shaking the can in front of each executive, a popularity contest for who steps up with the biggest donation to the cause, and an intimidation session for any weak-minded individual that doesn't conform. The brownnosing corporate survivors step in line. And, in a gallant display of psychokinesis, it's clear their trained minds have convinced their olfactory nerves that ACG's, Gerald's, and Jeff's shit simply doesn't stink. I'm turning as green as an ACG fleece vest.

Finally, the can rattling comes to me. The loyalty conversation is straightforward. The team and I have a test in market that conservative estimates show could deliver at least $15 million in gross margin improvements. The details are mind-numbing, but the facts are solid. Jeff does question the pre/post, test vs. control scientific lift methodology that's showing these improvements. He takes me to school on how he would run the test, but in a rare moment of acquiescence, allows the methodology to sit for now. Tristan's keeper of the tote board, Addison, is controlling the laptop displayed on the big screen. I see her enter "$15M+" into the slide titled "PwnShop Reboot Gross Margin Improvement Goals" in the row with the header "Loyalty Optimization."

Incidentally, $15 million is five times more than any other number that's been entered. I'll take revenue growth over cost cutting any day of the week.

In contrast, the innovation workstream conversation is about as pleasant as lancing a boil. Knowing it would be, I've come prepared with two visual aids that I pass around the table. The first describes the strategy, positioning, and customer experience goals for the Social Hub of Gaming (a.k.a. OKC).

The second, which looks a bit like a Fibonacci spiral, shows what we've called the Value Creation Engine.

The ACG kids are enthralled with my description and think the plan makes great strategic sense. The more they kiss my ass, the more the slight frown on Jeff's face deteriorates into a scowl.

"None of this makes any sense," Jeff fires. "This is all a bunch of ethereal fluff. This is and has been my problem with Oklahoma City all along. It's a wild goose chase. There's nary a KPI to be found in your presentation. This isn't a strategy. It's just bullshit slides. Again, I ask you, what is the quantum of the investment and what is the expected return on that quantum? We will make no investments without a thorough ROIC pro forma."

Quantum? This ain't physics nor are we speaking Latin in Ancient Rome.

"I presume by quantum you just mean the amount of the investment? It's about $3 million all-in to overhaul the twelve stores to our specs, so roughly $250 grand per store. But..."

"Do you know what our average store does in revenue?" Jeff interrupts. "If you did, you'd know how harebrained this scheme is."

"If you'd let me finish, I was going there. This is the cost of innovation. This isn't the rollout cost. Our average store does about $1.3 million in sales annually."

"And do tell, what's the operating margin of an average store?"

"About 6 percent. So roughly $80K. Let's assume we get a 50 percent increase in operating income. That's a six-year payback. And that's on the innovation budget of $250K per store. With scale economies, value engineering, and sponsorship/partnership, I think we can easily get that remodel cost down to about $100K per store."

"Fantasy land. $250 grand per store is a capital investment of $1 billion if we keep 4000 stores domestically. And no way in hell you're going to get a 50 percent improvement in income."

"Let me take the second point first. Our store traffic is dropping double digits every year. The income improvement should be measured against the declining trend line, not in absolute terms. The iceberg is melting at an increasing rate. So, you need to think of it like a 35 percent improvement in today's income, if it's dropping 15 percent per year. And, on the first point, if you were listening, it's not $250 grand per store, it's going to be $100K per store or less. That's $400 million, and based on the way the store dedensification project is going, less than that. Sounds like we'll downsize to a fleet of 2500 to 3000 stores, which puts it between $250 and $300 million. Instead, we're doing a share buyback, which, if I were an analyst, says we have no notion for the way forward, but instead we're going to spend our precious cash on buying an equity that has no story. And if I read that press release right, we're reserving the capacity to buy back up to 300 million worth of shares. Sounds like we have the money to invest, just not in anything but a reduction in the denominator of our EPS."[1]

"That plan will improve share price. Spurious store investments in a leaky business model is just throwing money out the window. No way we're ever investing that much in our stores."

"What if it works? I'm not asking for $300 million now. I'm asking for one measly percent of that to validate our hypothesis. The only

[1] Earnings Per Share is a standard investment metric to help understand the value of a company. Instead of improving EPS by growing earnings, share buybacks reduce the number of shares outstanding, and thereby can increase EPS without improving earnings. Simple example: Let's say a lemonade stand makes $1200 a year and four kids each own an equal share of 25 percent. Earnings per share would be $300. ($1200/4 = $300). If next year, the stand earns $1600, EPS would improve to $400 ($1600/4 = $400). But what if three kids buy out the fourth kid? And next year's earnings don't improve but remain flat at $1200? But EPS? It grows by $100 per share, since we're now dividing by a smaller denominator since there are now only three shareholders. ($1200/3 = $400). Share buybacks improve EPS by reducing the number of shares outstanding. Arithmetic as artifice.

capital we're risking is $2.5 to $3 million. If nothing else, there's option value on those learnings. Don't you agree?"

"Optionality is zero. It's a waste of time. Makes no financial sense."

"It has the potential to make plenty of financial sense. It's not just retail product sales. There are at least three potential new revenue sources: (1) Improved conversion rate on product sales because of try-before-you-buy. (2) Fees for hourly gameplay, league subscriptions, table top gaming nights, clinics, classes, birthday parties, and more, all at gross margins astronomically higher than retail sales, as the marginal cost of sales of these items are negligible, and (3) Media sales. Our stores become captive audiences for our vendors and any other advertiser that wants to reach the gamer (think energy drinks and snacks), with rich, digitally enabled, data-driven and measurable media and in-person activations."

"Not. Going. To. Happen." Spittle flees from Jeff's lips as he punctuates the Ps in happen. "Certainly not until I see a rock-solid business case with an ROIC that far exceeds our cost of capital."

"I sent you the pro forma last week. I got no response."

"That's because your assumptions are ludicrous."

"Do you remember the conversation we had not three days ago. I said I can send you the financials, and you'll simply challenge the assumptions. At the end of the day, we don't know whether it will work unless we put it in market. The only way off the beach is through those initial guns, a leap-of-faith investment. But only a moderate one. This is how innovation works. Risk first, reward later. Oh well. Okay. You all heard it here. Take it off the list. Not going to happen," I eyeroll like a petulant child who can't eat their cupcake before they finish their dinner. "Gerald, is this really what we're doing?"

"Let's take it offline," Gerald offers. "Emotions are running high. Leave it on the list for now, and we won't commit to any dollars. Regardless, we've spent too much time on this already. At this point, let's adjourn. Nick, Jeff, Dale, and Naomi, I need you to stay for an unrelated topic. Tristan, please stay as well."

While waiting for the others to gather their things and get out of the room and throughout the next part of the meeting, I unapologetically doodle a take on Edvard Munch's *The Scream*, only in my version, the guy's gouging an ice pick into his temple. Gerald gets up to close the conference room door as I'm perfecting blood spewing from Screamie's head.

"All right," Gerald begins. "Before we bring the larger group into the process for Naomi's organization optimization TO project, I think we need to land on a goal. We've already laid out the reductions at the stores. Most of the headcount cuts there will be part and parcel of the closures, but we're also talking about expanding the purview of our district managers. Most district managers manage six to eight stores. I'd like to eliminate 25 percent of them and move the rest up to ten to twelve stores each. But, I have you guys in here to start talking about the Support Center. As a starting point, amongst the corporate staff, I want a 20 percent headcount reduction and a 25 percent dollar reduction. We're too fat at the top, so we need to eliminate as many VPs and SVPs as we can."

"So will we be swinging our scythes at the same percentage across all the sheaves of wheat," I enquire, "or will some sheaves remain uncut, while others get scalped?"

Jeff facepalms, his muscly hand covering his gaunt face.

Gerald responds, after nodding in smirky recognition to Jeff, "Not sure I'm following fully, but I think you're asking if each of you needs to get 25 percent of cost out of each of your respective organizations. If that's what you're asking, my proclivity is yes, that's the simplest. But that's why we're all here. If you guys can agree that some portions of the organization need to maintain or grow, we'll need alignment on which other portions of the org pay for that."

"Mmm hmmmh. That's basically what I'm asking," I say. "And if that's the case, don't you think we need to align first on a go forward strategy so that it's then abundantly clear where we need investment and where we can deinvest?"

"We don't have time." Jeff can't help himself. "I've never seen an organization as bloated as this one. We can run much leaner in all areas. Hell, I'll bet we can subtract 50 percent and not even feel the difference."

"I agree," Dale says.

"Really? Dale, you think you can run your org with only half your buyers?"

"That remains to be seen, but I agree with Jeff that we're bloated."

"Oh, I agree with bloated," I say trying to get some level of consensus into the conversation. "Plus, at the exec ranks, we have a lot of folks still stuck in the old business model. But before we do any of that, shouldn't we get alignment on the way forward?"

"Asked and answered," Jeff upbraids me. "Do you not realize the Street is all over us to get our SG&A in line with our declining revenue? And did you not read Pestia and Hermit's nasty letter?"

"I'm aware of all of that," I retort. "I agree wholeheartedly we need to cut costs, but in a strategic way, not in an evenly spread peanut butter kind of way. We aren't going to save our way to growth. It never works. Are we trying to save the company or are we trying to ingratiate ourselves to a bunch of vainglorious activists?"

"Last I checked, those vainglorious activists are our shareholders. And don't you agree we exist to maximize shareholder value?"

"They're not shareholders. They're share flippers. Pump and dumpers. They're playing a trade. They don't give one shit about the long-term viability of this business. They probably have a standing limit order to sell the moment the share price doubles or triples their initial buy price. I'm sure they're thrilled with the buyback. I'm sorry, but getting a dead cat bounce because the Street rewards cost cutting is fool's gold. It does nothing to maximize real long-term shareholder value, much less our duties to our employees, our partnership with our suppliers and our service to our customers. In fact, if done willy-nilly, it could jeopardize us as a going concern.[2] We need a strategy."

"This is not an either/or. It's a both/and. That's why we're here," Gerald interrupts, shutting us down.

"I couldn't agree more," Dale chimes in. "We have to cut costs and plan for the future."

It's an "and" not an "or." Why don't we stick our heads six feet up a rhino's ass AND climb the watchtower. What a skull fuck. It's an "or." Make a goddam decision.

I suppress my vulgar thoughts. "I'm not saying we don't have to do both. I'm just saying it's a sequencing problem and a priority problem, in my lowly, and apparently lonely, opinion. Transforming should be more important than cost cutting. Cost cutting is a means to an end, a way to raise capital to transform. It's a shame we're getting ready to blow a chunk of that capital to buy back shares instead of spending time on a strategy. I'm just trying to get the discussion moving on what that end is, because it seems pretty terminal at the moment."

"You've beaten the horse to death. We're talking about org reduction. The way forward is another meeting at another time," Gerald admonishes.

The meeting lasts another twenty minutes. We discuss the timeline by which we need to come back to the TO with our headcount reductions and proof of at least a 25 percent expense reduction. By the end of the process, I've sacrificed all of my pawns, both bishops and a rook in the form of 25 percent staff and 30 percent cost reductions, but I've managed to keep my queen, Oklahoma City, as a laboratory, if not the way forward.

---

[2] Going concern is accounting jargon for a business that can meet its financial obligations. Auditors typically run tests to make sure a company has identifiable prospects to generate enough cash in any given period of time to pay its debts. Otherwise, it becomes insolvent. Instead of a going concern it becomes an expiring death rattle. That's not accounting jargon.

Intermezzo Terzo

"Sometimes you have to play a long time to be able to play like yourself."

—MILES DAVIS

Opryland Music Group
Nashville, TN
November 15, 1990

Whether I should turn out to be the captain of my own life, or whether I should surrender that decision to byzantanity, these pages must show.

I was wearing a boxy grey, Brooks Brothers suit with black Allen Edmonds cap toe oxfords badly in need of a polish. It occurred to me the last time I polished them was when I wore the same outfit to an interview with the recently created Andersen Consulting in the spring of my fourth year at UVA. This blandiose look landed me a job in Andersen's coveted systems engineering training program. Apparently, music composition majors made good systems engineers. I turned it down, along with three other sensible offers, two of them in the greater DC Metro area where my girlfriend Maura was working in private client services. Instead, I decided to move to Nashville to become a songwriter.

The "fammuhly teat" had run dry and I was living off bean burritos at Taco Hell. To pay the $300 a month to my college buddy for the room I was subletting in a slapped-up apartment complex on the Cumberland River, I was temping for Kelly Services, home of the "Kelly Girl."

In the waiting room, I steeled myself to meet Jerry Bradley at Opryland Music Group, the publishing company Gaylord Entertainment formed after its purchase of the seminal Nashville song publisher Acuff-Rose Music, whose copyrights include the entire Hank Williams catalog, as well as the oeuvres of the Everly Brothers, Lefty Frizzell and Roy Orbison.

Jerry Bradley, you might be curious to know, was the corpulent son of Owen Bradley, one of the pioneers of the "Nashville Sound," the commercial purification of our nation's white working class music, embalmed in the records he produced for Patsy Cline, Loretta Lynn and Conway Twitty. Jerry, through the bulletproof guild of nepotism, piloted the lucky sperm from his dad into the catbird's womb, the top spot at Opryland.

How I got a meeting with him is a lesson in preparation and opportunity. While getting paid eight dollars an hour for my temporary assignments, I moonlighted in an unpaid internship with Evelyn Reeves Management. Evelyn managed the wildly unsuccessful all-female country-with-a-bluegrass-slant quintet Bareback Flower. Though a low bar, Evelyn, who'd worked with some decidedly salty, but simple people, thought I was the smartest person with whom she'd ever worked.

After weeks converting her Red Chief Tablet accounting process into Lotus 1-2-3, she was astounded by how efficient computers could be at recordkeeping and exclaimed, "I never could have done this without you! You're so damn smart. I can't wait to see what you become." Since I was neither getting paid nor receiving equity for the groundbreaking transformation of her valueless operation, Evelyn paid me in favors. Not that kind, though it was more than a possibility that kind had played a role in her past. She was now a forty-something, beer-drinking, mom jeans–wearing tub of goo with a sweet face, who, in her prime, might have looked like an extra on *Smokey and the Bandit*. In one phone call she got me a meeting with Jerry Bradley.

Jerry's secretary let me into an office so ample it made his 270-pound rotund presence piffling. Gold and Platinum records adorned the walls.

After eyeing my barely pubescent, sensibly suited, 130-pound frame with a look that screamed, "No way in hell this guy's a songwriter," he invited me to sit on the black leather Eames couch flanked by two black belt leather Wassily chairs with tubular chrome. I guess design was within reach of rehabilitated rednecks.

The arrangement formed a U-shaped cul de sac. The inlet faced a low console supporting a sound system dominating the west wall of his office. A Macintosh amplifier sat at the helm. To the left was an Ampex quarter-inch reel-to-reel. To the right, a Nakamichi cassette deck atop a Nakamichi CD player. On either side, professional studio monitors. Black-stained wood. No grill cloths. Twelve-inch woofers. Three-and-a-half-inch horn tweeters. They rested on an inch of acoustic foam atop custom-made stands with four spikes at the foot of each to rise above the pile carpet.

"Evelyn sez you wanna be a songwriter," he belched.

"Uhm, yessir. I think so. I was a music composition major at the University of Virginia. I also took a poetry writing..."

"Hold it raht there, young fella. You think schooling qualifies you to be a good songwriter?"

"Well, I guess when you say it like that.... I'm just saying I have some training. I know I have lots to learn."

"I don't see ya brought along a guitar. Did ya bring a tape?"

"Yes sir. Right here."

I pulled a Maxell XL II sixty-minute cassette out of my outer suit jacket pocket with "Haller Song Samples" written on the label. Unable to attenuate my nerves, I handed it to him, shakily.

"I don't have access to a studio," I quivered. "These are simple guitar vocals that I recorded on my jam box. I'm not a very good guitar player, and I'm really not a very good singer. And the songs aren't...uh...well, you can be the judge of the songs, I guess. Do you think you can hear if it's a good song even if the performance and production are bad?"

"Son, do you really wanna be here?"

"Yessir, I think, I uh..."

"You ain't actin' like it," he interrupted, saving me from digging a deeper hole. "I ain't never been handed a tape with less confidence in my thirty years in dis bidness. And son, I wouldn't be in the position I'm in if I didn't have ears for a hit song. I've got golden ears."

Where the fuck did you get your confidence, you fat, falling up, fortunate son?

He slid the tape from its clear case, powered on the amplifier and the Nakamichi Dragon deck. He pressed eject. The armature whirred and the tape well opened. He slid my tape into the well, pressed another button, and the machine set the cassette into the tape transport. He pressed play and sat down on the chair to my left.

Silence. Then noise, wow and flutter. Then some shitty strumming of a guitar filled the room, followed by my shittier voice. Top-shelf sound system. Second-drawer sounds. The ironic contrast was as plain as my suit.

To his credit, Jerry took nine minutes and thirty-seven seconds out of his day to listen to all three songs in full. After some signal noise at the end, he looked up and said, "Is that it?"

I raised my shame-filled head and nodded.

"Son, I don't really know what to tell ya. Here's your tape. It was nice to meet ya."

"Thank you for your time," I said, extending my hand, as I unfolded myself from the uncomfortable couch and slunk out. I didn't have enough savvy or chutzpah to even ask for feedback, but he offered it anyway.

"Son, you're writin' filet mignon and we're lookin' for cheeseburgers."

Sony/Tree Music Publishing
Nashville, TN
January 1991

Bareback Flower never blossomed, and Evelyn realized there would never be a way for her to pay me. Good person that she was, she helped me land some project work with Booty Womar at Little Third Coast

Music, a boutique publishing company. Booty, like Evelyn, needed help computerizing some of his back office. He paid me $7.50 an hour plus free beers and industry stories to transfer all the pertinent information for each composition he managed—writer(s), performance rights agencies, copyrights, title, and more—from a painstakingly typed rolodex card catalog into a FileMaker relational database on his newly purchased Macs. He had about 800 songs, and it took me about three weeks to complete. Realizing how game-changing it was for him to have his data computerized, he, like Evelyn, felt he owed me a favor. He had heard from a fellow song-plugger at Sony/Tree Music publishing that they needed help transferring their massive library of quarter-inch demo reels to digital audio tape (DAT). Booty said he knew just the guy.

Acuff-Rose had Hank Williams. Sony/Tree had just about everybody else. It's authoritative. Tree International, as it was formerly known before being purchased by CBS (by then owned by Sony) in 1989, contains a treasure trove of the germs, sprouts and full-grown trees of American music. Its founder was Jack Stapp. He hired a guy named Buddy Killen to be a "song-plugger." Killen discovered a song called "Heartbreak Hotel," written by Tommy Durden and Mae Boren Axton. He convinced a man, whose Christian name rhymes with the pelvis he pivoted with ease, to record it. The rest is history. It was Elvis Presley's breakthrough hit on RCA Records and put Nashville on the map as a real songwriter's town for all forms of music, not just hayseed music. The Sony/Tree catalog included over 35,000 songs in 1991, and was *Billboard* magazine's leading publisher since 1973. Every time you hear a radio playing, or you stream or download "Heartbreak Hotel," "I Fall to Pieces," "Crazy," "King of the Road," or "He Stopped Loving Her Today," Sony collects a little toll. Hits were a helluva good business.

The entire Sony/Tree catalog was housed in the tape room—a mere chamber of some 400 square feet, with shelves lined floor to ceiling and spaced every eight inches with the seven-inch spines of some 10,000 reel to reel quarter-inch tapes containing the songwriter demos of every song in the catalog. Some tapes had one song, some as many as five or six. The tapes were all original "slaves," duplicates that were dubbed simultaneously with the mix down to the masters that existed in a vault offsite. During business hours, song pluggers—commissioned sales people who worked for the larger publishing companies to rep their company's songs—came to the Dutch doorway that separated this holy, yet workmanlike tape room from the rest of the offices. Song pluggers were up on all the Nashville recording sessions. If they learned from a producer friend that Garth Brooks was recording in three weeks, they'd search their personal memory banks of all of the songs written from their respective publishing catalog that might be a smash hit for Garth. They'd fill out a form to request the songs they wanted dubbed, and whether they wanted cassette or digital audio tapes (DATs), and the quantity of duplicates. The folks that worked in the tape room made these "dubs" or "dupes." It was one of the most mundane jobs in the music business, but, it was the motor oil of the engine that combusted a song into a hit.

Song pluggers carried these songs to the key decision-makers—producers, managers, label heads, artist & repertoire (A&R) personnel, the artist themselves, or even the artist's or producer's hair stylist or golf partner. If the right person fell in love with the song, the song may get recorded. And if it got recorded, it just might end up on the album—a "cut." The moment it was cut and sold, the publishing company got a piece of the mechanical royalties, the statutory micropayment they received every time an LP, cassette, or CD was sold to an end consumer. And some "cuts" might just become singles. Singles meant radio airplay. And radio airplay meant performance royalties. Smash hits meant massive royalties, many times for many years to come. But the odds of having a hit song as a rookie songwriter were basically one over one hundred factorial.

Interestingly, only the composer and their publishing company enjoyed performance royalties. Unless the artist was the writer or cowriter, they'd never see a penny from performance royalties. Same for the record label. Those parties only received royalties from direct sales, not indirect performances. The owners of the copyright—the composition's intellectual property—were the sole participants in performance royalties. The performance rights agencies that repped writers—ASCAP, BMI or SESAC—monitored radio airplay, bars, restaurants, and more, and created a formula based on that monitoring for how each rights holder was paid. Writers switched performance rights agencies like an impatient Walmart shopper switched checkout lanes. But when it was good, the tolls on a hit song were an almost infinite annuity stream. The elusive "mail money."

This was my first paying job in the music business. I was getting six dollars an hour to go into the very navel of Nashville's musical orchard, extract the seed from each wilting fruit, and freeze it forever in our frozen seed vault. Metaphorically speaking, of course. That seed vault was digital recording—the act of sampling a nuanced moment in time and converting it to a series of numbers so long the human ear can't really tell the difference, enabling storage on all kinds of media. My shift was from 3 PM to midnight, with an hour break for dinner. I was hopeful this would be the catapult position for my songwriting career, Jerry Bradley be damned.

The job was carefully extracting each piece of fruit-cum-reel from the branches-cum-shelves, weaving the tape through the heads on the TEAC X-1000R and onto the take up reel, fast forwarding through the song to find its peak signal on the VU meters, setting the Sony PCM-2700 rack mounted DAT record input switch to "analog," playing the peak part of the song and adjusting the input knob on the DAT deck to ensure the highest input level without clipping, rewind the reel tape to the beginning, and switch the machine to play and press record on the DAT machine. I was supposed to do this 35,000+ times, indexing each song on DATs that held four hours of music. Since we were converting analog to digital signals, each song had to play out in real time. Assuming the average song length was three minutes, thirty seconds, and the setup of each tape took five minutes, I'd be finished doing this in two years give or take.

"This is stupid," I proclaimed.

"What's stupid?" Mason, my twenty-three-year-old boss and aspiring song-plugger asked.

"Transferring these things to digital."

"It's fuckin' genius," he retorted. "Once you've converted this library to digital, we'll be able to dub off dupes at like 4X and 8X real time. Plus, I'm told we'll eventually be able to store these songs on fuckin' hard drives. As long as you don't fuck up and index these fuckers properly, eventually a song-plugger'll be able to call up whatever song and burn a CD straight from their own fuckin' computer."

"And then they won't need you."

"I'll be a song-plugger by then. But anyway, uh, soo that's why you think it's fuckin' stupid?" Mason mocked. "Because they're eliminating the need for a goddamn tape room?"

"No dipshit. That's progress. It's stupid from a business perspective. There's no generational loss on these things. The quality of pirated CDs will be as good as the original when dubbed from a DAT, unlike the muddy Chinese shit you buy at the flea market."

"Oh don't you worry your pretty little educated head about it. The RIAA[1] will make sure this shit is locked down as tight as a Catholic schoolgirl's pussy."

"Right. As if a Catholic schoolgirl has never lost her virginity. Hopefully the RIAA can do better than the DEA is doing with drugs. Demand for low-cost music will always outstrip the price controlled supply. It's why the government will never win the war on drugs. Until people quit wanting their fix, the black market will continue to feed the beast."

"That reminds me." Mason pulled out his vial of coke, dipped a little spoon into the powder that kept his half of the tape room humming, sniffed, snorted, wiped his nose and before screwing the cap on tight, tried again to bring me to the dark side. "Wanna bump?"

---

[1] The Recording Industry Association of America was the lobbying group in Washington, DC that represented the concerns of most of the participants in the record industry. Congress was notoriously slow to ensure legislation kept up with technology. The digitization of music presented all sorts of intellectual property compensation issues. The RIAA was attempting to get the laws to keep pace with the technology.

"Don't touch the stuff. I'm an Eagle Scout, remember?"

"Yeah. Pretty sure fuckin' Ted Bundy was a Boy Scout too. Doesn't mean shit. And, don't blame me when you fall asleep in here tonight and get fired."

"I won't. I'll blame shitty, corny music."

Just then, Greg, a song-plugger recently promoted from the tape room walked up to the Dutch doors. Behind him stood a bearded silver-haired gentleman in his fifties. In a darkly lit room, he might be mistaken for Kenny Rogers.

"Mason, Nick?" Greg greeted. "Do you know Tim DuBois?"

"Tim DuBois? Holy shit! So nice to see you again. I'm Mason. We met at the Shawn Camp showcase. Shawn and I are super good buddies. Do you think you'll sign him? Oh, and uh, congratulations on the Alan Jackson success. That guy's gonna be as big as Garth." The coke was coursing through Mason's blood stream, manifesting itself in a stream of lip licking, fawning flattery.

"Nahce to see ya again, Mason," Tim responded in his nasal Oklahoma accent. "I remember." His expression suggested he didn't savor the memory.

"Are you looking for more songs for Alan? I mean, you're at the county square of great country songs. We got loads of stuff that would be perfect for a neotraditionalist like Alan," Mason sniffled, revving up for another spew.

Witnessing the mania, Greg interjected. "Quit selling beyond the close here, Mason. We got it covered. We're looking for songs for a new duo, Brooks & Dunn."

"Oh, yeah. Kix Brooks got kicked off of Capitol didn't he? Guy was an animal on stage. Not the greatest singer, but looks like somebody I'd love to party with." Mason couldn't help himself.

Greg's body language said *shut the fuck up*, but instead he uttered, "Tim, over here is one of our new hires. Booty Womar referred him to us. Smart kid. He's converting our analog tape library to DAT. Nick, say hello to Tim DuBois."

"Pleased to meet you, sir. Nick Haller."

We shook hands firmly, neither letting the other get a firmer grip.

"So, Nick, whatcha doing here?" Tim asked.

"Honestly, I'm just learning all I can. Soaking it up. I thought when I moved to Nashville last August, I wanted to be a songwriter. I was a music composition major at UVA, and I thought that meant I'd be good. I've quickly realized I'm about the least talented writer in this town. And, to Mason's point, I'm told there are some well-crafted songs stored on all these tapes back here. I'm in the process of doing an analog-to-digital conversion of every one, which means I get to hear all of them. It's quite a baptism in the font of the art of songwriting."

"Meester, what's a graduate of the University of Virginia doing in the tape room of this ah-land of misfit toys?"

I laughed. Mason sulked.

"Yeah, my dad is super proud," I said, shaking my head in dramatic sarcasm.

"Well, stick with it. Ya never know. Hell, I was an accountant working for the Federal Reserve before I got the gumption to follow my own muse. Listen, here's my business card. The label is growing. Talk to my assistant Ramona and let's find a time to talk more."

I took the card, and Greg handed over his list of songs.

"We need four cassettes of these three songs. Highest quality."

As he and Tim walked back to Greg's office, I looked at the card. White with a cyan blue logo that reeked of '70s disco design. Arista Nashville. Tim DuBois. President.

"Who the hell was that guy?" I asked Mason.

"Tim Dubois. Supposed to be really nice. He's that rare combination of businessman and songwriter. Wrote, uh, let's see, 'She Got the Goldmine (I Got the Shaft)' for Jerry Reed, and, uh, 'Love in the First Degree' for Alabama. Before Clive got him, he ran Fitzgerald-Hartley here in town. They managed Restless Heart and Vince Gill. He cowrote 'When I Call Your Name' with Vince. And, he teaches accounting at Vanderbilt."

"Holy shit. And he handed me his business card?"

"Fuck you, man. I've been in this damn tape room for six years and nobody's ever treated me like that."

"I'm lucky I guess."

Mason turned his back on me, fiddled in his pocket, and took another bump.

Our First House
Nashville, TN
April 1995

I pulled the Camry into the driveway. Maura got out and headed to the front door while I went to the trunk to get our bags.

"Uh oh," I faintly heard her shout from the front stoop.

"Uh oh, what?" I shouted back, lowering the last bag onto the driveway.

"It's a big fat FedEx from Harvard Business School. I bet you got in."

We had just returned from a weekend trip to hang with her sister and my new brother-in-law in Atlanta. On the drive back, we got into a serious conversation about my plans to do the EMBA program at Vanderbilt's Owen Graduate School of Management.

I hadn't written a song in three years. Or painted a picture. Or made anything with my hands. Between marriage, immersion in the job, and frankly, a paralyzing fear of failure, I had my head responsibly above water, giving license to the waves and prevailing winds on the surface, allowing them to guide me, and freezing out the artistic current—the requirement to create—that flows consubstantial with my marrow. I lacked courage. I ran from me.

I didn't know it yet, but I'd begun the transformation. My soul was on its way to Coventry. Or at least to Cambridge, Massachusetts.

Restlessness with Maura's job + mutual desire to have kids + mutual desire for Maura to be able to stay at home with kids if we could have them + $27,000-a-year salary to support us if she were to exit the working world + liberal arts degree in music + four years of nontransferable experience pushing records + vexing fact that music was now being passed around for free on hard drives as compressed digital files called WAVs and MP3s with no generational loss + one brother who graduated from Harvard Business School and was killing it as the head of Dell's Japan office + another brother who'd just graduated from MIT with a joint degree in mechanical engineering and business administration and was killing it as a consultant for McKinsey & Company = time to apply to business school.

A few months before, after watching the label's first real failure at breaking a new artist called Dude Mowrey (you can't polish a turd), in a moment of vocational self-doubt, I took the GMAT and scored in the 98th percentile, with a perfect score on the math section.

I told Maura this, saying I should probably apply to business schools. She said, "Are you sure? You love the record business."

I did love the record business. At times, however, it felt like high school. Shouldn't I grow up? I wasn't yet aware that what I really loved were two of the best bosses anyone could ever hope for. Tim Dubois and Mike Dungan were each ridiculously talented leaders. Together, they were an unstoppable force that steered the company with care and feeding and a healthy dose of humor, playing the long game, eschewing soulless professionalism, quick fixes, and quick bucks.

Knowing Mike would never understand the desire to go to business school, I scheduled a meeting with Tim to get his temperature.

"Meester, if you think it's in you, I think you should do it. We'd hate to lose you, but ya gotta be you."

I applied to UVA's Darden School, Northwestern's Kellogg School, and in a strategic attempt to keep me at the label, Tim, who still taught at Vanderbilt, recommended me, at the not-so-ripe age of twenty-six, to the dean of Vanderbilt's Owen School as a candidate for their executive MBA program. (As an intense program that convened every other Friday and Saturday for sixteen hours over the course of two years with no summer break, they normally didn't accept applications without at least ten years of experience. I had less than four years at Arista.) Based on my test scores and the unassailable recommendation of Nashville's latest label head phenom, I got in. I also got into Darden and Kellogg.

I requested the application for Harvard when I requested the others, but set it aside, initially, as it was daunting, and with my imperfect 3.7 at UVA, I didn't think I had a chance. My procrastination meant I missed the January application deadline. I finally got my act together for the March pool deadline.

Two weeks before, I had decided on staying in Nashville and doing Vanderbilt's weekend program, which allowed me to keep my job. I filled out my declaration of intent and let Virginia and Northwestern know to give up my spot. Now, on the front stoop of our unassuming cottage lay a 9" x 12" FedEx envelope from Harvard Fucking Business School.

I extracted the wad of booklets topped by a letter printed on bougie, thick creme stationery, that began, "Dear Nick Haller, we are pleased to offer you admission to..."

"Harvard let me in?" I said without excitement, as a wary but audible dialog in my mind.

I peered at Maura, her eyes widening.

She inhaled about four gallons of air, and while exhaling, sighed, "How do you turn that down?"

Harvard Business School
Boston, Massachusetts
September 1995

Our Organizational Behavior professor, Cathy Ames, walked into the pit, removed her blazer, and rolled up her left sleeve while scanning the room. First, she rotated her head from left to right, examining the Worm Deck—the front row of seats that formed an arc around her focal point. Then, she moved her gaze up to the Garden Deck, the Power Deck (the tier of seating that sits perfectly at her standing eye level), the Warning Track, and, finally, the Skydeck.

I was in my assigned seat in the center section, sitting next to Danny O'Riordan from my study group. Super nice and keen individual. Went to UPenn undergrad. Not as cocky as most I've met here. Galway coloring. Jet black hair and piercing blue eyes, just a shade lighter than Tiffany blue.

Professor Ames moved her head along the Skydeck to the right aisle, rotated her head one or two more individuals, and while looking in the far right section, her gaze some 60 degrees from where I was sitting, began speaking.

"Donna Dubinsky. Steve Jobs. Dynamic manager at Apple who sees her domain shrinking. Mr., uhm, Haller..."

Her headlights quickly shifted to blind the deer with its head at a constant downturned angle. Me. Nick Fucking Haller.

"Wow, that was a head fake for the ages. Magic Johnson's got nothing on you," I offered defensively, hoping to buy a moment to gather my thoughts.

Some of the guys in the class chuckled.

This was my first cold call, the grease in the system that ensures most students come to class prepared. A section of first-years was ninety students. We were in Section E. You had a one in ninety chance of being cold-called. Odds were against it. Those odds escalated the less you participated in class. We'd been in school for two weeks. I had yet to make a comment. Fifty percent of one's grade was class participation.

"I'm glad I could be of service," she beamed with sadistic pleasure. "Would you mind opening the case for us."

"Uhm, yes ma'am. I mean, no ma'am, I don't mind. You know, uh, yes, I'll open," I said, my voice shaking a hair, at least in my own estimation. I fumbled in my notebook to find my notes.

On this day, we had to prepare for four cases from the set curriculum for all first-year MBA candidates: Accounting, Managerial Decision

Making (basically stats), TOM (technology and operations management), and OB (this class—organizational behavior).

"I'm not your madam, Mr. Haller." Eighty-nine students leaned in, all eyes on me, hoping for some drama.

"Huh?" I looked up. "I'm sorry ma'am. What did you say? I'm just looking for my notes here."

"Never mind. Apparently you have a hard time multitasking, Mr. Haller. I said I'm not your madam."

"That's what my wife says. Uh, I mean, the bit about multitasking. Not my strong suit. I, uh, don't think my wife has ever said she's 'not my madam,' uhm, to me."

I looked up briefly, hoping for a laugh. Instead, I saw stunned curiosity from my classmates and a piercing stare from my professor. Everybody was uncomfortable. I floundered.

"The case, Mr. Haller. Your thoughts."

"Uhm, yes." I looked to the ceiling for deliverance and then cast my gaze back down into the pit of hell.

"Well, you have on the one hand Steve Jobs. Super powerful, competent entrepreneur and executive. He's got an idea for how to make distribution run better. The problem is, for the girl in the case…"

A hiss built, first among the women, and then some of the men. I looked around desperately, not knowing what I'd done. I knew I looked like a fool but hissing seemed harsh. Fully exposed, I hit the eject button.

"I'm sorry, Ms. Ames. Why don't you let someone else open the case?"

Julia Weeks raised her hand.

"Yes, Ms. Weeks. Would you like to pick up where Mr. Haller left off?" She smirked before adding, "You know, basically the beginning."

"Yes, thank you, Professor. It seems to me the protagonist in the case, Donna Dubinsky, has a fair amount to learn in the area of emotional intelligence…"

Julia proceeded with a perfectly outlined, extemporaneous case opening, laying out the salient points of background, clearly stating the problem, and offering her explanation for the way forward. Textbook.

Problem is, we didn't have textbooks. That's the method. Business boot camp. Learn from the school of hard knocks. Tear us down so they could build us back up.

After staring into space for about three minutes, marinating in the echoing hiss in my head, and ruminating on why I ever thought moving to Boston for this was ever a good idea, I whispered to Danny, "Why was I getting hissed?"

"You called the woman in the case a girl. That's seen as demeaning. You're not in Kansas anymore."

Harvard Business School
Boston, Massachusetts
October 1995

Of all of the professors in my first semester at Harvard, each impressive in their own way, Elon Kolhlberg was my favorite by a country mile. And while advanced mathematics were his stock in trade, particularly Bayesian statistics and stochastic game theory, he possessed an innocent sense of humor that allowed him to impart wisdom in all areas, not just stats. He was one wise human. Wicked smaht. Folklore conjectured that he'd put his keen mind to work as an analyst for the Mossad as a young adult. Out of the blue, he requested a meeting, and I was anxious, despite my 95 average on his quizzes and tests.

"Meester Haller. I uhm so gluhd you came to see me dis day. Ow are dyou?"

"Pretty stressed if I'm being honest."

"Yes, I cuhn see daht. Em, daht is vwhy I vwant to tahlk to dyou dis day. I hahve a curiosity. De vwritten vwork dyou turn in, eet's en de top fieuhve percent of da class. Yet, dyou don't speak a vword. Vwhy is dees?"

"You noticed?" I eye roll. "I guess I've always been an introvert. Prefer book learning to the lion's den that is the case study method. Heh.

I probably should've made an attempt to understand that more before I came here."

"But down't dyou teenk dat's part of da process? To become more cahmfahrtable in dyour own skeen?"

"I guess so. I fear, however, I'm losing myself. I'm becoming less comfortable in my bare skin. I think the only reason they let me in this place is I'm a diversity candidate. There weren't a lot of lily-white rednecks with dads named Stonewall Jackson whose job experience prior to matriculating was hawking hillbilly records."

He smiled with sagacity, a cross between Alec Guinness's Obi-Wan Kenobi and the animatronic Yoda in *The Empire Strikes Back*.

"Doo dyou teenk dyou are somehow less qualified dahn dyour peers?"

"Definitely. I didn't work for Goldman Sachs or McKinsey or Bain or Morgan Stanley or PepsiCo or Procter & Gamble. I didn't go to some preppy boarding school or an Ivy League college. I'm not an expat whose dad owns some major manufacturing concern in Pakistan, or Kuwait or Chile. I left Nashville making $37,000 a year, a full five years into my career. Everybody in Section E seems to have been making three to four times that, and they're all like two or three years younger than me. Yes, I think I'm less qualified."

"Mmm hmm. I see."

He swiveled in his chair and grabbed a tiny paperback book, one of about eight of the exact same title.

"Do dyou know the Danish fairy tale audor, Hans Christian Andersen?"

"Yes, of course. You want me to read '*The Ugly Duckling*'?"

"Hehe. Vell, dat might help too. No, I want you to reread dis, assuming dyou've read it before.

He hands me the Scholastic edition of *The Emperor's New Clothes*, with a *Schoolhouse Rock* illustration of a nude, obese king looking at himself in a mirror.

As I flipped through it, he said, "Read it not as da adult dyou vant to become, but as da child dyou used to bee."

I read it on the T ride home. The child didn't know enough to not know the truth. He's the Wise and Holy Fool archetype, like Chauncey Gardiner in *Being There* or Forrest Gump in, y'know, *Forrest Gump*. My classmates were the charlatan weavers, spinning yarns that are invisible and unfit for those not of their office, or those who are just plain stupid. The emperor was HBS. The metaphor delivered me.

Arista Nashville Offices
Nashville, TN
November 1998

"Hey Page! Hey Dick!"

I looked up from my desk to see Lee Roy Parnell, one of our artists, straddling the wall between the Jack-and-Jill adjacent doors to my office and the office of Page Murphy, Arista Nashville's general counsel. Lee Roy was different than most '90s Nashville recording acts. (A) He could flat play. His slide guitar conjured visions of Duane Allman and Bonnie Raitt, and (B) he didn't wear a cowboy hat like most of Nashville's poseurs. His Stephenville, Texas upbringing formed the foundation of his accent, but he'd also interlaced a little playacting from spending his entire life in the music business, copping the grammar and attitude of famous bluesmen. And, unlike the over-aftershaved urban cowboys, he was a nice guy who admitted his shit stinks. His first CD was an unmitigated disaster. His second, off the strength of his single "What Kind of Fool Do You Think I Am," went Gold. His third album made money, but not much. His fourth album had just come out on a recently launched subsidiary label, Career Records, and was performing modestly.

Lee Roy addressing me as Dick is not a one-letter typo. After returning to Nashville with my highfalutin Harvard MBA, I became director of finance and operations for my old label and team. Graduating with an MBA in 1997 was good timing. I turned down seven offers, including a strategic planning job from BMG in New York under its new young chairman, Strauss Zelnick. But the Nashville of the early '90s, a "rocket sled on rails" (to quote the poet laureate of the Peterbilt, C.

W. McCall, songwriter of "Convoy,") was too compelling. I reentered the business as the specter of digital disruption loomed. MP3 usage was accelerating at the pace of a rocket unencumbered by the friction of rails—it flew in the ether. PCs came installed with Windows Media Player, which played MP3 files. Crafty kids were ripping CDs. New sites offered the ability to download thousands of songs. And though President Clinton had just signed into law a new copyright act, trying to shore up copyright infringement for a digital age, its soft underbelly was the limitation of liability for the tech companies that provided the services the pirates used. The platform wasn't the pirate. The illegal downloader was the pirate. Problem was, pirates were sprouting like a biblical weed infestation. Many former music purchasers were passing around hard drives with thousands of songs and copying those drives to their computers. In an hour or two, one could transfer the equivalent of a wall of LPs onto their own hard drive with a simple USB cable. Then, once they'd built up their library, they could email songs to friends or set up websites where strangers could download their collections.

In a period of two years, the very business model of record companies was under siege. And, we still had a year before Napster arrived. My pessimistic ass predicted this back in the Sony/Tree tape room in 1991. But, I couldn't deny the charismatic leadership of Tim DuBois and Mike Dungan.

Seeing the digital age coming, Arista Nashville entered a period of austerity. I gave a speech to the team, as the new bean counting sheriff, half-joking, with the refrain, "Stop the hemorrhaging!" I famously said that we were shutting down the supply room. "You can't get a new pen without turning in one that no longer writes. New pencil? Show me a stub and I'll give you a new pencil."

They knew I was kidding, but I was hopeful they got the point. The good old days were going fast. After that speech, my "Nick-name" became a dickname, and the team took great pleasure in calling me Dick.

I have an 8" x 10" headshot of Lee Roy, signed accordingly:

To Swingin' Richard,
Don't let your meat loaf.
Lee Roy Parnell

"Hey guys," Lee Roy continued. "It's awesome y'all's offices are ass to elbow. Y'all are just the two fellas I needs to see. Y'see, Kinky Friedman—uh, you might be innarested to know that I, me, myself, this Baptist Rube-boy toured as a Jewboy back in '76—wants me to play on his tribute album. I cain't say no. I'm gonna do it. And I'm gonna do it for free. If the label needs to make money off of it so be it, but that's on y'all."

Friedman—founder of Kinky Friedman and the Texas Jewboys, and court jester of country swing (his band's name a cheeky nod to the seminal Bob Wills and His Texas Playboys, the band incidentally that Lee Roy's dad played for)—was casting his tribute album, *Pearls in the Snow*, with all-stars and industry darlings. Since Kinky was with a different label, we had to either give Lee Roy permission to play on the record without compensation to Career Records, or negotiate a payment to the label, either a flat fee, or, if enough leverage existed, points—consideration for him temporarily breaching his contract with Arista/Career.

"Well, Lee Roy, this is a bit fun and uh, unorthodox, to be talking to you and not your manager. Is Robertson good with it?" I queried.

"And before you answer that," Page interjected, "has Kinky's label provided a proposal for how guest artists and their labels will be compensated?"

"Well, let me take these in the order I received 'em." His eyes lit up with a smirk when he said, "See, I've learnt sumpin' from all dat media trainin'. So, uh, Dick," the name seemed particularly engorged and stabbing all of a sudden, "yes Robertson's AOK with it. He don't think it'll sell shit. And we don't care. Kinky's a national treasure. Or at least a Texas treasure. And Page, seeing that he's releasing this on his own independent label, y'know, Kinkajou Records, nobody's really thought through any of dat bidness bowlshit. Dat's why's I'm here. Figured you bookworms would figure dat shit out. And anyway, Kinky has written up a crocodile contract. Said he gave the same thing to Willie."

"Nelson?" Page asked.

"Of course. They're old buddies," said Lee Roy as he walked into Page's office.

I got up and followed, curious to see what this was all about. He handed Page a loose leaf of yellow legal paper. Staring at the back of it, all I saw were loads of grey/black blotches bleeding onto the backside from large, angular Sharpie strokes. It took Page no more than two seconds to read this "contract." A buttoned-up lawyer, Page rarely let go. The laugh that bellowed from his fit frame had to be a PBR—personal best record—in terms of bare guttural glee. He handed me the sheet, still chortling and wiping tears from his eyes.

I had to collapse into a fetal ball in his little upholstered side chair to contain my snort-laugh eruption.

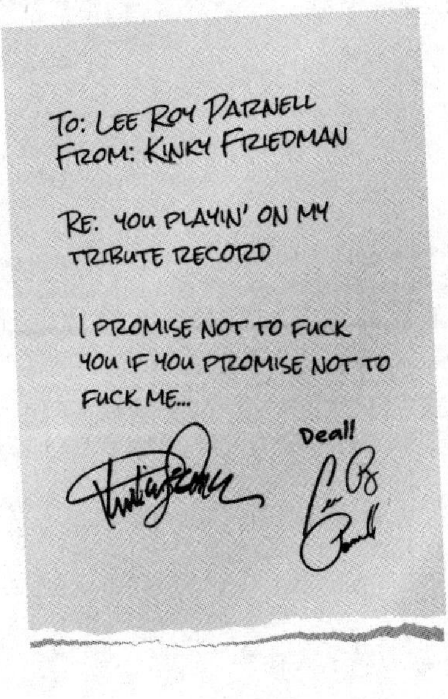
TO: LEE ROY PARNELL
FROM: KINKY FRIEDMAN

RE: YOU PLAYIN' ON MY TRIBUTE RECORD

I PROMISE NOT TO FUCK YOU IF YOU PROMISE NOT TO FUCK ME...

Deal!

SIDE B

Funkennovation
vs.
The Placebo Syndrome

PERSONNEL

The Band		
GamerTag	Instrument	Title
Nick Haller	Scat Vocals	Chief Marketing Officer
Maura Haller	Ostinato Vocals	Wife
Craig Spartan	Lead Guitar	CEO, Guitar Mart
Fred Rhodus	Geddy Lee's Double-neck Rickenbacker	Best Friend
Stephen Gossamer	Friction Harp	PwnShop Boss, EVP & Chief Strategy Officer
Talbott Jebson	Glass Armonica	Corporate Psychologist
Claude Prendas	Funeral Drum	Outgoing CEO
Harvey Handler	Dead Cat, Company Ink	Previous EVP & Head of International, Incoming CEO
Jack Floyd	Alpenhorn	CFO
Tom Testa	Zeusaphone	Chairman of the Bored
Lance Park	Synclavier	Bored Member, Interim CEO Nominee
The Pips		
Helen, Jackie		

Track 6: Let it Bleed

"Playing things too safe is the most popular way to fail. Dying is another way..."

—ELLIOTT SMITH

Between LAX and Westlake Village, CA
November 2010
3821 days to POSS
CSP: $14.08

I was somewhere around Malibu on the edge of the canyon when the shame began to take hold.

The guilt was a hopeless mess, all churned together and half crushed. Some of the shame had disintegrated into a pulverized forgotten powder of half-memories, but I counted about thirty-five or forty fuck ups still intact. My self-reproach had eaten all the sins of commission, but there was quite a bit of regret left from things undone. Not enough for anything desperate, but a careful rationing of the indignity would probably keep my marriage intact. I'd been commuting the last six months to California as the new EVP and general manager of e-commerce and marketing for the leading domestic retailer in the MI (Musical Instrument) industry, Guitar Mart.

e-Miles/e-Rewards Offices
Dallas, TX
March 23, 2010
3970 days to POSS
CSP: $14.08

Several months ago, I was staring at my computer trying to fix an investor presentation that my boss had just called a "fucking abortion." Not a lot of ambiguity in that phraseology. I wondered if he was coaching me or getting ready to fire me when my cell phone vibrated with a text from the headhunter at Russell Reynolds.

"Hey Nick! Time to get on Realtor.com!"

I texted back, "Does that mean I got the job?"

"Sure does."

"Wow."

The job was EVP and general manager, e-commerce and marketing, at Guitar Mart. I got the call to interview about two months ago. That call came on another particularly bad day at the office—a vitriolic argument with the boss over me not being hard enough on the salespeople—initiating an intense round of phone interviews, then trips to California and Boston for a gauntlet of interviews with the executive team and the lead partners at Maine Capital, who had purchased Guitar Mart in 2007 to take it private.

Not even really agreeing with the premise of e-miles, three weeks into it, I knew I had made the worst decision of my career. I'd now been at it three years.

The Guitar Mart news represented deliverance. The job was perfect. How could anyone draw up a better job for me than running e-tail and marketing for the world's largest retailer of musical instruments?

I took a screen shot of the text and forwarded it to Maura. She, who rarely traveled, happened to be in Houston at MD Anderson, the number one hospital in the world for cancer treatment, as it was her dad's quarterly oncologist visit. In portending coincidence, the day I received my big job offer, she received the news that his cancer had returned with a vengeance.

I knew she was there, but the last few visits had been ordinary. I didn't think to preface the text with "How's your dad?" My text arrived within minutes of Maura learning that he was terminal. Houston's hospital of hope gave their final recommendation—palliative care and hospice.

Within seconds, I got a return text.

"Dad is dying. I can't even begin to think about moving to California."

I waited until she returned home to discuss further. After learning the full story, I realized she was in no emotional state to pack up the truck and move westerly. Career vs. family. Family's gotta win.

I dialed the headhunter to ask if I could get a call with the CEO to see if he'd consider a commute scenario. He was a super solid guy. But he was also practical. I'd be the only individual on the executive team commuting. He was willing to take the call in thirty minutes—good sign.

"Craig, Nick Haller here. Look, first off, many thanks for the exciting offer. Not sure I'm worthy."

"Are you kidding me? You rose head and shoulders above the other candidates. You are the guy. We're super excited to have you. What's up?"

"Well, Maura and I just received some horrible news. Her dad has been fighting stage 4 colon cancer for the last five or six years. Has lost his gall bladder, had his liver resectioned twice, and gone through intense regimens of chemo and radiation therapy. He's been able to keep it at bay for the last three years or so. As poetry would have it, the day Russell Reynolds texted me that I had gotten the job, Maura was receiving the news that MD Anderson had run out of options. He was terminal."

"Wow. Tough news. That's a great hospital. I'm sure he wouldn't have made it this far without them."

"True that."

"So do you need to delay your start date?"

"If only it were that simple. He's a tough guy and won't take this sitting down. He's already exploring some radical blood washing treatment in Germany that the FDA hasn't approved. The problem is, we can't predict when or if he's going to die. But Maura, strong-willed as she is, has said she can't even fathom, y'know, the emotional upheaval of finding schools for three kids, selling a house, finding a house and moving, all while her dad is either dying or undergoing experimental treatments. In short, she can't move anytime soon. So, uhm, would you guys entertain an indefinite commute scenario?"

"Indefinite? No. Can you put a timetable on it?"

"Well, I think it would be at least a year."

"Look. Tough situation all around. But I have a company to manage and you have a duty to your family. My initial reaction is not only no, but hell no. I don't see how it will work. I commuted for four months when I was in management consulting, and it almost killed my marriage. I could possibly entertain this scenario but for no more than six months. The reality is, I'm mostly worried about you burning out. The burden will be on you."

"And what happens if he's still fighting after six months?"

"You move."

"Okay, let me talk it over with Maura and I'll get back to you tomorrow."

"Look, Nick, I don't want you to get the wrong impression. We really want you here. But the job is here, and we can't have you halfway. It's all or nothing. There's a lot of work to do."

"I understand."

I knew Maura's answer before I even asked.

"How could a company be so callous?" she posited. "My dad is fucking dying. And they think it's just super easy to find schools for my kids, find a house, sell a house, move, make new friends, all in a state that represents the antithesis of family values. Who are these people? Look dear, you can go, but I ain't going with you. You married the wrong girl if you think I'm going to kowtow to the almighty company. What if you hate the job like you do every two years anyway?"

I didn't sleep that night. She was right. Cons: marriage risk, bitter children risk, company risk, boss risk, location risk, job satisfaction risk, private equity micromanagement risk, debt leverage risk. Pros: Music was my passion and this was my first C-level opportunity at a $1 billion-plus company.

Because I was on Central Time and Craig was on Pacific, I waited until 10 AM to call his mobile.

"Craig, it's Nick," I said mournfully.

He read the tone immediately. "Tough night with the wife?"

"Indeed. I'm going to have to pass. Thank you for what would have been a dream opportunity. Unfortunately, I can't make the timing work."

"Well, super disappointing. Back to the drawing board on the search. Best of luck to you."

"And to you too. Seriously, I can't thank you enough for the opportunity. Sorry to waste so much of your time."

"Comes with the territory."

e-Miles/e-Rewards Offices
Dallas, TX
June 23, 2010
3878 days to POSS
CSP: $14.96

I turned my phone over to see a text from the headhunter at Russell Reynolds, who I hadn't heard from in three months.

"Hey man. Hope you're doing well. Let me know when you have a minute to discuss Guitar Mart. They want to pick up where you last left off."

I dialed the guy. He answered.

"Not sure I understand. Where we left off was I turned down the job. They were none too keen about embracing a commute scenario."

"Yep. That's where you left off. They're willing to consider an indefinite commute."

"Really? What changed?"

"Two things. One, I put every qualified candidate in the world in front of them. Loads of people want that job. They couldn't get you out of their mind. Nobody else measured up. You should be flattered."

"Wow. I am. Who knew? And what was the other factor?"

"Your wife called the CEO."

"You're breaking up. Not sure I heard that right. My wife did what?"

"She called the CEO. She didn't tell you?"

"No! Incredible. Let me talk to her and figure out what the hell has gone down."

I speed dialed Maura.

I almost started in immediately, but instead led with her dad. Once bitten. Twice shy. "Hey, what's the news on your dad?"

"He's definitely going to Prien, Germany for that transfusion blood cleaning thing. It's crazy, but he won't listen to me. I wish he would just be at peace with this and enjoy his last months. I think the doc in Germany is a quack or at least a charlatan, and Dad is grasping at straws."

"Don't know how you get in the way of a man's will to live. I can't imagine him traveling there in his condition."

"Well, I was hoping you could go with them. They're not very experienced in international travel. And neither am I. Plus, there's the kids."

"Say no more. It would be an honorable duty."

"That's nice of you. Means a lot. I'm just so damn forlorn and raw. He's such a complicated character. I love him to pieces but he's got some major flaws. The whole third wife thing makes this triply difficult."

"I'll bet. Is she ruling the roost?"

"No, but she's not my mom. She's not even my stepmom. This isn't love. It's desperation. Why would Dad remarry when he's terminal with cancer? It's been a year and a half and I'm still having a really hard time getting over that. And who the hell would marry someone knowing they're going to lose them immediately?"

"It's hard not to believe she simply married a guy almost twenty years older to quickly cash in. She certainly doesn't look like Anna Nicole

Smith, but she is a nurse. Neil Young needs a maid. Your dad needs a nurse. It ain't love. It's transactional."

"I know. But it's my dad. The guy I look up to. He's supposed to be my hero. He now just comes across like a lech. Why do I have to spend the last years of his life with this money-grubbing candy-striper?"

"I'll let that remain rhetorical. Hey, so I just got a call from the headhunter at Russell Reynolds. Says Guitar Mart wants to talk again. Anything you'd like to share?"

"Uhm, yeah." Her voice revved up. "Probably the dumbest thing I've ever done. No. Definitely. Stupid." I could feel the temperature rising through the tiny iPhone slit. "I called the CEO because I'm so fucking confused about everything right now. I hate this job offer. I hate that you want this job. I hate that you hate your current job. I hate that my dad's dying. And haven't I told you? I HATE California. I am not raising kids in that godforsaken Gomorrah of self-centeredness. I am NOT. Do you hear me?"

"Yes, I hear you. I feel you. That's why I'm confused. They say they're willing to discuss a commute. How did you get his number? What did you say?"

"I don't know," her voice clutched, holding back rare tears.

Maura, at 5'2", is one of the biggest people I know. She shed all her tears years ago as a teenager during the era of her parents' divorce. She had few left. Just a stiff upper lip and a mountain of grit. But, I could hear her fighting them back.

"I just googled their headquarters, got the number, and asked for the CEO. They asked who's calling. I said 'Maura Haller, wife of Nick Haller, the guy you were talking to a few months ago about a marketing executive position.' Craig called me back within an hour."

"And what did you say?"

"Basically, 'you know and I know there isn't a more perfect candidate for your silly job than Nick Haller. And if you think he's married to some drooping flower who's going to wilt the first weekend he's away from home, you don't know Maura Haller.' I said, 'I am not going to be the reason a commute won't work.'"

"Wow. Really?"

"Yes."

"Why?"

"I'm an idiot."

"Well, that's a courageous act of love is what it is. Probably the greatest I've ever received. I'm not worthy."

"Well, don't put me on any pedestal. I instantly regretted it. Are you really going to abandon your family for a job? Not even a good one. A retail job? Retail is dead."

"I'm not abandoning my family. I'm providing for my family."

"Oh bullshit. Grow up. You really think this is a good move? How does this end well? I am NOT moving to California!"

"The exit plan isn't yet clear. It's like invading Iraq. We know I need a career change just like Iraq needed a regime change. I guess we'll make it up while we're screaming. But it really puts me in the C-level game, and at a company that operates in an industry that I not only know a lot about, it so happens to be my passion. Music is everything to me."

"Yep. Apparently it means more to you than your wife and your kids. Peter Pan and his artistic Neverland. My dad's dying, you dick. Can't you see that's tearing me apart?"

"That's why I turned down the fucking job. What part of that do you not understand? Perfect job. Colossally imperfect timing. But… And… YOU called them back to say YOU were supportive of a commute. Not ME. YOU picked at the scab."

"For the last three months you've been moping around like the saddest sack I've ever known. And let's be real, YOU've been one hell of a sad sack on multiple fucking occasions!"

"I couldn't be more confused right now. This situation is impossible. If I take the job, I'm a selfish dick. If I don't, I'm stuck at a company with no prospects that's simultaneously siphoning my life blood. Yes, I've been a sad sack. Maybe that's because I've spent my whole life trying to be the man in the grey flannel suit for you and the kids. I fucking hate it! It's not who I am. We're getting nowhere. Let's talk when I get home."

"Oh boo hoo. Wittle artist boy has to fucking man up."

She hung up on me.

I walked in the door, set my keys and wallet down in the little leather monogrammed catchall somebody gave me one year for Christmas, and saw Maura cooking. My daughter was at the counter. It was clear I'd interrupted a serious conversation.

"Hey," Maura said.

"Hey," I replied. "Am I interrupting something?"

"No. We were just talking about this godforsaken situation. You can't make this up."

"No you can't. Look, I'm sorry that phone call went off the…"

"No, I'm sorry," she interrupted as she's prone to do. (It's her impulsive personality. Ready. Fire. Aim.) "I'm just stressed beyond belief. You should take the job. We can do this. But I have one condition."

"What's that?"

"I want a blood oath that you will NEVER make me move to California."

"Can I convince you to move to California over time if it all works out?"

"Doubtful. But possible. But you have to promise you will never force me to."

"As if I can ever force you to do anything. You're the one with the power and control gift. I'm just a wittle artist boy, remember?"

She smiled knowingly, powerfully.

I went to her office nook next to the kitchen, grabbed a sheet of printer paper, a blue Sharpie out of her pen cup, and rifled around in the junk drawer to find a safety pin. I wrote a note, signed it, pricked

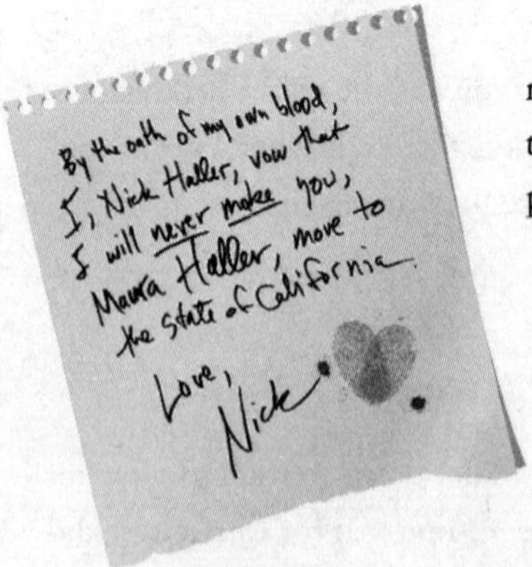

my thumb with the pin, and pressed the burgeoning blood twice against the paper to make a heart.

e-Miles/e-Rewards Offices
Dallas, TX
June 24, 2010
3877 days to POSS
CSP: $14.24

I dialed Craig Spartan's personal cell phone.

"Craig, Nick Haller here. Russell Reynolds said you wanted to pick up where we left off?"

"Yessir." He chuckled, "Against Brain's and my better judgment, we're willing to let you commute indefinitely."

"So I heard. I talked it over with Maura last night. It's ain't gonna be easy sledding, but we're more than willing to do it."

"Listen, I am taking a mighty risk betting on you. Not only do you have to perform, but you cannot flake out on this commute."

"You have my word, sir. Scout's honor. I can't tell you how much I appreciate your willingness to take such a risk. And, I'm convinced at least for the first six months or so it will be better for the company, as I will be 100 percent committed to the business when I'm in town."

"Yes, but I'm not worried about the first six months. We both know you can't implement any of the change we need for at least two years.

Then you need to operate the changes. I need your head wrapped around this being a five-year commitment."

"I'd be willing to sign a contract if that's what it takes."

"We need to leave it as employment at-will, but I would like you to think about your commuting cadence, and send me a proposal for how you plan on doing it."

"Well, I've already thought through that. At least initially, my plan is to work three straight weeks, fly back to Dallas on the third Thursday night and work from Dallas for one week, and then fly back to Westlake Village for another three weeks. We'll see how that works for a few months, and tweak the cadence accordingly. I'll put together a calendar for the first few months, making sure I'm in Dallas for major events in Maura's and the kids' lives—birthdays, recitals, sporting events."

"Do you plan on getting an apartment out here?"

"I don't think so. For multiple reasons, not the least of which is my own mental frame of mind, I'd prefer to stay in extended stay hotels, ship my car out, get a plastic bin or two and fill them with clothing and other essentials, and go about it that way. If I'm in a hotel, I think I'll feel like I'm always on a business trip, doing my job. If I get an apartment, it might start to feel like I'm living a separate life."

"Well, that sounds crazy, but if that's what you want, assuming it's cost neutral, I'm not going to micromanage. I've also talked to HR and our travel department about getting you an AAirpass on American, since you're coming from Dallas. I think it will make it a lot more flexible for you."

"Sounds great. Craig, seriously, I can't thank you enough for the opportunity. I am completely pumped."

"I am too. It will be fun. But, and I mean this will all of its gravity, I need you to swear on your mother's grave that you WILL NOT flake out on this commute."

"I hear the gravity and I hear the grave. I swear to you I WILL NOT flake out on the commute."

Track 7: A Sort of Homecoming

"Two of the hardest words in the language to rhyme are life and love. Of all words!"

—STEPHEN SONDHEIM

Guitar Mart Offices
Westlake Village, CA
October 1, 2012
3040 days to POSS
CSP: $14.72

Craig Spartan was dressed for the marine layer conditions normal to the Support Center in the Conejo Valley. A golf shirt and Kjus wind vest enclosed him, as he stood at the door to my office—a door he rarely darkened. I loved managing by walking around. Craig preferred to have his team come to him. A principled, teetotaling man, Craig, at fifty-seven, stood 6'5", was chiseled, rode his road bike in the Malibu canyon some twenty miles daily before work, and over fifty miles every weekend between his mandatory golf rounds. He carried maybe 6 percent body fat. The only nick I found in his armor was his debilitating claustrophobia, predominantly a fear of elevators. I attended meetings in downtown LA with him where he walked seventeen flights of stairs to avoid getting in one. We left a hotel for another when the late check-in clerk informed us his ground floor room wasn't available, but they could get him a room on the sixth floor. His command of most situations is as assured as Marko

Ramius's grip on the Red October, but nonetheless, Craig would make a horrible submarine captain. Too tall. Claustrophobic.

As our collaboration and tenure together had progressed, I'd become more daring in ribbing him about a neurosis over which a man as in control of himself as he, ironically, has no control. I was baffled how he could rationalize riding with his executive team in the close quarters of a six-seater corporate jet. I watched him fidget if the pilots didn't immediately take off after closing the door. And I watched him become downright agitated if the first thing they did upon landing was anything but open that door. But when the thing was in the air, no problem.

A year or so ago, after Maura's dad finally succumbed to cancer, Craig exclaimed that it was completely irrational that she would choose to stay in Dallas with the kids all week as a single parent rather than move to California. I asked, "Is it any more irrational than you not getting in an elevator?" The outworn topic never came up again.

Our working relationship had blossomed into a bit of a friendship, or more correctly, a foster brother kinship. Our personalities weren't super similar—he was planful and measured while I was spontaneous and unfiltered. But, my puerile superego appreciated his strengths, and his suppressed id appreciated mine.

By his demeanor, I could see he'd sauntered up to my second floor office in search of a little brotherly advice from his recruited little brother.

"Is Maura moving here yet?" he winked.

"As if. I thought she enjoyed the apartment we rented in Malibu this summer. The kids definitely did. It was so nice to have everybody here. But alas, she was more than happy to return to the more structured land of child-rearing and family values in Dallas. You know, the kids' hair got too long, they started calling her MFB (mutha fucking bitch), and they started asking about getting tattoos, high colonics and psychedelics. Back on the chain gang."

"Yeah, we always had concerns raising our kids here. I get it. How long have you been commuting now?"

"More than two years. It's getting a bit old, but I'm hanging in there."

"Man, I thought for sure you would flake out on us. Impressive that you're able to keep this up."

"Working for a guy like you makes it all worthwhile," I said sarcastically but with enough softness that he knew it was heartfelt.

"Well, that's nice to hear, and I know you're being a bit sassy. But, I do appreciate all you've done on both the brand front and on the digital transformation. The e-tail business is killing it."

We exchanged a few more compliments, like the Goofy Gophers, the overly polite and civil Looney Tunes critters with British accents that most people confuse with Disney's cheekier Chip 'n' Dale. Eventually, Craig got to the heart of the matter. "So, uhm, if this were your company, what would you do with it?"

The phrase "So, uhm?" is the tell of the weakest of hands. Almost as egregious as double-checking one's hole cards. As a lifelong kid brother, it was rare that an older male sibling sought advice from their younger blood. When they did, it was typically with a glancing question, never directly stating the problem. I'd learned to be careful in the presentation of my response. Don't bruise the male ego. Knowing, as the older brother in the relationship, that he probably wouldn't answer, I said anyway, "Why do you ask? The 'Maine-iacs' putting pressure on you?"

"No more than usual. Just feeling a bit philosophical."

Bullshit. They're lighting a fire under your ass.

"Well, the way I see it is the business needs a fair amount of investment, but the Maine guys' bet is getting long in the tooth and they don't feel like doubling down. Sound about right?"

"Hmm," he equivocated. "Any more clichés you'd like to toss in there?"

"Naw, Craig, I'm just being a troll."

No reaction. His undergraduate degree was in business administration. Not a liberal arts bone in his body.

"Anyway, here's how I see it," I said as I moved to the couch. I picked up the T bucket acoustic bass the Fender guys let me demo, and began to slap out, whitely, the quintessential lick in Larry Graham's seminal and sublime contribution to the wellspring for modern electric bass, "Hair."

"Are you going to tell me how you see it or are you going to play that funky music white boy?"

"Aha. I see what you did there. Need to do something with my hands to think. But, I also don't multitask well. So, reconcile that shit for me," I smiled.

"There's a lot about you that will never be reconciled," he winked.

I rested the bass on the sofa , realizing, in a rare moment of maturity, that it might be a distraction for me and an annoyance to him.

"As I was saying, I feel like we're running a family-owned bed and breakfast, metaphorically, of course."

"Of course," he nodded while taking a seat in the slouchy chair across from the slouchy couch.

"It's been some eight to ten years since we've done any real maintenance. The faucets are leaky, the carpets have been shampooed one too many times, the shower curtains are moldy, not to mention the pattern is no longer fashionable. We don't have enough plugs for electrical devices, much less good Wi-Fi."

"I get it," he prodded impatiently, "the inn is run down."

"Not only is it run down, the Hatfields just opened an inn across the street with all the modern amenities, and we're starting to lose customers. And so, as your little brother, metaphorically, of course…"

"Of course," he smiled and nodded in a "go on" sort of way.

"…I'd come to you and the rest of the family and say we're not distributing any cash this year to anyone. We need to reinvest in the business and the capex needed exceeds our annual retained earnings. In other words, we're going to capital call the family partnership. We need a major remodel to not only bring us into the modern era, but also to invest in some meaningful points of differentiation from the Hatfield's new place, like a kickass workout facility with steam rooms and saunas in the locker rooms."

"Yep. Ever since Maine bought us in 2006, we've had to deinvest in our stores and inventory, with all of the available cash we generated going to pay interest to the debtholders, since they levered this business to the hilt."

"Ain't that the truth. Anyway, if this were my company, that's what I'd do."

"Well, I don't disagree. It's a shame when capital structure informs strategy."

> Guitar Mart Offices
> Two weeks later
> 3026 days to POSS
> CSP: $16.24

"Hey Rhodus, I gotta go. My boss is at the door. But think on it."

Fred Rhodus is my bestest sidekick from my youth. He and I and our buddy Lucia Weaver forged our characters on a road trip we took around the western US upon graduating from college. We dubbed it Tour '90. At an open mic night at a bar in Lawrence, Kansas called the Bottleneck, Rhodus and I played music in front of more than one hundred people. It was a glorious disaster. As I had been reading Cornelius Ryan's D-Day epic *The Longest Day* on the trip, the act of facing our fears, taking the stage amongst scores of drunk college kids, forged my mantra: The only way off the beach is through the guns.

I greeted Craig, saying, "Sorry, I was just on the phone with a good buddy from home. Do you know what your crack marketing team has lined up for me?"

"No, what?"

"They're letting me interview Rush when we induct them into RockWalk."

"Well good for you," Craig chuckles. "I, for one, can't stand Rush. Hate them in fact. It's the most self-indulgent pap that was ever created. Plus, that lead singer, what's his name?"

"Geddy Lee."

"Yes, Geddy. His singing is about as pleasant as that abrasive noise my modem makes when it's trying to establish a connection."

"Ha. You're dating yourself with that comment," I teased.

"I'm dating MY self? You're dating YOUR self. I'm eight years older than you and I think Rush is old."

"Well, I'm excited. Don't make fun of me. We're each entitled to nerd out in our own way. Where are your bike shorts, by the way?"

"Cute."

"Anyway, what's up?"

"You might want to sit down."

Fuck. What did I do? "Uh, okay." I grabbed my obligatory spot on the slouch couch, he in the slouch chair.

"Some news is going to break tomorrow that I'm resigning."

"Oh man. No! Are you kidding me?"

"Nope. I've always wanted to be CEO of a public company. And you know how most of my past is in the restaurant and food business—House of Blues, California Pizza Kitchen and PepsiCo?"

"Yep. You're leaving musical instruments to go back to pizza or salty snacks? BORING! Who with?"

"I can't say yet. It's a public company and they're working through exiting the existing guy. Suffice it to say it's a major restaurant concern."

"Do you have to move?"

"No, it's in Southern California."

"Taco Bell? You're leaving us for Taco Hell?"

"No, it's not Taco Bell. You'll find out in due course."

"Well, that's a big bummer. I hope my conversation about how we've kicked the can on investment to continue to service debt on this business wasn't what swayed you. I presume this was going down when we spoke a couple of weeks ago?"

"Indeed it was."

"I could tell something was up. Just wasn't sure what. So when do you announce and when do you leave?"

"We'll announce internally tomorrow to the team. I'm sticking around for a few more weeks, at which point my new employer will be made public."

"Well, it's been a benediction. Have you named a successor?"

"No, but you should toss your hat in the ring."

"No way. They'd want me to move here." I looked him in the eye. We both smiled with our eyes. "Well, this is bullshit. I hope we get somebody who understands the capital structure problem. No way anyone should take this job unless they refinance and pay down a shit ton of the debt. I guess I have some serious thinking to do."

"I can't tell with complete certainty, but I don't think there's a lot of appetite for paying down the debt with anything but retained earnings."

"Seriously? They levered the shit out of this thing and its management's problem to solve? Yes, it makes me cynical," I opined. "Nobody ever takes the fall for a bad investment. Guitar Mart has a right to exist. It was doing fine until unbridled greed strapped it with so much debt. And then, instead of adding more equity to the investment, which would reduce but not eliminate their ROIC, we lay off employees and constrain inventory so all the small dick fat cats get paid. It ain't right."

"Man. You are getting cynical. Don't go there. You're too talented. This is a good company, and they need your creative thinking."

"So good you're ditching us for a public company?" He raised his eyebrows. "Sorry, I guess I should say congratulations. I get it. These private deals are impossible to exit when you're management. I guess it's easier to make the big bucks and see liquidity as a CEO when it's public."

"At least in this situation I'm afraid so. But that's where I am in my career. You haven't been in the seat. If you want to be a CEO, this could be a good opportunity for you. You know the players, you know the constraints. You should come forth with a plan to run it. I don't think they'll find a better candidate who's more passionate about the product and the people."

"Or a candidate who's more cynical about the Sisyphean task of peddling faster for a bunch of coldhearted private equity masters of the universe. Plus, I'll get organ rejection from Maura. No, I fear I've got some serious soul searching to do. With you leaving, not sure who I can trust."

"You can trust yourself."

"Ha! If only. By the way. Do you remember when I took this job, you made me swear that I wouldn't flake out on the commute? Well, you rat bastard, you flaked out on this deal before me, much less my stonewalling wife."

"Ouch! Fair. But ouch!"

Guitar Mart Parking Lot
Westlake Village, CA
May 22, 2014
2442 days to POSS
CSP: $26.80

I snuck out of my office after telling everyone I was going to get a late lunch. I connected my phone to the car's Bluetooth, drove out of the parking lot, and turned right onto Westlake Blvd. The phone rang at precisely 1:30 PM Pacific Daylight Time. It was an 817 number, the area code for Ft. Worth and most of Tarrant County, including the inaptly named Vineland, Texas. I pushed the green phone receiver on the steering wheel.

"Nick, Stephen Gossamer. How are you today?" he said somewhat robotically.

"I'm doing well. It's 72 and sunny in the Conejo Valley. How are things in the Texas wine country?"

"You do know that Vineland really isn't the Texas wine country don't you? If there is one, it's the Hill Country—Fredricksburg and the rest of LBJ's old congressional district."

"Yes, Steve. I'm aware. Just trying to be cute. I guess I failed. My apologies. Can I call you Steve, or do you prefer Stephen?"

"Either is fine," he said unemotionally.

"I'm just used to Steve. My kids sometimes call me that."

"Is that your middle name?"

"No. I'm just a big Steve Earle fan. I took the boys to see him one night at the House of Blues. They say I talk and act like him."

"Don't know Steve Earle."

"You've never heard 'Copperhead Road?' 'Guitar Town?'"

"Don't think so."

"Anyway, back to Vineland. As you know, I grew up in Dallas. I just always thought naming that town Vineland was a bit ironic for a mid-cities suburb that once served as a secret picnic location for Bonnie and Clyde and their families."

"I guess so. Listen, I must get to a meeting away from the office in twenty minutes. What was your reaction to the offer letter?"

"Well, I'm flattered, and I think the comp is mostly fair. I appreciate you going back to the team to make me whole. The big outlier question for me is still title. It doesn't look like we made any headway there. I'm not a big title guy. Couldn't care less, actually, as long as the culture of the company isn't hierarchical. That said, my offer from Neiman Marcus is an SVP title, and I'm leaving an EVP title at Guitar Mart, reporting to the CEO. Here, I'm reporting to an EVP, which I'm 100 percent okay with as long as I have a seat at the table. I mean I haven't had a VP title in at least ten years."

"Look Nick. I have gone to bat for you. This is the most we can do. You will be the highest paid vice president in the company."

"I imagine that's because my peer set are substantially EVPs and SVPs at most corporations. I'm not asking for money. I'm asking an organizational behavior question. Can you at least tell me if I'll have a seat at the table? Do my peers that have a comparable span of control have an SVP or VP title? In a lot of companies, only certain titles get invited to certain meetings. It seems weird to me to be a chief marketing officer in a company with numerous SVPs and only be a VP. Not sure it's sitting right, and I want to feel good about this."

"The offer is the offer. You have twenty-four hours to make a decision. Sorry but I have to run."

He hung up before I had a chance to respond.

What the fuck kind of mob negotiation tactic is this? I thought he said this was a collaborative place to work. Sounds pretty fucking Machiavellian to me. Dare I say bullying?

I dialed Maura.

"Hello dear. Are you moving back to Texas? God I hope so."

"Technically, I never moved away, but to answer your question, maybe? I was feeling really good about PwnShop, but the guy who's going to be my boss just hung up on me, saying I have twenty-four hours to decide before the offer explodes."

"What did you say that pissed him off?"

"I just asked some honest questions around title. I got the revised offer and it has the title as vice president, chief marketing officer. Seems bizarre to me to have a chief title and the responsibility it implies, that it wouldn't be an SVP. And then the strong-arm *Mission: Impossible* offer explosion bullshit."

"Yeah, but it is back home. And, I'm sure they're just tired of going back and forth on it."

"You're right. Can't have your cake and eat it too. But something smells bad. I'm sure I'll accept, I just don't like the way that conversation went."

Track 8: Poor, Poor Pitiful Me

"When people start asking you to do the same thing over and over again, that's when you know you're way too close to something that you don't want to be near."

—NEIL YOUNG

Home
June 15, 2016
1694 days to POSS
CSP: $23.32

They shoot the marketing guy first. Despite all the time I'd spent with Stephen Gossamer's shrink buddy Talbott Jebson, I was getting the sinking feeling Stephen and PwnShop President Joe Engel were growing weary of my defiance toward their covert plan to cash cow[1] the core business.

"My God, Maura. I've had unrealistic bosses in the past, but this guy takes the cake."

"What do you mean?"

[1] Another B-school business jargon bingo phrase. Cash Cow was one of the four quadrants described in the Boston Consulting Group's famous Growth-Share 2 x 2 matrix, developed in 1970, where market share is the X axis and growth is the Y axis. Companies occupying the quadrant with High market share and Low growth are said to be "Cash Cows." Typically, the strategy for these types of businesses is to "milk" them (yes, even grey flannel suit-clad business consultants use metaphors), cutting costs to maximize cash flow and plow those available funds into High-share/High-Growth "Stars."

"First of all, he completely dismissed the IDEO project."

"Is that the group in San Francisco you met with two weeks ago?"

"Yes, the ones who designed the first Apple mouse. He basically said it's a waste of time and money to perform any innovation on a mature business that should be cash cowed."

"And you don't think so?"

"No. We have only two defensible points of differentiation: (1) the store associate, who reflects our customer, and is an expert fanboy or fangirl in the whole video game space, and (2) the stores themselves which are a hyperlocal gathering place for the gaming public in every community. It's only a slight exaggeration when we say that we have a store within a skateboard ride of 85 percent of the US population. We just need to reimagine what the experience can be."

"Seems a bit dreamy, dontcha think?"

"Et tu, wifey? I mean, maybe. But do you think rolling up AT&T authorized resellers is the solution?"

"Oh god no. I just know you're probably too out there for the harsh reality of your situation."

"You're probably right. He made me get with a corporate psychologist."

"Well, you could use a shrink."

"That's what this guy thought. After a fairly productive first meeting, he asked me in the second meeting about my relationship with my father. Don't you think that's a bit out of bounds for an executive coach?"

"Depends on the context."

"It's how he started the call."

"So what'd you tell him?"

"I told him I always wanted to murder my father and fuck my mother. That Oedipus, the original muthafucka, got nothing on me."

"You didn't."

"I did. That's a bullshit question in a business setting."

"And your answer wasn't inappropriate in a business setting?"

"Once he went there, I felt like a little Homer meets Freud joke was fair game. It took him a bit but he laughed. And he got the point. He didn't ask again about my dad. But that's all water under the bridge. The situation is just weird. What's your advice?"

"Maybe back off your edgy humor. Just don't get fired. Count to ten before you let your passion get hold of you. We now have a kid in college."

PwnShop Offices
June 9, 2016
1693 days to POSS
CSP: $21.56

"Good morning, Helen!" I said to the heralded assistant I shared with Claude, Joe Engel, and my boss, Stephen Gossamer.

"Good morning, Nick," she said rotating her hand and wrist and moving her head back and to the left, the universal signal to come closer so she could say something to me in private.

I shuffled closer and leaned over the counter of her cubicle.

"Listen," she whispered, "Stephen came in this morning and said for you to come see him the moment you got in."

"So why are we whispering?" I said with my typical smartass inflection.

"Because he was acting kind of weird. He and Joe were in a closed-door meeting when I got in and as he was walking out, that was the first thing he said to me. He normally at least says good morning."

"Hmm. Wonder what's up. Never good when those two get to talking. Thanks for the heads up."

I walked three doors down to Stephen's expansive office, one of only six with a window in the low-budget warehouse/office. The door was open, and he was at his desk, typing away. I lightly knocked on the door frame.

He looked up, making rare eye contact. "Oh Nick, good morning. Come on in," he said in as jovial a manner as he could muster, one side of his mouth in a half smile, the other creased in determination. He stood, walked out from his desk and shook my hand, an atypical gesture for him, but his handshake was limp as ever.

"Should I close the door?" I asked.

"No, no. Not necessary. This won't take long."

I sat at the head of his conference table. Normally, he'd sit with me, but, this time, he went back behind his desk. I couldn't help but notice the vacant saggy ass of his obligatory boomer Levi's 501s as he turned around. He almost looked street they were so baggy. He sat in the Aeron chair and pushed his frameless glasses back into the notch at the top of his nose.

"Listen," he said, his eyes skirting all over the ceiling. "After you left yesterday, I've been thinking about our conversation. And, uh, I'm just wondering," his eyes immediately darted from the ceiling and squared upon my own, "Are you happy here?"

"Uhm, what do you mean? That's kind of an out of the blue question," I responded.

"No hidden agenda. Just curious. Do you find this job fulfilling?"

"No less fulfilling than any of the other executive jobs I've had. Happy is probably not the adjective I'd use, but I don't think I've used that adjective for any job I've had except my early days in the record business. For me, these jobs are a shit sandwich. But the more bread you have, the less you taste the shit, if you know what I mean," I smiled at my poor excuse for wit.

He chuckled politely, but it was clear he found the statement juvenile if not nonsensical.

I doubled down. "I guess what I'm saying is I never really thought I'd find myself in a job like this. I was a music major for crying out loud. I'm super grateful for the opportunity, and I'm making more money than I ever thought I would."

"But you're not happy, are you?"

"It's nice of you to be concerned, but you should talk to my wife. In her opinion, I've never been happy in a job. Let's just say, I find moments of happiness that keep me going, and that's all I need. I have enough hobbies and avocations that keep me happy."

"Well, I don't think you're happy. I'd like you to take the day off to think about what might make you happy."

"What do you mean?"

"Just that. Contemplate what drives you and whether this job is fulfilling your inner drive."

I didn't stop to think, I just yanked my now rapidly beating heart out of my sunken chest cavity and displayed it, like a trained sommelier, in all its fragile, bloody glory on my red and white gingham sleeve. "I thought you hired me to be chief marketing officer, but all we've done since I've gotten here is take every red cent of retained earnings from PwnShop and plow it into purchasing AT&T reseller stores, businesses where we don't own the brand or the customer—AT&T does. And we're doing it under the guise of running small box retail as a core competency. We suck at small box retail. We're only good at video game retail. You can't do what we do in normal retail. We pay our employees at the fifth percentile of average retail wages because we know they would rather take a dollar or two an hour cut in pay from selling soulless cell phones to sell something they're passionate about. And, we rent stores in the dingiest, crappiest strip malls because we know our customer thinks of us as a destination. And, we've never invested in our systems, or e-tail, or any form of digital in any meaningful way. We say we're good at small box retail but we refuse to invest in the required experience. You want me to be excited to market stores where we don't own the brand or the customer?"

"As I suspected."

"I'm not unhappy. I'm just frustrated."

"There are things we can do to alleviate your frustration," he says, his eyes darting all over the shitty acoustic tile again.

"Like what?" I asked. "I don't understand."

"Just take the day off. Go home and think about it. Talk to Maura. And let's talk about it tomorrow after you've had a chance to reflect."

"Okay, but I want you to know, I'm not unhappy. I just want a little latitude to take a moderate amount of risk investing in the game business, not the phone business."

"I understand," he said.

I grabbed my backpack and headed back out, past Helen's desk.

"Where are you going?" she whispered.

I leaned again over the counter. "I think I just got fired."

"No. They wouldn't fire you. You're too loved around here. What did he say?"

"He asked if I was happy here, and to take the day off to think about it."

"I know Stephen can be kinda mysterious at times, but he's a good guy at heart. I don't think he's firing you. I think he deeply cares about you and wants what's best."

"I wish I were as optimistic as you always are," I responded. "But my spidey sense says I just got fired."

I pushed the backpack strap more squarely into the saddle between my right shoulder and collar bone and skulked out. I connected the phone to the stereo and typed "Run to the Hills," tapped the little repeat arrows that looked a bit like the recycling symbol, turned the volume knob 60 degrees clockwise, and waited for the telltale riff and galloping drums of Iron Maiden's opener from *Number of the Beast*. Bruce Dickinson wailed as a Cree, lamenting white man coming across the sea bringing pain and misery, and wondering whether they'd ever be set free. The only answer? Run to the hills. Run for your life.

I galloped in my steel coach powered by 300 horses through the concrete Texas prairie back to Dallas.

Haller Household
June 16, 2016
1693 days to POSS
CSP: $22.56

"Wait, it's 11:20 AM. What are you doing home?" Maura asked.

"Oh, I just thought I'd work the rest of the day from home. Wanna go to lunch?"

"I can't. I have Middle Eastern Summit[2] at 12:30 PM."

"Maybe I should join?"

"Yeah right. You'd wilt under the uh, disorder, you know, the galaxy of estrogen sunbeams."

"Ooh. Nice metaphor. True that. I guess I'll just go get a burger at Burger House or Goff's."

"What's up? You seem weird."

I wanted to quote Napoleon Dynamite's standard line when he came home from school, "Worst day of my life. What do you think?" Instead, I dropped all protective sarcasm.

"I think I just got fired, but I'm not quite sure."

Maura was strung tightly. Like mandolin tight. And the money dysfunction that ruled her life since her parents divorced when she was sixteen was only amplified by the untimely death of her father that left her and her sister an illiquid taxation mess for the ages. In short, the potential of financial instability was her kryptonite.

Without knowing it, I plucked the note (C8 in scientific pitch notation) two octaves above the female high C (C6) that sits two ledger lines above the treble staff. And, speaking before thinking (it runs in the marriage), her nerve tension quivered, and a cacophonous fugue of

---

[2] Euphemism for Maura's lunch group with her besties that takes place at an old Dallas institution owned by a Lebanese immigrant called Food from Galilee. As tradition has it, Food from Galilee has become the only place they'll dine for their get-togethers. Hence the euphemism. Nary a sentence is finished, nor does anyone open their mouths unless someone else is also speaking. Interruption isn't rude; it's required. What is finished—rather licked clean—is the best and most ridiculously reasonably priced shwarma, hummus, and baba ghanoush in one of the least acculturated cities in America.

unloaded anxieties spilled forth like the monster attack sequence in Stravinsky's "Danse Infernale" from *The Firebird Suite*.[3]

"You CANNOT get fired! You know we have a daughter in college and another that will be there in two years. Don't you? I told you last night not to let your passion get the best of you. Please oh god tell me you do know we have a daughter in college? Look me in the eye and tell me you're not getting fired." Her voice stabbed my soul.

"Whoa now. Not fair. I'm already stressed and you're going to amplify the stress?"

"I'm sorry." She immediately retreated, an action that has happened maybe once before in our marriage. Her typical MO was to add stress where none existed. "It's just that I paid bills this morning, and I don't know where it's all going to come from."

"I understand. I'm worried too. Look, I've never ever even come close to getting fired. Most of the time I'm being fought over. This is a first for me. But, if I'm going to get fired, I can't believe they won't give me some sort of glide path."

"Well, they damn well better. But wait, sometimes you tend to rush to doom and gloom scenarios. What happened?"

I related the conversation with Stephen and my subsequent optimistic attaboy from Helen.

---

[3] I did my senior thesis on Igor Stravinsky, my favorite composer. *The Firebird Suite*, a ballet, put him on the map. The opening of the 5th movement, the "Danse Infernale," is a tone poem musically expressing an attack of mythical creatures on the protagonist, Prince Ivan, by the evil wizard, King Kastchei. It is the marquee example of a modern "orchestra hit" followed by double-tongued trumpets jumping up two octaves to their uppermost register to palpate the listener's nervous strain. The fury the movement portrays is often imitated, if not completely ripped off. Compare the original to the overture in Andrew Lloyd Weber's *Jesus Christ Superstar* or the acceleration of tension in Paul McCartney's "Live and Let Die" for popular derivative examples using an actual orchestra. Now, most modern keyboard workstations have a sampled patch called Orchestra Hit as part of the standard "General Midi" sound set. It has become a cliché in modern hip-hop. For any youngsters that have stuck with me this long and haven't TL;DR'd me, a great example is Cardi B's remix of Bruno Mars' "Finesse." And, for fuddy-duddy white guys like me, the use of the keyboard patch in Yes's "Owner of a Lonely Heart" and Duran Duran's "A View to a Kill" might be more familiar. (The latter was also produced for a James Bond movie and is derivative of "Live and Let Die," albeit with a keyboard sample, which in turn is derivative of Stravinksy's seminal work. But I digress. Yet again.)

"Well, I see why you might think you're going to get fired, but I choose to side with Helen. I think Stephen just wants you happy and realizes he may have put you in an unfair situation. For now, so I can go to Middle Eastern Summit unburdened, that's my analysis."

And then she stopped, looked into space and said, "For now. Until I go to bed and can't sleep. Dammit, Nick, I don't need this stress right now."

"You think I do? I'm sorry. Maybe I'm just being pessimistic. Anyway, there's nothing I can do about it today."

PwnShop Offices
June 17, 2016
1692 days to POSS
CSP: $22.00

I entered with my backpack on properly. A few years back, a chiropractor told me I had slight scoliosis, and that driving too much and wearing a backpack over one shoulder aren't helping the situation. Most of the time I forget. Today I remembered.

As I walked upstairs to my office, the executive suites were deserted. Even Helen was missing. I proceeded down the corridor and made the right U-turn at the first available cross hall into my office. There, seated at my small round four-seater conference table, was Stephen and the angel of death herself, Jackie, the director of employee relations. Every time I'd fired somebody, Jackie, who was super sweet and performed her role with the utmost professionalism, had been my HR partner. It was not the most uplifting work, but she disguised any unhappiness by remaining steadfast in the act of duty.

Whenever a dismissal occurred, it was done in the Riggio conference room outside the main area of the building that requires badged entry, presumably so any violent reactions remained away from the rest of the employees. Jackie in my office with a big legal folder led me to believe I was getting fired. But that it was my office and not Riggio, led me to believe that might not be the case. Or, at least they didn't think I'd become violent.

I sat down at the small table, forgetting to remove my backpack. I just sat there on the edge of the chair, leaning forward awkwardly to make room for the massive hunch on my back.

"Good morning, Stephen," I uttered. "And uh, good morning, I think, uh Jackie?"

"Listen, Nick, I think you know what this is about. Per our conversation yesterday, you're being separated from the company. Jackie will walk you through the terms of your separation, along with the procedural next steps. I want to thank you for your service to PwnShop," he said, standing. "In all seriousness, you're one of the smartest people I've worked with. I'm sorry it didn't work out." He walked toward me, extending his hand. "But if there's anything you need during the transition, I'm more than happy to help out in any way I can." We shook hands, me sweatily, he lifelessly. "I mean it," he said with his eyes cast to the ceiling.

What the fuck kinda skull fucker are you? "Go home and think about if you're happy?" "Per our conversation?" What a passive aggressive con. Subterfuge. Well, yes! Unhappy? Goddamn right. I am now. Really fucking unhappy, you dead-fish-handshaking-can't-look-me-in-the-eye psychological predator. Fucking Rasputin. Goddamn Littlefinger.

"Thanks for the opportunity, Stephen." I said, my voice quivering like Link Wray's tremolo guitar in "Rumble."[4]

Jackie opened her folder and started passing me papers. I'd seen this movie too many times, but I'd never been the star of the film. I was in a brain fog and didn't hear a word she said. We exchanged pleasantries. I grabbed the folder of COBRA drivel this and Outplacement tripe that and stood.

---

[4] A paean to juvenile delinquency performed by Link Wray, a seminal surf guitarist, employing a distorted tremolo effect in its guitar tone.

"Oh wait," she said. "I almost forgot. Your laptop is over there, right?"

"Yes, I left it here last night," I said, pointing to the MacBook on my desk.

"Okay, then I just need your badge, your keys, and your corporate card."

I pulled out my wallet, removed the PwnShop credit card, unclipped the retractable badge holder from the coin pocket on my five pockets, and ripped a fingernail while clumsily fishing the key off the steel keyring. I set them all in a haphazard pile in front of her.

"Just call me when you want to retrieve your personal items."

"Will do."

"I'm sorry," she said.

"You're not supposed to say that. Ever. That's off script. And, it's not your fault."

"I know. I'm just sorry to see you go."

"Me too."

I waddled around the U-turn out from my office back into the main hallway. I passed by Helen's still vacant cube and made eye contact with Claude, who was just arriving.

"Hey, man," he said. "Come here for a second."

I stood in the vestibule of his massive office and couldn't help but stare at the 32-inch—presumably life-size—resin Yoda statue, replete with its woolen cloak, resting upon a bookshelf in the back corner, overseeing all activities in "the room where it happens." I forced my gaze to Claude's, who was staring me squarely in the eye. He extended his hand. We shook. Solidly. Steadily.

"Listen, I just want you to know you're a talent. I'm super sorry this didn't work out, but given my fight over the last eighteen months, I feel like I have a lot more perspective on things. Just about every executive in this building has been through something similar."

"Really?" I questioned. "It's definitely a first for me."

"I know you don't want to hear it right now, but it's something you need to go through to clarify who you are, what you stand for, and to find the resolve to pursue the career that's best for you. I've been through it. Joe and Stephen have been through it. It sucks right now, but take your time—I think we've given you some—to really self-reflect and figure it out. And please know, I'm 100 percent referenceable. Happy to help in any way I can. You're a talent. I know you're going to do great things. Sometimes we have to step back to move forward in the right direction."

"Well, uhm, that means a lot," I said, swallowing. "Especially from a person of your character, who's been in the fight, literally, for their life. You are one of the good ones, Claude, and I can't thank you enough for the opportunity. I'm sorry I wasn't a good fit."

"Not your fault. Ours. We sort of knew it when we brought you in. You need a growth opportunity that allows you to be creative. This is a hunker down and diversify situation. Go dream big. You'll find it. And listen, call Helen in about six weeks and let's set up a lunch once you've had time to reflect and redirect."

"Thank you, Claude. Means a lot. I guess I just said that. Anyway, I just might take you up on that lunch. I wish nothing but the best for PwnShop. Protect the family."

"Indeed!" he exclaimed.

As I was walking out, I passed Jack Floyd's door.

"Hey Nick. Do you have a minute?"

"I find myself with more than a minute it seems."

Jack sniggered loudly, then uncomfortably. "I'm sorry to see you go," he whispered, "I've never worked with a marketing person who understood finance and accounting as well as you. You will be missed. I hope our paths cross again soon."

"Well, that's nice," I said while working through the cognitive dissonance.

I guess that means I failed as a marketing wonk. Maybe I would have been better funded if they thought I didn't understand economics, finance and accounting? And, oh, pretty sure our paths will never cross again.

I walked out to my car. Connected the phone. Typed "Johnny Cash Hurt" into the Spotify search bar. Tapped the repeat icon. And drove home, preparing myself, if that's even possible, for the looming shame that awaits in admitting to your spouse of twenty-three years that the breadwinner might now be on the bread line. The song had become a comical cliché for depression, but for a good reason. The regrets of a frail man dying from the complications of diabetes, reinterpreting the lyrics of a much younger man's figurative suicide note to shake his heroin addiction,[5] transported me to the place of failure I always feared: my empire of dirt.

> Home
> June 10, 2016
> 1692 days to POSS
> CSP: $21.00

"Told you so. I finally win an argument. I was right. I got fired," I blurted as I saw Maura after walking through the front door.

"Are you serious? Fired?"

"That's what I call it. Gossamer's memo to the company calls it a 'resignation to pursue other opportunities.' They gave me nine months' severance."

"How can they fire you? You got a four out of five on your last review. And nine months? For the chief marketing officer? Shouldn't it be at least a year? Do you have a lawyer?" The stress in Maura's voice was like an ice pick to the temple.

---

[5] "Hurt" was written by Trent Reznor, the iconoclastic leader of Nine Inch Nails, who commented that Cash's cover in 2002, released just seven months before the legendary troubadour's death, gave the song an entirely different meaning, but "every bit as pure." Incidentally, Reznor recorded the song and the album on which it appears, *The Downward Spiral*, at 10050 Cielo Drive, the "Manson Murder House" in which Sharon Tate and others were maliciously murdered by brainwashed followers of the charlatan Charles Manson. Needless to say, the tune has a heaping helping of gloom and doom.

"Yes I have a lawyer but I'm not going to engage them. I'm a not-yet-fifty-year-old white male. Texas is a right-to-work state. It is what it is. That's plenty of runway."

"So what are you going to do now?"

"Right now, I'm going to go play my bass. Maybe take a nap. Maybe brood."

"Well don't brood too long. You have a family to support."

"Thanks, love. I'm well aware. I just need to crawl inside myself and be swallowed by this reality. Its substance. Its shame. I hate to say it, but I always knew this was my fate. I've spent my whole career trying not to get fired instead of putting my ass on the line. What a dumbass I am."

"Oh lord. That's pretty poetic, but don't get all depressed on me. And don't start the self-pity. I don't think I can handle that."

"You can't handle it? What about me? Can you please just empathize for one single fucking moment?"

"I'm sorry. You're right." She patted me on the head, pulling it to her shoulder. "I'm sorry you got fired, baby. That must suck." Her voice was trapped between compassion and mockery. "By the way, the light bulb over my sink is out. Do you mind changing it? At least that will give you something to do. I'm off to a school board meeting."

Really. How are those two thoughts even remotely related? Who gives a shit about a shitty-impossible-to-grip-recessed light bulb at a time like this? Something to do? How about sympathy sex? Or a heartfelt hug. I don't need something to do. I need deliverance.

"Sure. I'll change it," I forfeited.

She left, her slingbacks clapping away on the hardwood floor like the castanets in *Carmen* that entice Don José to abandon his duty.[6]

You do know José killed Carmen in the end, don't you Sweets? Oh yeah. You hate *opera.*

Home
June 18, 2016
1691 days to POSS
CSP: $22.00

Last night I dreamed I was at the bingo parlor. I brandished the red blotter in my left hand to dot the bingo card and the purple blotter in my right to daub my sunken eyes. The game at hand was blackout. The red diaphanous ink bled into every square but the free space, making each number more vivid, more sanguine. The purple ink bruised my eye sockets in the manner of bad Halloween zombie makeup. I kept waiting for the caller to call the free space. He was an impish, short-banged man wearing a Sergio Tacchini track suit and Dansko clogs. I'm 99 percent sure he was Napoleon reincarnated. I'm one percent sure he was Kip from *Napoleon Dynamite*. He never called the free square. There was no one else in the parlor. He called all seventy-five balls while I sat. Bing-no. Bin-going. Bin-gone.

Maura and I were seated in our requisite Edith and Archie chairs in the family room. Were both drinking our coffee. Mine had a splash of milk. From cows. Hers had been in the blender with cinnamon, cashew

[6] First performed in Paris in 1875, *Carmen* is Georges Bizet's wildly popular opera that, predominantly through the emotion of its music, diagrams the downfall of Don José, a weak-minded soldier seduced by the manifest wiles of the gypsy Carmen. Bizet, a French composer, is credited for bringing Spanish flamenco music, along with its requisite castanets, to a much wider audience. The gypsy Carmen is a classic example of the seductress archetype: the femme fatale from whose tractor beam we of the penised patriarchy are incapable of escaping. As such, we watch Don José transmogrify from an honest, dutiful soldier to the tortured murderer of his lover, simply because self-control is out of the question. I mean, when a hypnotizing cocktease swipes left on you and swipes right on a flamboyant yet manly toreador, murder is the only option, right?

milk (*I didn't know nuts had udders?*), coconut oil, and ghee. Some crazy keto thing.

"What are you going to do today?" Maura pecked the thin, cracking ice.

"Well, I broke that light bulb off at the socket that you wanted me to change. I guess I gotta deal with that. I'm also thinking about emailing Stephen Gossamer."

"Really? What for? Going to ask for more severance?"

"No. That is what it is. But, he told me that he would be happy to help in any way possible. I just want him to tell me the short, pithy sentence that I can say that makes headhunters think I'm not damaged goods."

"Oh that's good. You're already talking to headhunters?"

"No, Maura. My body's not even cold yet. I haven't talked to anybody. I think I need a day or two to process all of this, dontcha think?"

"Well, spring is almost over. Before you know it, we'll be in the summer lull, vacations and whatnot, and nobody will be hiring until the fall. We could be in a recession by then. And you do remember we have a daughter in college and a son who will be there in two years?"

Spring almost over? The vernal fucking equinox was just ten days ago. And holy shit?! I have a daughter in college?! Well spatchcock my scrotum and call me Varys.[7]

"I know. I know. You're right."

"I've got a meeting at school and then tennis this afternoon. Please fix that lightbulb while you're doing whatever you're going to do."

"I will."

I went to the electrical panel, cut the switch to the kitchen circuit where the broken socket awaited, went to the garage and grabbed a stepladder and a pair of needle nose pliers, walked back into the house, climbed the stool, and painstakingly turned the bulbless socket in quarter turns with the pliers until I got enough metal upon which my

---

[7] Varys was the eunuch in *Game of Thrones*. Internally at PwnShop, we jokingly called Microsoft's rumored digital-only console (eliminating the need for a disk drive) "Project Varys." Get it? Diskless.

fingers could find purchase. I sliced my thumb slightly, but was successful in removing the socket. I climbed down the ladder, got the new bulb, twisted it in and found that it was defective. Damnitalltohell. I climbed down the ladder again, got another bulb, stepped up the ladder, almost lost my balance raising my arm and head up and backwards, and finally got a successful lodgment. I climbed down the ladder, went upstairs to the electrical panel, flipped the circuit back on, walked back down the stairs, turned on the wall switch and saw a glorious halo of light emanating from the recess in the ceiling. Satisfied, I folded up the step ladder, and made the mistake of looking at the oven to check the time. It showed a scrolling message: P-L-E-A-S-E S-E-T C-L-O-C-K. Shitfucksunovabitch. In cutting the circuit I realized I now needed to reset all the clocks in the kitchen. Finally, I progressed in getting the kitchen back to square one, which was really no progress at all, and thirty-seven minutes of my life had passed.

I sat down at the kitchen table with my personal laptop that I didn't use frequently since I'd been using company-owned laptops in the main for the past fifteen to twenty years. This begat a password crisis. Another twenty-five minutes frittered away with me finally getting logged into the laptop after six failed attempts and requisite waiting periods, and then the mind-numbing rigor of resetting my Yahoo password for my personal email, upon realizing I had it cached in the company laptop and couldn't remember it either. The morning of the first day of the rest of my life slithered away thusly, a vapid, henpecked scrotum, a replaced light bulb, synchronized kitchen clocks, and two new forgettable passwords as my trophies. I should have ignored the circuit breaker panel and just stuck my tongue in that socket.

After standing at the fridge and noshing my way through lunch—three lacto-fermented pickle spears wrapped in Tillamook Swiss cheese slices, a few celery stalks as vessels for almost a cup of roasted red pepper hummus, cold dark meat with congealed fat pulled from the left quarter of a store-bought rotisserie chicken, two pita crackers with a heap of crunchy peanut butter and blackberry preserves, a few guajillo peppers and Manzanilla olives (two-thirds of the famous Basque gilda pintxo), a gulp of 1 percent milk from the carton, fourteen pistachios, two of which I had to pound with a knife to get the shell to split, and three heaping tablespoons...no fuck it...the rest of the pint carton of Graeter's "Midnight Snack," the most sublime expression of food love ever created—I sat back down at the kitchen table, full of Breyer's remorse, to self-immolate my lack of discipline after my snackcident, and eventually, to craft the email to Stephen Gossamer.

To: sgossamer@PwnShop.com
From: boogerhaller@sbcglobal.net
Subject: Need your counsel/Favor

Stephen,

First of all, thank you for the gentlemanly way you handled my exit. I've returned the signed paperwork to Jackie, so we should be all good on that front.

Since my departure a couple of days ago, I've had a chance to reflect. I'm fortunate yet naïve about the situation I'm in, as I have no point of comparison in my almost fifty years on this earth. I've never been fired, asked to pursue other opportunities, or "promoted" to customer. I've only been promoted. This is uncharted territory for me.

As I begin my search for the next thing, may I take you up on your offer to help out? I'm not asking for a reference, nor for introductions to any of your network. I just want your counsel. What is the short, pithy sentence that I can tell prospective employers and headhunters that prevents them from reading into my PwnShop experience that I'm damaged goods?

That's it. Many thanks in advance for your help in this matter. Best of luck to you, Claude, Tom and the entire team as you pursue the diversification strategy.

Warmest regards,

Nick

I reread the draft email and removed the bit about being promoted to customer. I hit send. And waited a full month for a response.

Home
July 19, 2016
1660 days to POSS
CSP: $23.72

And on the twelfth day of July, my ex-boss gave to me...

12 angry men-dications,
11 clocks tick-tocking,
10 little injuries,
9 hives,
8 my twin in the womb,
7 deadly tailspins,
6 pack of fear,
5 senses jerking overtime,
4 crying out loud,
3 sheets to the wind,
2 despair is human,
...and a cartridge in a Glock 33. (For me.)

He also gave me a response to the email I sent over thirty torturous days ago:

To: boogerhaller@sbcglobal.net
From: sgossamer@PwnShop.com
Subject: Re: Need your counsel/Favor

Nick,

I was delighted to receive your email. My apologies for the delay in my response. As you may remember, we were in the middle of closing the acquisition of 13 AT&T stores owned by an entrepreneur in Tacoma, WA. Not an overly problematic diligence/closing, but a diligence/closing all the same.

Your question about what to tell potential employers, if that's the route you choose to go, is a good one. My two cents—you shouldn't work for a large company. You're not built for it. You should do something more entrepreneurial in an endeavor for which you have a passion. But, if you're truly deciding to stay in the game, before I answer your question, I want to share that I was in the same place you were before PwnShop hired me in 2011. It's not a fun place to be, but in a few years, you'll look at this with the perspective of hindsight and realize it made you better. I know I have.

In the summer of 2010, I walked into my boss's office with some hard data...[...blah blah blah...gory details of the injustice of his firing at his former employer...yadda yadda yadda...soul searching... ba dum bum bum...serious reflection, mindfulness, and prayer...and so forth and so on...self-acceptance...woo woo woo...self-discovery... whooptee fucking do...self-actualization...et cetera...]

And now to answer your question, I think there's a simple answer that you can say in all honesty: "I resigned for strategic differences because I believed there was a way forward in the core business through transformation. My bosses, however, wanted to cash cow the core business and plow those retained earnings into a comprehensive diversification plan."

That's it. You can add that I'd be happy to serve as a reference. I would. You may not believe or trust me, but as I stated on your last day, you're a smart guy and you'll be just fine in the long run.

Don't be a stranger. I know I won't. I'll reach out in a few months for lunch. Please let me know how else I can help.

Sincerely,

Stephen

Now there's a skull fucking of the worst disorder. In writing. They wanted to cash cow the core business and plow those earnings into a silly diversification? That's all I ever wanted them to admit. And they fire me and then tell me what I wanted to hear after I'm gone. For real? Didn't we have that conversation umpteen times and he denied, denied, denied? Unbelievable.

After processing the email for about an hour, Maura walked in.

"Come here," I said, "and read this. This has been messing with me all day."

"What is it? I have to change and shower really fast. I'm late for a birthday lunch."

"Stephen finally responded to my email. It's lengthy, but you don't have to read it all. Remember how I asked him for help on what I might say to potential employers about the conditions of my departure?"

"Yes."

"Just read his answer to that. Right here," I said while scrolling up on my laptop screen.

She leaned over my left shoulder, asked to borrow my glasses, and scanned the email for all of three seconds.

"That's really nice," she exclaimed. "I thought you said you got fired? What he wrote makes total sense to me and sounds like an easy thing to say to, um, headhunters and such."

"That's it? Don't you see, that's what I was trying to get him to admit when I worked there? It takes me getting fired for him to admit it?"

"I love you dearly," she said while kissing the top of my head. "But it must be difficult to be such a pessimist. Listen, I really am late. We can talk about this later."

Why can't she ever take my side?

Track 9: Keep Coming Back

"Be honest. Brutally honest.
That is what's going to maintain relationships."

—LAURYN HILL

Sheraton Hotel
Trophy Club, Texas
June 8, 2018
971 days to POSS
CSP: $13.28

The corporate race, to which so many of my characters belong, has been playing at reindeer games from the beginning and probably will till the end, which is a nuisance for the few people who grow up.

I still hadn't grown up. I'd just grown older. In twenty-seven days, I'd complete fifty trips around the sun. As my life was equidistant between thirteen and eighty-seven, I found vexing comfort in these extremes, simultaneously basking in irreverent adolescence and masking the remorse of roads not taken.

After getting fired from PwnShop, instead of a period of soul-searching followed by an intensive "exploration of other opportunities," I took the path of ceased existence—another job at a tired, disrupted, bricks and mortar retailer, with a weekly commute to California. Namely, Tailored Brands, Inc. (TBI). You might better know it as the stitched together merger of Men's Wearhouse and Jos. A. Bank. Yep, that Men's Wearhouse, the suitery that the least interesting man in the world but the most megalomaniacal haberdasher in history, George Zimmer, guarantees "You'll like the way you look." And yep, that Jos. A. Bank, the shop for which *SNL*'s spoof spot touts, "These suits are so cheap I use them to clean my kitchen counters!"

Yeah, not the most solid career management. But I was panicked. And, the job met three criteria I'd come up with in the brief moments of downtime between episodes of changing lightbulbs. (1): Does management view the solution for disruption as a strategic transformation? (The last team at PwnShop viewed diversification as the solution). (2): Will I have a seat at the table? (Despite promises to the contrary and all the BS about title not mattering, I was never invited to the room where it happened.) And (3): Will I be working for an asshole? (I suppose asshole is in the eye of the beholder. But if it looks like a brown eyed hamflower or a rusty starfish, talks like Rush Limbaugh or Kanye West, and smells like shit or bleach, then it must be an asshole.) And no, I wasn't seeking a "yes" to each question. I'm not a masochist.

After about a year at TBI, Harvey Handler, the newly appointed CEO at PwnShop, left a message while I was in Tahoe skiing with my son. He said Claude had collapsed in a board meeting back in November, was hospitalized, and succumbed on March 5 to the brain cancer he'd fought so valiantly. The board, in all their foresight, didn't have a succession plan in place.

Let me repeat, Claude had stage 4 metastatic brain cancer with three glioblastomas, and the board didn't have a plan for replacing a dead man walking. There's a reason we called it the Bored Room.

After Claude died, the board hired a personnel firm to do 360 degree reviews of the four remaining senior executives: President Joe Engel, CFO Jack Floyd, my old boss and Chief Strategy Officer Stephen Gossamer, and EVP of International Harvey Handler, with orders from the board to promote from within. The outcome of the review process exposed the diversification for the fiasco it was, and the board terminated Joe and Stephen without cause. Jack got his wrist slapped for not fully divulging the poor performance, but remained as CFO. Harvey was named CEO, and he wanted to talk to me about returning, this time as an SVP.

Before returning his call, I got Grady on the line to fill in on the back story, leading with my assumption that every executive had disqualified themselves and Harvey was merely the last suit standing.

"Bingo!" he said. "Joe and Stephen were selling the board a bill of goods on how great the diversification acquisitions were doing, and then AT&T drastically cut our commission. It was a ticking timebomb. And with Think Geek, we're up to our eyeballs in excess inventory. Two huge egos who are impossible to work with. That came out. Jack got to keep his job, but I think he's been damaged by the way the board was led to believe everything was hunky dory with the acquisitions."

"So…Harvey? I barely knew him. The guy was omni-absent. What's his M.O?"

"Hard to tell," Grady waffled. "Remember those ZING Pop Culture stores they launched in Australia? That business is doing okay, but it isn't going to fix the hole in the ozone layer. He's an operator from what I can tell. He's already rolled out his own slogan: 'The future's in the fundamentals.'"

"Oh. God. Classic old school retail. We're not being disrupted. The only problem we have is that we aren't stacking the cans on the endcaps efficiently."

"Hahaha. Such a smartass. Man I miss you. Do you think you'd ever come back?"

"Dude, I have a fair amount of trauma from that toxic place. Pretty happy to be out of the madness."

"So, how's it going out there in California?" he asked.

"The CEO at TBI is a good guy. A genuinely solid human being. Now, of course, I'm starting to wonder if the board is attempting to set the nice guy up to finish last, but I can't tell you how much of a pleasure it is to go to work every day and not have to surmise where and in what position I'm going to get fucked. Regardless, it's nice not feeling like I've got to put on my trench coat and negotiate with terrorists every day."

Harvey was relieved I'd called him back. After some back and forth, I ran my criteria by him, and after this neo-CEO slathered me with a thick slab of wocka wocka, mah ná mah ná and a dollop of verbazuma's revenge, I interpolated his politically noncommittal answers to be "No," "Perhaps," and "Probably not."[1] He was dead set on operational excellence over strategic transformation as the way forward. He was thinking about creating a president of the United States business and have the CMO report to that individual, but he wasn't sure yet about that structure and said he would consider having the CMO report to him. And, based on how the conversation went, he didn't have the ego or lack the empathy to be Webster's second definition for asshole (the first being "anus"): a detestable person. That said, I wasn't sure if he wasn't one of the alternate definitions, an annoying dolt specifically, but I tend to use the term jackass for this ilk, as they're sometimes lovable and quite distinct from anuses and assassins.

I told him my current position met my criteria more than what he was espousing, but he asked me not to dismiss him out of hand, and could we have dinner the next time I was back in town, three weeks hence. On the

[1] You avid gamers might've thought wocka wocka was intended to be the onomatopoeia of the sound Pac Man made when gobbling pellets. Perhaps, perhaps, perhaps. It was also the nonsense catchphrase the Muppet Fozzie Bear used to indicate when he'd delivered a joke's punchline. And, you avid Muppet fans might've thought the nonsense song "Mah Ná Mah Ná" was originated by the Muppets. You'd be wrong and possibly outraged to learn it was written for a 1968 Italian documentary, *Sweden: Heaven and Hell*, about Sweden's wild sexual mores. The song accompanied a sauna scene. Hmm. Think the PBS and ABC censors knew that when The Muppets performed it on *Sesame Street* in 1969, and again on the debut episode of their eponymous TV show in 1976? Both Benny Hill and Red Skelton spread the "Mah Ná Mah Ná" love in their television shows, and Hot Butter, best known for their song "Popcorn," did a Moog synthesizer cover in 1973. My favorite version was by the great Cake. You can find it on their 2007 release *B-Sides and Rarities*. Incidentally, their rendition of the Doris Day classic, "Perhaps, Perhaps, Perhaps" can be found on their 1996 album, *Fashion Nugget*. But if you think Doris was the first to do it, you'd be wrong. It was originally written as "Quizás, quizás, quizás" by the Cuban songwriter Osvaldo Farrés and performed in Spanish by Bobby Capó in 1947. Famous Cuban American Desi Arnaz was the first to record it in its English translation in 1948, some seventeen years before Doris Day made it famous on her album *Latin for Lovers*.

day I was flying out, I called his assistant to make sure we were still on only to be told that "something's come up" and rescheduling probably wasn't in the cards.

I immediately called the town gossip to get the goods, and Grady informed me of a nasty rumor floating about that Harvey, six weeks into his illustrious promotion, may have attempted to seduce one of PwnShop's event staffers at the annual President's Awards banquet for high-performing stores.

"How the hell would you like to be Tom Testa right now?" I asked Grady about the aging board chair, now well into his seventies.

"Oh. My. Gawd. Can you imagine?" he asked.

"He finally found the heir apparent to take over his Wall Street darling, only to have him get sick with brain cancer, so he allowed the inmates to run the asylum, and then the prodigal son up and dies just when they thought the cancer was in remission, and oh yeah, he then forgets to double click on the extracurricular activities of the next guy he put in the seat, and now he finds himself holding the bag again. Just when you think you're out, they pull you right back in. I just feel sorry for the people there. The leadership can't get out of their way."

Never a dull moment at PwnShop. A month later, I received a call from Jack Floyd inviting me to dinner at the very same restaurant where Harvey and I were to meet. We got it scheduled a few weeks out. He, and his SVP of accounting and the head of HR met me. I gave them the three criteria, they gave me the very same wocka wocka, and mah ná mah ná and slathered me with a heaping helping of Nick Haller adoration. The answers to the first two came out again as "No" and "Perhaps." They agreed with Harvey that the future was in the fundamentals. And on having a seat at the table, they said if I came back as CMO, I could interview for the president role Harvey was planning once whatever CEO they found next was in place. I pointed out that the next one might not even like me, or Harvey's plan. And then I asked whether they would take the job if they were me.

"Frankly, that's why we're here," Jack said. "You're a hard guy to figure out. There are a ton of folks that would be doing back flips if you came back. I didn't know how much of an impression you'd made until you left."

Thinking he didn't really answer the question, I responded, "Only the good die young." After beholding bewildered looks all around, I continued. "Well, I think I've heard what I need to hear. Gentlemen, I don't want to waste your time, but I also don't want to be a wet blanket. It's great to see you all, and I'm flattered you're thinking of me."

"You are the right answer for us," Jack responded. "I realize this is bad negotiating, but you're the only candidate we're talking to."

"Clearly, I need to count to ten and sleep on it," I said, "but if you put a gun to my head tonight, I'd have to say 'not interested.'"

After a sound night's sleep, I called Jack and confirmed my lack of interest.

Two weeks passed before I got a call from Tom Testa's assistant saying the chairman of the board wanted to meet with me for breakfast.

Well now we're getting somewhere. The Chairman of the Board himself. They must be desperate.

As I pulled into the circular driveway of the Trophy Club Sheraton, the pitch and percussive character of the banjo and mandolin from "Where is My Mind?" punctured the sanctuary of the car's cockpit. This was the Trampled by Turtles 2011 cover of the Pixies' signature song, the production unfussy, allowing enough elbow room for me to take notice of Dave Simonett's calloused and iron vocals reciting the Black Francis-penned lyrics. They were elusive, spinning yarns about feet "on" the air, head on the ground, collapsing, empty. It was a strident question. Where is my mind?

It was already 82 degrees, not yet 7:30 AM. A guy about my age, with a blue merle beard and the valet company's baseball cap on backwards, opened my door. Lost in the music, I forgot where I was for a moment.

"Love that song, dude. Saw the Pixies at The Vatican, in like '90 or '91."

"The Pixies played for The Pope?"

"No, the club in Houston, back when music was actually live."

"Oh man, you're singing my song. You know, I think my buddy followed Soulhat there when he was living in Austin. Or maybe that was The Abyss."

"Same place. Somebody bought The Vatican and changed the name to The Abyss. It was an old church originally."

"Ahh. Cool. Old church becomes a rock club. Name it The Vatican. Irony."

"Exactly. Yeah, I grew up in Houston. Great memories. Saw a bunch of good shows there. Mudhoney and Urge Overkill. Social D."

"Wow. Mike Ness is a hero. Like he said when I was at Guitar Mart, 'All my heroes are outlaws and junkie guitar players.'"

"Word. I don't want to judge, but you don't look like the typical Social Distortion fan."

"Whaddya mean?" I said as my hands danced in the air like one of the showcase models on *The Price Is Right*. They spotlit an inconspicuous outfit—a lightly starched grey and white gingham check shirt, navy chinos, and suede Clarks Desert Boots. "I'm a fucking hipster," I winked, handed him my keys and headed into the restaurant.

As I approached the hostess stand, I saw Tom Testa sitting at a booth next to a guy who, seated, was a whole head taller than Tom.

They were both on one side, almost like a cute couple, leaving the other unoccupied with room for all sorts of conjecture. The other man appeared to be about fifteen years Tom's junior, and, with jet black hair and almond eyes, clearly had some Asian in his heritage.

"Tom! Good to see you!" I exclaimed as he stood, more slowly than when I last saw him almost two years ago. I gave him a handshake before we pulled in for an awkward half hug with the requisite shoulder pats.

"Good to see you as well, Nick. I'm glad you could join us."

"My pleasure." I caught the eyes of the other gentleman, who was stuck in the booth, rising above the seat in an awkward, impatient squat, his thighs pressed against the underside of the laminate tabletop.

"Hey, Nick. How are you?" he said, extending his hand. I untwisted from the hemi-bro hug with Tom and shook it. "Lance Park," he continued.

"Nice to meet you, Lance," I emoted, with perhaps too much feigned affability and too much waggle in my shake.

As we sat, Tom started right in, skipping the customary small talk, "Listen, Nick, I know you've talked to Harvey and then Jack, Chuck and uhm, uhm, uh, you know, the accountant..."

"Colt."

"Yes. Colt Woodford. Senior moment."

"It happens to me all the time."

"They tell me you aren't interested in coming back. I'm here to tell you, you are."

"Okay then," I chuckled. "Let's commence the convincing."

Lance laughed. Tom looked a bit confused and annoyed.

"Don't you think we should at least let Nick order before we beat him into submission?" Lance smirked.

Ah, a fellow smartass. Who is this guy and why is he at the table with the OG Chairman of the PwnShop waterboard?

"Sure. I guess so." Tom allows, his impatience outweighing any decorum.

"Uhm, even before that," I chimed clumsily, "uhm, I don't know that Lance and I have ever met. Mind if I ask who you are?"

"Of course." Lance said. "We met once at a PwnShop board meeting dinner. I think Stephen Gossamer brought you along."

"Oh wow. That's embarrassing. I remember having to go to that dinner..."

"Having to go? Was it that painful?" Lance continued to lilt in his sarcastic manner.

"Haha." I courtesy laughed. "Anyway, I'm ashamed I don't remember meeting you."

"A six-foot two smartass Korean American? That's not memorable enough for ya?"

"See Tom, I didn't remember Lance. Senior moments happen to the youngest of us," I doubled down.

"Ho ho ho," Tom said, more Scrooge than Santa, as if he were saying "bah humbug." "Anyway, Nick, Lance has been on the PwnShop board for five or six years..."

"Actually seven, Tom. I joined in 2011. Time flies when you're having fun doesn't it?"

"I guess so," Tom dismissed. "Anyway, Lance volunteered to come along, as he's particularly interested in meeting you."

"Well, thanks for coming Lance. I'm having a hard time getting over the fact that I don't remember meeting you. What's your background?"

"You didn't spend last night memorizing the bios of all the board members? Shame on you!"

I thought he was kidding, but couldn't really tell. *Big ego or couldn't give two shits?*

"Heh heh. I didn't know anybody else would be in attendance."

"Tom, I can't believe you're talking to this guy. He should be disqualified for not knowing my background." He stabbed, allowing the words to pierce my thin skin. I'm pretty sure my eyes widened. "Oh, I'm just messing with you, Nick. I can't think of anything less boring than the bios of this illustrious board."

"That's why we call it the B.O.R.E.D room," I spelled the cheeky spelling that hangs outside the largest conference room in the PwnShop Support Center, venturing into the barren patch of obvious puns and dad humor.

"Haha. Yes we do. Literally, right?" He nodded, smiled and turned his head to Tom. "That's how it's spelled on the sign outside the big conference room, right?"

The waitress came, I ordered a bowl of oatmeal—the encroaching cholesterol reading from last month's physical still fresh on my mind. After I handed back the menu, feeling a bit judged by my prudish order, Tom started in, his voice conveying renewed crabbiness, as if any levity was a venial sin, worthy of confession but pardonable in the end.

"Lance, briefly please, tell Nick your background."

"Fifteen years at Microsoft in the Xbox business. Was most recently in strategic planning for Microsoft Game Studio, and was in charge of the *Halo*, *Gears of War* and *Forza* franchises."

Holy shit. Somebody from the actual gaming industry and not some can stacker. And strategy? Wha?

"Prior to that, and please don't hold it against me, I went to Harvard Business School."

"Ahh. HBS. Where it's two-thirds BS."

"I've heard that one before. You're just jealous," he winked.

"Actually not. Graduated in 1997. Two years that messed me up completely," I deadpanned.

Here we go again. Two HBS graduates who have mentioned the fact within three minutes of meeting each other. As much as I run from it, I'm still a fucking hypocrite. No better than the rest of those type A masters of the universe.

"Tom, you didn't tell me this guy was so self-defacing," Lance jested.

"Don't you mean self-effacing?" Tom corrected questioningly.

"It was an intended pun. Sorry it fell flat. Anyway, Nick, didn't they teach you about power and influence in the late '90s or were they already going soft by then."

"Oh, they did. But somebody had to be the poster child for, uh, I don't know, mediocrity and career oblivion."

"Haha. Tom? Why are we interviewing this guy again?" he mocked, in an older brother kinda way.

"I'm told Nick was thought of pretty fondly by his peers..."

"So fondly I got fired," I winked at Lance. He smiled knowingly.

"You do know we've ended our relationship with Engel and Gossamer, your uhm..."

"Executioners," I interrupted.

Tom gave me a fatherly stare. "Well, you do know Claude spoke highly of you."

"He was a good man. So sorry to hear he couldn't beat it in the end."

"You don't know the half of it. So were we.... So were we." He paused in vacant reflection for a four count, and then continued, "It's been a rough few months."

"So I gather. I can't imagine. I'm sure you thought you'd have left this thing in good hands at this point in your career."

Too forward and honest.

Another four count.

"Yes, but it is what it is. And so, we persevere. Anyway, back to the topic at hand. Jack says you weren't interested in CMO. Can you please tell me why?"

"Well, sir." I paused, confused by the confounded nature in which he presented the question. *Did these people not talk to each other?* "I think I was pretty clear. First off, I like what I'm doing, the people I'm working with, and the challenge of differentiating a house of similar brands, and modernizing them with mass customization."

"But the job is in San Francisco, right?" Tom dug for the hometown discount.

"Yes, but the kids are much older now. John will be off to college in the fall and George is exhibiting some interest in boarding school. If that happens, it doesn't really matter where I work."

"What does your wife think?" Lance asked the right question.

"She doesn't love it, but she also knows that everybody is happier when I'm happy in my job."

"Mmm hmm. I see," Tom said, visibly cogitating.

Then, I listed off my three criteria, enumerating and illuminating each. "For number three, it looks like you got rid of the assholes in the main. That's a positive. But, number one and two are what leave me empty-handed. It's where the job you're proposing, which I might mention I've done once, shrivels up like a grape-cum-raisin on the vine. I don't care to repeat that experience."

"Eww. Vivid." Lance smirked. "That bad? Old, dry and shriveled?"

"If it looks like a raisin and is shriveled like a raisin…"

"…then it must be PwnShop?" Lance bantered.

I smiled. This guy got it. "You said it. Not me."

"Enough repartee, you two." Tom pressed. "Help me understand. It's chief marketing officer of the biggest company in gaming. We're, what, at least four times the size of Men's Wearhouse?"

"Not to be argumentative, but after the merger, they're about half the size of PwnShop. More importantly, it's apparel. The IMU[2] is like 90 percent. As a result, the marketing budget I'm managing is over $300 million. At PwnShop, domestically, which is apparently the only scope of the job you're proposing, it's about $50 million, and declining every year. At TBI, I can put in play some pretty creative stuff."

"Don't you think a smaller budget actually allows you to be more creative?" Tom submitted this zinger in a manner of plain truth, leaving no room to expose the incongruity of the statement.

The wrinkle between my eyebrows eroded into a gulch as deep and dry as the Copper Canyon in the lawless Sierra Madre Mountains of northwestern Mexico. It said, *"El apego emocional a tú argumento es directamente proporcional a tú falta de conocimiento sobre el tema."* (The emotional attachment to your argument is directly proportional to your lack of knowledge about the subject.)

Lance, witnessing the frown, redirected. "I get why you don't think you have a seat at the table, but I'm not following you on your third criteria. Something about the problem at hand?"

---

[2] A standard retail metric—Initial Mark-Up. It's the difference between the sales price of an item and how much it cost to purchase or manufacture it, expressed as a percentage. In the case of PwnShop, most of its inventory was purchased. In the case of Tailored Brands, most of the inventory was either custom manufactured or sourced with a manufacturing partner in the Far East. A suit made in Indonesia costs the company between $30 and $50, depending on the fabric, and sells when it's not on sale for $300 to $500—a 90 percent-ish IMU. That margin can pay for a lot of marketing, or a lot of promotion.

"Exactly. Let's say we're running a circus. If you'll pardon the, um, insipid metaphor, can you tell me which side of the spectrum you're on? Over here on the right, you're looking for a circus ticket promoter. You think the problem is simply unimaginative marketing, and you're looking for a clever person to improve traffic and retention with slick, crafty promotions. And over here, on the left side, you think you'll never be able to drive any more traffic with promotions, because you think your fundamental selling proposition is broken. In the terms of a circus, your clowns aren't funny, the acrobats are injured, and the societal mores have shifted from thinking taming a lion or riding a bedazzled elephant is cute. They now think it's cruel and unethical. And in PwnShop terms, you don't believe we can drive traffic with physical software anymore because of digital disruption."

"Well, I still think lion tamers are entertaining. I'm leaning more toward a better circus ticket promoter," Tom said as he pointed toward my right hand.

This time, Lance rolled his deep brown irises upwards. He leaned over Tom and pointed farther left than my left hand. "I'm sorry Tom, but as you and I have discussed, I think this is a complete reinvention."

I nodded. Finally somebody here was willing to say the baby was ratchet. Not a yes man.

"As you can see, Nick, Lance and I have been debating this. We got rid of some of the other executives because diversification was a complete waste of time, money and resources."

"I totally agree," I said.

"Really?" Tom said, puzzled. "I thought you were all about reinvention?"

"I am. But I agree that diversification is a third rail, and ain't the way. And, I'm in agreement with Lance that the old way is all but dried up. We have to find a new model for driving traffic."

"And what do you think is the answer?" Tom asked, without adding, but clearly implying, "smart guy."

"Community, media revenue, and entertainment slash esports. You may or may not know this, but I had IDEO lined up to work with us when I worked there to help think through reinventing the stores to become the local church of gaming."

"Not aware. Don't you think we've become soft? We just need to block and tackle and delight customers like we did when this business was humming," Tom said with a hint of nostalgia.

"You mean, the future is in the fundamentals?"

"Exactly," Tom said, taking the bait.

"To be resolved. It's a needed, healthy debate." Lance said. "Tom, are you okay if I pull him into the cone of silence?"

"Yeah, sure," Tom conceded.

"Look Nick, I've thought long and hard about this. This company is in a bad way. I've agreed to take on the role of interim CEO, while I evaluate the situation and the board looks at other candidates. I know I don't want to do this without other smart players on the team who are willing to challenge the status quo, and it's clear you think for yourself."

"I've been told that's sometimes a problem."

"Bullshit. We have a tough problem to solve. People around that building apparently love you. You seem like a smartass to me. I have a soft spot for smartasses. Just know I'll out smartass you. Anyway, I'd love to have you sit at the table with me and help fix this thing. Gaming as a category is phenomenal. We just have to reinvent the mousetrap. Will you join us?"

"By sitting at the table with you, does that mean I'd report to you?"

"I agree the US business needs one throat to choke, but I think marketing is much more strategic than just the US operations. I'd want this position reporting to me. In all transparency, things are moving very fast and we're still working through the details of my job, but I'd like to have you on the team, and I'd like to have you reporting to me."

"So SVP then? Reporting to CEO?"

"Yep."

Shit, should have said EVP.

"Well, now you've finally given me something to think about. Assuming comp package is competitive, when were you thinking you'd want me to start?"

"Yesterday."

"I'm sure, but I'm serious. I have great respect for the guy that hired me at TBI, and I don't want to leave him in the lurch. I need to give him adequate notice."

"Two weeks?"

"More than that. If I do this, which I'm not saying I will, it's contingent on me not burning a bridge with TBI."

"Wait, what?" Lance interrupted. "I know TMI and FBI, but what's TBI?"

"Oh sorry. Tailored Brands Incorporated."

"Ahh, yeah. Sorry."

"I need to do the gentlemanly thing."

"Jesus. You UVA guys. Chivalry is dead. I'm serious. As a heart attack. I'll put together an offer letter with a start date of July 1. If you need to move it a little, fine, but this can't drag on into Q3. We've got titles to release and a transformation to launch. The best time to plant a tree was twenty years ago. The second-best time is today."

"I like the way you think."

"So do I," Lance smirked.

We spent the rest of the breakfast small talking, with me probing him for asshole tendencies. He was cocksure, but not impenetrable.

Upon departing and agreeing that he'd get me an offer letter before Tuesday the following week, I got back in my car. The phone connected to Spotify, and the tune resumed. Where is my mind? Way out in the water. See it swimming?

Home
Dallas, Texas
June 9, 2018
970 days to POSS
CSP: $13.28

My youngest son and recent skiing partner George overheard me and Maura discussing yesterday's conversation with Tom and Lance.

"Dad, are you really thinking about going back to PwnShop? I thought we talked about this? I want to go to college. We're going to be in the poor house."

"Haha. I heard your bit about *Fortnite* killing the company. It's not a done deal; I'm working through it. But wouldn't you rather have me back home, or am I too much of a miserable wretch to be around full time?"

"Are you kidding me? But, there's no way to fix that company. It's toast."

"Jeez. Those are doomsday words from a fourteen-year-old. Are you shorting the stock? Sounds like it, if you're in the business of spreading rumors of a premature demise. That said, I have an idea on how to fix it."

"What's that?"

"I might not be home as much as any of us like, but I've observed a weird phenomenon amongst you and your buddies. You know when P.J., Archer, and Andy were here two weekends ago?"

"Yeah."

"You played basketball in the driveway for a bit, and then you went up to the attic and watched each other play *Fortnite*."

"P.J. is unbelievable. He's been asked to play for an esports team."

"That's amazing, and that's part of the idea."

"You think PwnShop should buy an esports team? That's your idea?"

"No, not exactly. Anyway, after watching each other play for about an hour, do you know what y'all did?"

"I don't remember."

"You asked me to give all three of them rides home so you could play *together*."

"You can't play together in the same house. You have to log on from your own console to play as a team or against each other."

"That's the observation. You want to play together."

"Uh huh."

"When I was a kid, Intellivision and Atari had four controllers. We could all sit on the couch and play each other on the same screen. And then, as a family, we did it when the Wii came out?"

"Yeah, but those games suck."

"I know. To play the games you guys play, you need a lot more computing power for each player. So, you each have to have your own console, right?"

"Right."

"Well, what if I remodeled the attic with a badass internet connection, four gaming chairs and four consoles. Would your buddies go home then?"

"No way! That'd be awesome. They'd never leave."

"Exactly."

"Are you really going to do that?"

"You spoiled entitled shit." I winked. "I don't want you delinquents grab-assing here all day. What if I did that at PwnShop?"

"Oh. Hmm. I mean, yeah, I'd probably go. Definitely more than I go now, which is never. You mean they'd have multiple consoles and we could hang out there, away from our moms telling us to 'get off the PlayStation and go play outside.'"

"Exactly."

"Okay, I feel ya. But, don't screw it up."

"Son, nothing meaningful ever happened without taking some risk. There's a lot more to be worked out, but I'm seriously thinking about it."

SIDE C

Transcendental Coups

PERSONNEL

The Band		
GamerTag	Instrument	Title
Nick Haller	Groan Tube, Lead Vocals on "Murray with Fringe On Top"	EVP, Chief Customer Officer
Gerald Meade	Metronome	Chief Executive Officer
Jeff	Brake Drum	EVP, Chief Financial Officer
Dale Spivey	Wheelharp	EVP, Chief Supply Chain Officer
Eli Geller	Otamatone, Background Vocals on "Murray with Fringe on Top"	Director of Innovation
Garv Pastor	Tesla Coil	Founder and Former CEO of Chompy
Quint Haddad	Theremin	Former CMO of Chompy, New Bored Member
Suprit Shetty	Timbales	Bored Member
Maura Haller	Slide Whistle	Wife
The Wrecking Crew		
Fred Rhodus, Lucie Raines		
Creem Magazine		
Rebekah		
The Swampers		
Binks Toole, Tess, Naomi, Helen, Jim		

Track 10: Brick House

"Making the simple complicated is commonplace; making the complicated simple, awesomely simple, that's creativity."

—CHARLES MINGUS

PwnShop CBI
Vineland, TX
August 1, 2019
552 days to POSS
CSP: $5.00

On this first and greatest lie, that profits now are always better than profits later, more and more lies are based in necessary consequence.

The day goes by just as years go by. A slug through scree at the time. A single beat of a hummingbird's wings in retrospect…

…I don't know how it comes about, but I, the hapless Haller, the solitary, the hater of employment's petty conventions, always take up my quarters in just such companies as this. It is an old weakness. I dwell neither in fast speculative ventures nor in blue chip stalwarts of predictable tediocrity, but instead and deliberately in these well-known but disrupted bourgeois specialty retail behemoths, that reek of mold and bleach, where panic ensues when you bang the door of transformation or deign to enter the building with befuddling conclusions or dirty shoes.

We're at the eighth closed session of the PwnShop unicameral senate's discussion of mass layoffs. Figuratively, of course. The chambers are in the offsite meeting space across the parking lot from the main PwnShop building. Claude created the space and named it the CBI: the Center for Big Ideas. Literally. Laughably. These chambers haven't witnessed a big idea since the company thought about purchasing Steam some nine years ago.

Today, the senate is discussing "organizational optimization"—with paper blacking the windows to prevent would-be voyeurs from seeing their heads on the chopping block. The whole company knows it's coming. Along with our twenty-something ACG "experts," we are debating how deeply to cut into the staff. A healthy pruning to make the company more efficient, or cutting to the bone to meet the activists demands for significantly rationalized SG&A? It's not much different or less chaotic than George Lucas's *Star Wars* prequel trilogy's Galactic Senate.

Gerald Meade, a.k.a. Chancellor Palpatine—his countenance not dissimilar to the features of the celebrated Scottish Shakespearean thespian Ian McDiarmid, the actor who portrayed Palpatine cum Darth Sidious—is now in control. Like Palpatine, he seems to have accepted his emergency powers with feigned reluctance. Checks and balances have been thrown out the window. But the legislative process, like most autocracies, is now much more efficient. His vice chair, Jeff , by day, is the presiding senator, zooming around in his repulsorpod, veins bulging out of his neck, forearms, and biceps like tiny earthworm-sized asps, repulsing any argument that mentions the fact that work still needs to be done and customers still need to be served. By night, I guarantee you he puts on a Darth Maul costume. He espouses one goal—a demonstrably smaller cost structure for the sake of the shareholders. Never mind that saving one's way to growth is an impossible M.C. Escher optical illusion.

It's a clumsy tragedy. If only Billy Shakespeare or Stevie Sophocles had their hand on the pen. The characters would be more sympathetic, their downfall more tragic. Instead, as *New York Magazine*'s critique of

The Phantom Menace so aptly put it, "being human has never been more humdrum."[1] Jobs be damned. The shareholders need returns now. Future be damned.

In the midst of all this gleeful decapitation of hapless stormtroopers is a more subtle reorganizing of the back ranks. In my promotion to chief customer officer, Gerald told me my domain would include traditional marketing, the loyalty program, and, most importantly to me, strategy and innovation. Under Lance, the entire e-commerce P&L reported up through me as well. Gerald, in a rational, gentlemanly conversation, had discussed splitting the responsibility for merchandising the site from the responsibility of marketing the site. I was okay with this, knowing I would keep strategy and innovation. Dale Spivey, the chief merchandising officer, would have the site platform and merchandise. I would have the responsibility for marketing the brand overall, which included the budget for all digital marketing.

Today, we're each presenting the org charts outlining the post-layoff organization in each of our domains. This is the second such presentation, as the first attempt was dismissed for not adhering to the rules of the game: a flattened organization with no more than five levels. Level I is the CEO. Level II are his direct reports: mostly EVPs like myself, Jeff, and Dale, and SVPs like the head of stores, the general counsel, the interim CIO, and the head of HR. Level III are VPs and directors, eliminating the title senior director. Level IV are managers. One could not occupy level IV unless they manage at least three people. Level V comprises everybody else. Each level has a pay range, and no occupant of that level can exceed that range. In the main, I was for these rules. Yes, the structure presented problems. What to do with senior directors? Grandfather their title? Demote them to director? And what about the knowledge workers like coding engineers and marketing specialists who had manager titles for pay reasons, even though they had no direct

[1] Rainer, Peter. "Cause and FX." *New York Magazine*. Accessed April 21, 2025. https://nymag.com/nymetro/movies/reviews/64/

reports? The Level V pay range didn't accommodate experts with no direct reports who would be otherwise unrecruitable. I felt like I could work through most of those and ask for forgiveness rather than permission on others. In all, I agreed that a flattened hierarchy is a much more efficient way to run the company. A dramatic layoff like this does, in fact, enable a firm to fix org structures that, like a garden, become weedy, messy things if left untended.

We go around the room. I, in a surprising role reversal, am the biggest rule follower. I've eliminated two VPs, and cut my team by 20 percent. I've never been good at these reindeer games. In past lives, I've played the game like a tiresome flea market haggler. But in reflecting on every instance, I'd have saved a lot of hard traveling had I just gone in with the full cut, because logic never prevails in these efforts. Pints of blood are the currency of the realm.

Spivey, the chief merchant, who's gerrymandered the e-commerce platform team from my org, keeps his overall headcount flat, as he's planning on dramatic e-commerce growth.

Claggart, the Sith-like CFO, shows cuts of all the old guard, but replaces most of these roles at a lower level. Same responsibilities, but at lower salaries, as if every quality finance person wants to take a pay cut to work at this disrupted company. Curiously, he's added a VP of strategic planning. I have a VP of strategy and business development, as Gerald ensured me the function resides in my domain.

"Any questions?" Claggart states, without a question inflection at the end of the phrase. It's clear he doesn't want any.

"Uhm, yeah. I have one," I buzz into the ointment. "Part of the reason we're all here is to make sure we don't have any redundancy across functional organizations. Correct?"

"Yes. Mee-see,"[2] Claggart proffers some business buzzword bingo.

---

[2] Mee-see is the phonetic form of the acronym MECE, made tiresomely famous by every management consultant the world over. It stands for Mutually Exclusive. Collectively Exhaustive.

"Well, at least we should go for mutually exclusive orgs," I continue. And then I can't help myself. "With the depth of cuts here, I doubt we'll ever get to collectively exhaustive. I think we'll be leaving a lot of tasks on the table."

"Not if you hire quality people," Claggart patronizes. "Is that your question?"

"No."

"Get on with it. There are a lot of people in this room. We can't waste time on conjecture and speculation."

Cue John Williams' foreboding "The Emperor's Theme."

"My question, if you please, is about your strategy role. I have one in my org as well. Strategy reports up through me. If the role in your org is a financial planning role, I don't think we have redundancy. But if you're envisioning that role to be exploring which lines of business we'll pursue in the future, and as importantly, which we'll jettison, that's the intent I have for my role. My question is what is your plan for that person?" I ask with a note of derision I can't disguise.

"Build the five-year strategic plan. Set goals and build the blueprint for our future. Your role is customer strategy, not business strategy."

"As I understand it, my role is strategy. Mutually exclusive of finance and operations. Collectively exhaustive of customer strategy, business strategy, innovation strategy, partnership strategy. You know, Mee-see. Strategy."

Claggart's tic materializes. He quickly dips his ear to his large, left trapezius muscle, which connects directly to the bottom of his jaw, bypassing the notion of a neck. Did I just hear the ignition of Darth Maul's double bladed saberstaff? Nah, maybe that was just the A/C fan firing up.

"Your role, and Gerald correct me if I'm wrong," Jeff tics his head to the opposite shoulder, "is deploying the capital we approve to drive sales. Marketing. Traffic. Customer lifetime value. Nothing more, nothing less."

"Uhm, I suppose I don't disagree," Gerald evades in his best Pontius Pilate Palpatine, making himself scarce while shuffling off to Naboo, just like Palpatine's false peace initiative.

"Neutral" Switzerland, after all, was complicit in the Holocaust.[3]

"And what if, God forbid, the strategic problem we find ourselves in means there is no efficient way to move those metrics without fundamentally overhauling our strategy?" I continue.

"That's for me and my team to figure out," Claggart parries.

"That's great alignment of role, task, authority and accountability," I say, my delivery dripping with sarcasm, the protest of the powerless. "Basically, I'm accountable for sales, traffic and CLV,[4] but I have no authority to make the strategic changes needed to have any chance of keeping those metrics from falling off a cliff. The iceberg is melting. Don't you see?"

"You have the authority to spend the money allocated to you to affect those metrics. Anything else is outside of your swim lane."

"A mighty catch-22, innit, Mr. Claggart? Accountability with no authority."

"No. It's not. It's the situation we're in, and you are to stay in your lane. I thought you were creative. You need to do more with less."

"Strategy is *my* lane. It's in my offer letter. And, there's a massive difference between imagining the possible and irresponsibly indulging in reverie. It's marketing, not magic. We *are* dealing in reality, right? Or are we dealing in some mystical fantasy land of alchemy and sorcery where the laws of nature don't apply? Where less is more, and cost cutting improves the top line. 'In which lion and hyena come together,

[3] A classic catch-22. An ostensibly neutral country, Switzerland, and its famed banking system gladly accepted deposits from both Nazis and Jews. Jews, at the onset of the war, parked assets in Swiss banks thinking they would be a safe haven. After the holocaust, Switzerland would not release the funds to the families of the deceased, since the Nazis never issued death certificates—duh. Moreover, there are numerous theories surrounding Swiss banks abetting the financing of the Nazi war machine, including knowingly accepting deposits of gold that Germany plundered from Jewish prisoners and occupied countries' central banks. Of course, there are also theories that the holocaust never happened. Hmm. Good people on both sides.

[4] Customer Lifetime Value.

in a great glorious future!'"[5] I emote in my best Jeremy Irons imitation. "You can't fix this problem without strategically changing the game. There is no magical promotional potion or eliminative elixir to save us."

"The reality is this is the most childish display of insubordination I've ever witnessed in my career. Alchemy. Elixirs. *The Lion King*? Really? Grow up. This is reality. Not kindergarten. Like all marketing guys, you're all talk and no action. Worse, you're out of line."

"A. I'm trying to take action but it appears I'm being cockblocked. B. I don't work for you, so I fail to see how I'm being insubordinate."

His eyes narrow. He twists his head deliberately to the left and then the right and then...he holds his tongue.

I don't. Don't have the self-control gene. "So does this mean I shouldn't fill my role?" Sucking at politics, I stupidly lead the witnesses.

Why am I asking? I should take a page out of Mr. Claggart's "Hitchhiker's Guide to Gaslighting", *or, if I were even more clever*, "Mr. Spivey's The Seven Habits of Highly Effective Double Agents", *and just shut the fuck up and do whatever I want. Why am I ALWAYS seeking permission?*

Finally, Gerald enters the fray. "Let's leave it there for now, and we can discuss exact roles and responsibilities for each of your positions as we evaluate potential candidates."

August 28, 2019

PwnShop, the world's largest video game retailer, laid off over 120 more people in the latest sign that it's struggling to adapt to a changing market

[5] Excerpt from the coronation speech of Scar, played by Jeremy Irons, to the surviving lionesses in Disney's *The Lion King*. Spoiler alert (as if you, dear reader, have never seen *The Lion King*). Scar, a metaphorical player of the short game, murders his brother Mufasa. Mufasa was a beloved and benevolent king, smart enough to play the long game, respecting the circle of life, and taking full responsibility for his kingdom and subjects. Upon committing fratricide and assuming the throne, Scar's desire for instant gratification turns the Pride Lands into a wasteland.

November 25, 2019
PwnShop Headquarters
436 days to POSS
CSP: $6.60

We come to the point in the weekly Monday business review meeting where I and my teammates present the customer and marketing metrics.

"I'm pleased to report that every store in Oklahoma City will be open by this weekend. By the hair of our collective chins, we've met the goal of having the entire market remodeled and reopened before Black Friday. Uhm, let's see. There are countless people in this building to whom a huge debt of gratitude is owed, but it wouldn't have happened without Eli Geller, our head of innovation, who stepped in after the layoffs to take on full project management of the effort."

"That's *director* of innovation. It's critical that we're intentional in our word choice. We must be careful to not inflate titles nor stray from the realignment purposes of the overall Reboot initiative," Claggart interrupts while furiously typing on his iPad Pro, mostly ignoring anything else I have to say.

This guy wants to step on my dick at every turn. We can't even congratulate a team on a job well done, even if it's on an initiative he's been belittling since he joined the company. "My sincere apologies," I eyeroll. "Eli Geller, our, uhm, lowly director of innovation, uhm, worked tirelessly after our, uhm, what shall I say, our, uhm, most noble and magnanimous project to optimize our formerly unruly, uhm, and shall we even say, flaccid organization into the highly motivating model of rigid efficiency it has become today." I stress the words flaccid and rigid and smirk like an adolescent who has just drawn a hairy boner on the bathroom stall. I dart my eyes at Claggart, who's not smirking. He's strengthening his resolve, and his tic.

"Highly unprofessional. I'm just going to ignore that. Where are we on charging for the gaming bays?"

"Seriously? Before we dig into that, can we at least pause for five seconds to congratulate the folks who worked many long hours to get this thing over the finish line?"

"Sure. Congratulations. Well done." Jeff doesn't dote. He "antidotes." And asks again about the gaming bays.

"Jeff, we went over this in last week's OKC deep dive," I implore. "Have you approved the software vendor we're going to use for accepting payments?"

"No. I'm not approving it, as discussed, until I see a business case. Moreover, since we're embarking on the initiative to migrate all our back office onto Microsoft's ERP and POS, it makes little sense to integrate with some fly-by-night payment processor for a mere twelve stores."

"Look, I don't think we should waste everybody's time here relitigating the fact that you have a business case but you're holding me hostage until I'm able to magically read your mind. And, it's the problem of innovation. Our back-office systems don't presently support the functionality that OKC requires. We can either integrate quickly or wait for eternity. The fact of the matter is it's a risk. The business plan is moot the day we reopen these stores and have actual data. Moreover, since it's my ass on the line, I'm adhering to a simple innovation principle—we're not going to pave any sidewalks until we see where people walk. Metaphorically, of course. Charging for gaming on day one is asinine. We need to build a pattern of traffic behavior before we put a paywall in front of it. The experiment first and foremost is, do people want to hang out and play games at PwnShop? I have no idea. I think they will. If they're willing to do it for free, then the question is how many and how frequently? And if the answer to that is that the demand exceeds supply, we can use price and the laws of microeconomics to regulate supply and demand. But first, we have to see if we have any demand."

"I don't understand a word you just said," he says, lighting his gas lamp. "Your metaphors miss the mark. This project is a waste of time if you don't charge for gaming on day one."

"I don't disagree," Gerald rejoins.

"Guys, everything you're asking for is antithetical to the art of innovation. With OKC, we're pursuing blue ocean, what-if type analysis. As we've discussed, what if the gaming bays generate so much traffic that we don't ever need to charge for gaming? What if people come to the store so frequently to hangout, they shift a larger share of wallet to us from their in-console purchases? What if they buy more collectibles? What if they buy food and drinks? We don't necessarily need to charge for gaming for us to make money on this. And, if we charge too much too soon, we run the risk of killing the seedling before it's ever had chance to take root," I preach. Perhaps too preachily.

"What if, please, for the love of God, you quit using metaphors? You obfuscate the discussion. Look, it would be great to tell the Street that we're testing a new revenue stream—charging customers to sit in our gaming bays and play games. But, because you're refusing to charge, we don't have a new revenue stream, do we?"

"We need to capture the Street's and our customers' imaginations by relating a story. A narrative. An experience that doesn't yet exist. When it exists, we'll know when and where and how much we can charge for it."

"Fantasy. Fiction. We need facts. Gerald, let's make sure we take Oklahoma City out of the script."

"Agreed," Gerald concurs.

PwnShop Bored Room
December 17, 2019
414 days to POSS
CSP: $7.52

Fifteen minutes before the earnings call, Gerald, Jeff, Dale, and I, with our head of investor relations, gather in the Bored Room. Gerald is reviewing his script and the potential questions analysts might ask, along with the recommended responses. Gerald looks up from the document, and queries "Nick, what is the latest on the loyalty improvements?"

"No different than what you have in your notes. Still quite positive. Single digit improvements in traffic in loyalty test markets and double-digit improvement in basket."

"Gerald, we must be very careful about making misleading statements. My team hasn't fully vetted these results, and I'm concerned we may be overstating the impact," Jeff overpowers.

"Not to be relitigated here with five minutes before the call," I say, "but we've been through that test vs. control group methodology three times, and ACG has confirmed the results. Can't we call a win a win?"

"Not to worry, Jeff. I won't oversell it. We'll say the results are early," Gerald affirms.

"So, Gerald, do you want me to comment on loyalty or Oklahoma City if they come up?" Why do I even ask such questions? I already know the answer that won't be mentioned—I'm too much of an unfiltered loose cannon.

"I'll take any that come up. Thanks for offering," Gerald smothers.

The Q3 earnings call progresses as it always does—a twenty-minute, antiseptic recitation of the amazing strides we've made in cutting costs and deploying all available capital to buy back shares while willfully ignoring the melting iceberg in the room. Sales are tanking. Consumers aren't buying used games and consoles anywhere near the rate of our glory days. The business model is broken. But, don't look there. Look at how great we are at generating free cash flow by closing stores and driving inventories down to nothing. And look how much EPS has improved, not from increased earnings but from fewer shares.

Of the 4360 words and fifty-three paragraphs in the script, 80 percent is devoted to cost cutting, store closures, the winddown of our Northern Europe operation, inventory reductions and share buybacks. The changes to the loyalty program, albeit a tactical win, get one paragraph. Oklahoma City, the thing store managers think is our only hope, that gets repeated standing ovations at town halls and conferences, gets one sentence.

"We've reimagined twelve stores within our Oklahoma City market, and while it's too early to share specifics, we are encouraged by what we are learning from the numerous customer immersive experiences being tested."

> February 26, 2020
> Oklahoma City, Oklahoma
> Arena Concept Store
> 343 days to POSS
> CSP: $5.16

Singing to the tune of "The Surrey with the Fringe on Top" from Rodgers and Hammerstein's *Oklahoma!:*

"Bears and puts and shorts better scurry
When we've had a call with Eiffel Murray.
When you've had a call with Eiffel Murray
It'll make the stock go Pop!"

"Cut! Dude, you can't say that, much less sing it. Ridiculously funny, but we don't want you to get fired," exhorts Tess, director of PwnShop TV.

I'm on camera with Eli Geller who is with me in Oklahoma for our first public unveiling to the press and the industry of our laboratory stores. Before the VIPs arrive, we're filming a piece to be broadcast to all stores, showing them the various innovations with which we're experimenting.

The Eiffel Murray bit is fresh on my mind. Just a week ago, I learned Gerald and Jeff had a call with the famed investor, who minted money by convincing Goldman Sachs to sell him credit default swaps against the riskiest collateralized subprime loans in 2006 and 2007, effectively predicting the 2008 meltdown and enabling him to short the entire US housing market. Apparently, he told them PwnShop may have a short squeeze opportunity. More than 120 percent of our shares are being shorted. Duh. The harder question is how do you drive up the stock price to scare off the shorts? Mr. Murray, despite hobbying as a seven-string death metal guitarist, proffers the same level of creativity and funeral drum dryness as our CEO and CFO—cut costs, buy back shares and beat next quarter's consensus.

I'm 6'1", wearing a futile brown bandana to look like Curly in *Oklahoma!* Next to me is Eli, all 5'6" of him. The height contrast beckons a Penn & Teller comparison. But, that's the only similarity. We're not nearly as funny as the Vegas magic duo. Plus, unlike Teller, Eli has a speaking role—the resident millennial roasting me whenever I open my Gen-X mouth.

"It's nice of you to be worried about my job security, but I'm afraid I've already dug myself a six-foot hole," I comfort.

"This should help you climb out of it, not lie down in it!"

"Fair enough! Let's continue. Onwards!" I say, rolling my hand over and over in a forward propelling motion. "We got a long way to go and a short time to get there!"

February 28, 2020
Oklahoma City, Oklahoma
Retro Concept Store
341 days to POSS
CSP: $5.04

"Do you believe gamers really want to hang out in a PwnShop?" Rebekah, a reporter from *GamesIndustry.biz*, queries.

I had to beg Gerald for permission to do a press junket, as he, rightfully, is concerned I'll make misleading forward-looking statements, overstate its importance to his overall strategy, or worse, be critical of our current situation and make us look desperate. I promised I wouldn't invite financial press, only gaming press, and assured him I'd be on my best behavior. His final wish—"Please don't use that church metaphor."

"It's a good question," I respond to the reporter. "I'd rephrase it slightly, though I get your intent. The experiment is, do people want to experience in real life the same social phenomenon they're experiencing virtually with modern gaming? I believe they do. I believe there is a latent, innate human desire, based on what you see at E3 or Comic-Con or PAX, where folks want to consort in real life with other folks in their gaming community, a much more powerful notion than doing it over your headset. Virtual is a great way to fill the gaps in between, but if you can have a local place that you can do this together on a regular basis, it seems to me a very worthy experience. We shall soon see."

Geller rejoins, "The goal is for PwnShop to become a social and community gathering place. It fits well in Oklahoma City given the rural communities that surround the urban hub. This is a typical PwnShop market. Outside of OKC, internet isn't always reliable, so centers like internet cafes or get-togethers like LAN parties aren't feasible for everyone. But if a nearby PwnShop has the facilities, it can function like a YMCA for games. These new stores can really embrace the digital ecosystem rather than actively fight against it. And, interestingly, non-digital experiences have been popular here as well. The popularity of tabletop gaming has surprised the hell out of us. *Dungeons & Dragons* in particular. In just six short weeks, we've massively increased our tabletop offerings, scheduling employees or hiring freelancers to be Dungeon Masters at hosted games."

"I'm just a suit, not a core gamer," I rejoin. "When I entered this industry, let me tell you how much I didn't know. Like most non-gamers who haven't seen the light, I stereotyped gamers—hidden in a basement, eating Cheetos, never interacting with others. But, I've changed my tune completely. Returning from E3 in 2014 I said, 'We are missing out on an enormous opportunity.' Pardon my political incorrectness, but, if E3 is the Vatican, why is PwnShop not the local church? I pitched the notion of this starting back in 2014, which meant doing a deep dive into understanding who our customers are, what customers we are not acquiring, and what is a retail experience that truly embraces the modern digital gamer."

Oh shit, I said it. It just came out.

"Interesting," Rebekah says, nodding apprehensively.

"This is a living, breathing experiment. We can't strangle it with preconceived notions. I often tell the team, 'We're not building any sidewalks until we see where people walk.' I mean, who would have ever thought you'd see people playing *Dungeons & Dragons* in a PwnShop? That's been one of the happy accidents. If we had paved a purely digital sidewalk, we never would have learned this."

"Mmm hmm," she nods with a look that says either this guy may have something or he's the most full of shit interviewee she's ever encountered. "But back to the point Mr. Geller was making, do you think this concept will peacefully coexist with established LAN lounges and esports centers in big cities? Do you plan on putting them out of business?"

Geller goes first. "It's the gateway drug theory. I don't think we're ever going to have the depth of a really good, local hobby shop. I think people will come here, do a one-hour adventure in *D&D*, then they'll go buy their minis and paint them and get really ingrained in the culture at a hobby shop. I think both can coexist peacefully."

Oh great. I've already pissed off any puritans by comparing gaming to religion. I've pissed off the left by omitting the Wailing Wall or Mecca, and now the right as my little boy wonder has invoked recreational drug use. We're going straight to hell.

To deflect going down the drug rabbit hole, I add, "My perspective is, the more people, the more places, the better it is for all of us. It just hasn't permeated yet.... Right now, the way people hang out with their buddies is on headsets in their own homes. Do they want to do that regularly in real life? That's the question. If they do, there's going to be a place for us, a place for the big arenas, all those things."

"Okay," Rebekah exhales. "Thanks. On to something perhaps a bit controversial. PwnShop is notorious for training the humanity out of its associates and turning them into transactional robots. What is the upselling you're forcing onto your associates here?"

"Oooh! Goody. I'm so glad you asked," I jump in and then wander into a bit of a daydream. I actually couldn't agree with her more. I better temper my thoughts as we still have 30,000 employees held at a figurative gunpoint by senior and field management to deliver on their daily sales metrics.

Geller looks at me, sees that my ADHD has kicked in, and responds first. "Stores still have important KPIs they have to hit. That's all I can say." If only this reporter knew how firmly Claggart has shoved his foot up our respective unmanageable asses.... "But I hope you'll see the environment feels different, more social, more fun. It's less transactional. Transactions are always good, we always want transactions, but we're trying to get away from the 'transaction first' mentality," Eli smirks.

Finally, I snap out of it. "What the employees are creating here is a week in, week out beehive of activity," I say. "It's a different construct, like being more of a cruise director. They're becoming an expert guide to shepherd the guest through whatever gaming experience they're seeking. Fundamental to this is the belief in the associate, who is an expert, working closely with a customer, who happens to share the same passion. Let's let that relationship lead. That's the input. Transactions and shareholder value hopefully follow. That's the output."

"Speaking of shareholder value..." Rebekah sits up.

Why the fuck did I mention shareholder value? Doh.

"...Let's call it what it is," she continues. "PwnShop is struggling. Your diversification venture with AT&T failed, in the past six months you've closed hundreds of stores, and you just had mass layoffs."

Jesus. I thought this was the games press. I know they hate us, but can't they see we're trying something different? Why ya gotta be such a hater?

"Is there a question?" I interrupt. "Wait, before you answer that, can we go on background here?"

"Sure," she says, exhaling through her nostrils and leaning in.

"I thought this was a customer experience piece," I petition, "not a financial performance piece. I want to be as candid as I possibly can, probably to a fault. That's my 'nick.' My mother named me correctly. In truth, I wanted to try this a long time ago, after attending E3 in 2014. That's when I suggested this experiment's fundamentals. It got rejected because we were cash cowing the core business and plowing all available capital into the phone store diversification plan, something I was not personally thrilled with. So much so that I departed in 2016. They called me back in 2018, saying they were ready to refocus on the core business. You're right, the best time to plant a tree was twenty years ago. But the next best time is to plant one today. So back on record, is there a question here?"

"Yes, there is," she says, her official, affected reporter voice *subito con brio*. "This whole Oklahoma experiment seems like something a thriving business tools around with when it has the freedom and capital to do so. Given the difficulties you're facing, isn't this just an act of desperation? A Hail Mary if you will?"

I guess woke reporters can invoke the Catholic Church but I can't? The ADHD kicks in. I hold my hand up to gather my swirling thoughts. My mind's eye flits to Jack Nicholson in *A Few Good Men*. "A Hail Mary? Ya goddamn right I ordered the Hail Mary!" Nah, I don't think she'd see the humor in that. What about the response Spinal Tap's manager gives to a reporter when asked if the band's popularity is declining as they're playing tiny venues when they used to play massive arenas? "Oh no. No, no, no, no, no. No, not an act of desperation at all. I just think that our customers are becoming more selective." Nope. Aging myself even more. Instead, I lie like a politician. "It can't be a Hail Mary. A Hail Mary is a notion of desperation. We're not in that situation. We just don't believe we're in that situation," I stress, perhaps too strongly. "The urgency of it is finding additional ways to generate traffic. Then the unanswered question is, does that traffic generate the revenue lift we would expect relative to the investment? It's a classic return on investment business question. The rumors of our demise are overexaggerated."

Her slightly shaking eyes and face say, "No they're not."

My frenetic brain agrees, but, I sally forth. "And certainly with the onslaught of the new consoles there's urgency where we believe we need to transform the way we interact with the gaming community. There are myriad notions of how you could innovate and continue to invest over time. We're planting seeds here, seeing which orchards bear fruit and to what degree, and then let them grow and bear the appropriate fruit." *Whatever the fuck that means*. And then I conclude, "We're approaching this from a customer-centric standpoint, not a miserly one. The risk of rushing this out is that the business would have the hubris to think it knows what's going to work, and we would just plow full steam ahead into the wrong concept. That would be a massive mistake and only speed our demise."

Speed our demise? Doesn't the mere phrase make the world think I know we're doomed? Not a good poker player. Ever.

February 29, 2020
Oklahoma City, Oklahoma
Arena Concept Store
340 days to POSS
CSP: $5.04

Sony's head of North American sales grabs my hand and shakes it. "Thank you for a wonderful tour. This is just what the industry needs from PwnShop. Super, super exciting stuff," he says.

"Yes, indeed," says Activision's chief digital officer. "Couldn't agree more. I thought this was just going to be a redecorated store. You're revolutionizing the game. Let us know how we can help. I want to make sure all our games are loaded in these gaming bays and the couch coop areas. What an amazing place of discovery. This is exactly what you guys should be doing. Also, I need to put you in touch with DC who runs marketing for the Call of Duty League. He'd love your 'Pop Warner League' esports plan. Thanks for the invitation. Definitely worth the trip."

There are so many smoke blowers in this industry. Are they just being polite? Or are they genuinely impressed?

"Oklahoma is not the sexiest destination, particularly on a Saturday, so, seriously, our sincere thanks for coming. And look, there are so many fantastic people in this company that worked their asses off to make this happen, case in point, this guy right here," I say, pointing at Eli who gives a cocky little millennial bow. Then, huddling the VIPs with a wave of my hand, we step away from the gathered glad-handers. "I'm probably way out of line and definitely out of school here," I murmur. "But for the life of me, I can't understand why I'm not getting Gerald's and Jeff's buy-in. I know we don't correspond much, since most of your relationship with us is through the merchant team, but Dale was here Thursday and was blown away. I trust he'll put in a good word for what we've done. You know corporate politics. Nobody wants to get behind something unless it's politically expedient. I don't know why Gerald is tentative. Maybe he thinks I'm a flake and it's too expensive. And Claggart hates my guts and this whole concept. Again, I don't know why. I thought it was just a 'not invented here' thing, but it's more deep-rooted than that. For the life of me, I'm just trying to put forth ideas that help create a narrative for a new way forward. We can't even have a collaborative discussion on it. Again, I know I'm out of line here, but any good word you can send back to Vineland would be much appreciated."

"Have they been here? Have they seen these stores?" the Sony executive asks.

"I'm trying to get Gerald here in the next week or two, but his schedule is ridiculous. And I don't think Jeff will ever set foot on Oklahoma soil."

"That's a shame," he continues. "I'll definitely put in the good word for what you've accomplished here. Was going to do so anyway. I'll also tell them they need to see it for themselves."

"Thank you," I say again, in all humility.

I wave goodbye to the group boarding the bus back to the OKC airport then nod to Grady to come over. Since he's the video game vendors primary contact, I comment to Grady, who flew in for the industry store tours to help entertain and host. "It seems to me they like it."

"They are completely blown away," he says. "They were like, 'Where has this kind of thinking been in the last ten years?' Dude. I'm serious. You nailed it."

"We've nailed it," I say, pointing to his belly and back to mine. "Couldn't have done it without all the support of you and your team."

"Aw shucks, Nick. You're nice to say that. But, look me in the eye. I know you suffer from all kinds of self-doubt, but this would not have happened—I repeat—would NOT have happened, if it weren't for you putting your ass on the line to make it so. This place aborts all babies in utero, killing all cross-department initiatives like this the moment it means investing even an ounce of time much less money in any real risk-taking."

"Wow, aborted babies in utero? Pretty politically incorrect for a black gay guy, dontcha think?"

He chuckles. "Learned from the best. But I'm serious. It's hard to get anything like this off the ground in this company. You've nailed it. Our vendors, and you know this, think PwnShop hasn't had a creative thought in decades, but they're jazzed with the possibility of this. This is exactly what the industry wants and needs us to be doing."

"Well, thank you," I demure. "You're nice to say all this."

"Damnit Nick. Don't be so friggin' modest. I'm not being 'nice,' I'm telling you the truth. You should be proud, INCREDIBLY proud, about what you've pulled off here."

"Too bad our fearless leaders won't see it that way. Hell, they'll probably never step foot here. They see it as a fool's errand, and I'm the fool."

"Dale came. And while he doesn't show his hand unless he has to, he saw the vendors' reactions. And I saw his reaction when he walked into the first store. Whether this ever gets rolled out in a meaningful way isn't the point. You've illustrated the art of the possible. But, yes, I share your pessimism with getting Gerald and Jeff on board. I'll help you make sure Gerald gets out here. He'll come. He'll get it. But Jeff is Jeff. Not to be a pessimist right alongside one of my favorite pessimists, but you're right. He'll never visit. It gives him plausible deniability to never experience it."

"I fear you're right. It's not creditmongering. I'm looking for the rest of the company to claim it as their own and take the ball and run with it.

Jeff, for all his rule by fear flaws, could be a hero on the Street and the best executive this company has ever seen if he'd just open his mind a hair. I mean, come on, free your mind and your ass will follow."

"Little white privileged boy is quoting Bootsy Collins?"

"Hells to the yes. Keep it on the one, Grady."[6]

Grady looks at me quizzically. I say nothing. He shakes his head, signaling half the shit I say is claptrap anyway.

March 12, 2020
Oklahoma City, Oklahoma
328 days to POSS
CSP: $4.96

"Look, Nick. I'm glad all of you kept nudging me to get to Oklahoma. Super impressive. The thing I can't get my mind off of, more than any of the gameplay, is just how open and accessible these stores feel. Will definitely congratulate the team on a job well done," Gerald says to me after we complete his personal tour of the OKC stores.

"Thank you. A lot of hard work, tough decisions, et cetera, all around. I sincerely appreciate you making the trip. I know how busy you are."

"I fear busy will be something we long for. This coronavirus thing seems like it might be real. Will be interesting figuring how to operate if everyone gets sick. You saw where the CDC says it's heading toward pandemic status?"

---

[6] Bootsy Collins is one of the pioneers of funk bass. He cut his teeth in James Brown's band before becoming a founding member of Parliament-Funkadelic. I met Bootsy during my tenure at Guitar Center at the NAMM Trade Show—The National Association of Music Merchandisers—as we were collaborating with his charity that gives instruments to the underprivileged. His catchphrase, "Free your mind...and your ass will follow," is a personal affirmation. After meeting him, he told me to "Keep it on the one," a reference to funk bass vs. rock bass and most other forms of popular music. In non-funk, the backbeat, the two and the four, are everything to the feel. In funk, a massive exclamation of all instruments in unison on the first beat is all-important.

"I did. Never a dull moment at PwnShop," I commiserate.

"Never a dull moment," he nods, with the weight of the head that wears the crown.

Track 11: Castles Made of Sand

"Only the pure in heart can make a good soup."

—LUDWIG VAN BEETHOVEN

Makeshift Home Office
9 AM Business Review Call
April 6, 2020
303 days to POSS
CSP: $4.64

The worst thing about knowing that Binks Toole had been sacked for a month was seeing him every day on the Microsoft Teams call.

Binks was the SVP in charge of the supply chain and the ROC, the refurbishment center where PwnShop repaired thousands of consoles and resurfaced hundreds of thousands of game discs for resale. Bald, with a shortly trimmed goatee stippling his chin, he was an aging fitness nut and carried that energy, misplaced, into the workplace. He looked a lot like Disney's Tigger, a salty, popularized and bastardized representation of E.H. Shepard's[1] more humble and human original.

[1] A.A. Milne's illustrator for the *Winnie-the-Pooh* series from 1924 to 1928. It is said much of Milne's ideas for story and character came from the exquisite incarnation of the imaginary friends of Christopher Robin in Mr. Shepard's drawings. More interesting to me, however, is why so many authors and illustrators for children's, young adult, and fantasy fiction use initials rather than their given names. Off the top of my head and in alphabet soup order: E.H. Shepard, A.A. Milne, J.R.R. Tolkien, C.S. Lewis, E.B. White, J.K. Rowling, George R.R. Martin, S.E. Hinton, and R.L. Stine. Maybe I should go by F.M. Hamlin. Actually, M.F. Hamlin might be more appropriate.

He acted like Tigger too. Boundless, earnest, and clumsy. Binks "Tigger" Toole focused with passion on small problems that didn't matter in the larger scheme. Most of these problems were in areas that weren't under his purview. He loved to throw stones in the form of "ideas" at all the merchants, store operators and the entire marketing and innovation team. Meanwhile, his glass house was exploding in shards around him.

From the moment they met him, it was clear Messrs. Meade, Claggart and Spivey had zero respect for Binks. He survived the 2019 layoffs only because, heading into the holidays, Dale, his boss, felt we couldn't withstand the disruption to the supply chain. Now it was just a matter of time.

Two weeks ago, California's Governor, Gavin Newsom, issued a stay-at-home order to stop the spread of COVID-19 in our most populous state. Upon the CDC's stated desire to "flatten the curve" and not overwhelm hospitals, thirty-six states followed suit. These orders typically included language for "nonessential" businesses to close their doors. The orders weren't law, and the definition of nonessential was nebulous at best.

Since we're barely staying afloat, we've taken a position, spurred on by Claggart's hawkish, ready-fire-aim, storm the castle proclivity to exercise our right to make a buck. That because we sell used smartphones, a few computer peripherals like gaming keyboards, mice and Wi-Fi boosters, we are essential in helping Americans work from home. *Right.*

I don't disagree that we should be open. I'm just forthright. First, two of our largest competitors, Walmart and Target, clearly pass muster for essential businesses. In fairness, however, they're open because they sell food, appliances, computers, routers and other stay-at-home necessities. They happen to sell video games and systems. If the world were fair, they would have to shut down selling nonessential categories—video games, sporting goods, cosmetics—just as they are required to shut down alcohol sales on Sunday in puritanical southern states still observing blue laws. Instead, because they're cross-category generalists, they enjoy an unfair advantage. Specialists like PwnShop, Dick's, and Sephora, are under order to shut our doors. As a result, Walmart and Target see double-digit increases in same-store sales, along with triple-digit increases in e-commerce and curbside services, selling all the stuff the specialists are prohibited from selling. Elsewhere, profits plunge, regardless of massive increases in e-commerce. The store business is just that much more important to overall profitability. Only the broad survive.

But back to forthright. In a global pandemic, video games are the opiate of the masses, enabling folks to stay connected and shelter in place happily. It's a special elixir for these tortured times. Just be honest and take that PR position. But taking the position that because we carry a few mice we're essential? C'mon.

Overruled. As usual. Let the bad press start flying. Haters gonna hate. Claggart rips PR authority from me and my team, hires his own firm, and insists on controlling the narrative. It backfires tremendously. Hating PwnShop from the gaming press is just good sport. And hating PwnShop from the financial press is de rigueur. The shorts want to feed the market with as much bad news as possible to accelerate our demise and stoke their returns. But now, the national consumer press is getting involved:

- PwnShop claims it is 'essential retail' to remain open amid coronavirus shutdowns
- PwnShop reportedly told employees to wrap their hands in plastic bags while they continued working during the coronavirus outbreak
- PwnShop to employees: Tell law enforcement that we're an essential business

Amid this backdrop, tensions are running about as high as the G string on Tiny Tim's soprano ukulele.[2] Now that e-commerce is essential, the imperfections in our freight, fulfillment, and shipping vendor relationships are front and center. Claggart, assuming UPS wouldn't want to lose a customer of our size, and, being neurotically incapable of backing down in any negotiation, watched the world's largest freight carrier walk out of the building a week ago with their middle finger waving in the air. They were increasing their rates across the board. That's what one does when demand exceeds supply. Claggart refused to accept the laws of microeconomics and told them we were paying the old rates come hell or high water. David slung his little stone at Goliath's forehead, hit the mark, and watched Goliath laugh, then toss David like a ragdoll into the Dead Sea. The next day, UPS quit sending trucks to our warehouse. Binks Toole was left to take the blame and play the hand Claggart had dealt him.

"Binks, has FedEx agreed to our terms?" Claggart asks the beleaguered supply chain operator. "You know, given we're ready to make them our single source for outbound e-commerce shipments?"

"They're balking at our last offer, so, for the moment, we're just getting one truck a day. The warehouse is now backed up with over five days of shipments."

"Unacceptable answer. Utterly. Do you not understand how mission critical it is that we get them to understand our position?" Claggart jabs.

"Yes, but they have so much business, I can't convince them to send us more trucks for a rate well below their benchmark."

"Do you not understand that's your job? That's what you're paid to do."

---

[2] Herbert Butros Khaury, known professionally as "Tiny Tim," was a walking oxymoron. He stood 6'1", weighed well over 220 pounds, played the smallest and most tightly strung ukulele—a soprano—and sang in an absurd falsetto. Frizzy haired with a face somewhere between Weird Al Yankovic, Alice Cooper, and the child napper in *Chitty Chitty Bang Bang*, farcical, comical, and ironical, his regular appearances on *The Tonight Show Starring Johnny Carson* and *Rowan & Martin's Laugh-In* provided a prude foil to the acid-laced music of the late '60s. His signature song was "Tiptoe Through the Tulips," in perfect dissonance with his stature and mass.

We can all see Tigger's little bald head gyrate in the Hollywood Square it occupies on the Teams screen. "Can't you see you've put me in quite a predicament? I can't play them off against UPS, because they know UPS is no longer working with us."

"How did I put you in this predicament? Aren't you our head of supply chain? What are you doing to solve the problem?" Claggart gaslights.

Binks rubs his eyes with the heels of his hands. "I don't think it's appropriate for me to get into that in front of all these folks, do you?"

"What's not appropriate is you not doing your job. This is weak. Ridiculous. Dale, Binks works for you. What do you have to say?"

"Totally agree, Jeff. Binks, we discussed the latitude you have with FedEx. This is unacceptable. I'll give FedEx a call right after this. We'll get this done."

"Well, Dale, I offered them the highest rate you said I could go to yesterday, and they haven't budged."

"Not to worry, Binks. I'll get it done," Dale says.

There's a pregnant pause. All our sheltered-in-place eyes are on the long-suffering Toole, his head shaking back and forth in resigned frustration.

"Another thing," Claggart lights up. "Where are we, Binks, on accelerating the production of refurbished PS4s in the ROC?"

"We had a COVID outbreak in the ROC and only 40 percent of our workers showed up for this morning's shift. We're trying to figure out ways to incentivize more folks to come in, but it's a challenge to accelerate production with such dramatic absence."

"Try ain't good enough. Do. Something." Claggart shakes his head in disgust.

"That's news to me." Gerald, who has been silently staring at his phone for most of the call, finally weighs in. "60 percent of our ROC team is out with COVID?"

"No sir. They're not all sick," Binks accedes in what's starting to look like an orchestrated Tik-Tok workplace satire. "Remember, we discussed this? We gave them the option to stay at home if they had health concerns. I guess a lot of folks have health concerns."

"Who gave them the option?" Claggart cross-examines.

Binks face palms. "HR. I think they said that's what Gerald ordered us to do. Give everyone the option to stay at home if they weren't comfortable coming into work."

"Dale, is this right?" Gerald queries his lieutenant.

"Is what right? That you told HR that it's okay for ROC personnel to stay at home?" Dale directs to Gerald.

"No, not that." Gerald evades answering. "Is it right that 60 percent of our team there are no-shows?"

"It's not right that they're staying home, if that's what you're asking. But yes, and Binks correct me if I'm wrong, 60 percent of our people didn't show up, well, actually 62 percent to be completely transparent. Gerald, I totally agree, we need to do a better job communicating how safe we've made it in there," Dale kowtows.

While we're all working from the sequestered comfort of our homes? Not to worry Freddy forklift driver and Donna disk resurfacer. Just because you must show up in person, you'll be wearing a mask. And we're providing hand sanitizer that smells like reposado because we sourced it from a tequila company. The real stuff is on indefinite backorder. So is toilet paper. And we recommend you stay, oh, let's say three- to six-feet away from anyone. You're safe. Things are not as they appear. Kinda like a 6'1", 220-pound man naming himself Tiny Tim and singing in an improbable falsetto.

"Uhm. I was talking with my direct reports about this yesterday. What if…uhm, and I'm sure you'll say this is a bad idea…uhm…but just a thought…and maybe not this idea exactly…but, uh, what if we, uhm, I don't know, uhm, incentivize our warehouse and ROC folks to come in?" Binks proffers with all the nervousness of a long-tailed cat, or a Tigger in this case, amid a warehouse full of a flying fleet of forklifts.

"Do you mean pay people extra for merely doing their job?" Claggart cackles heartily. "They should be glad they still have jobs. Ha ha ha! Incentivize attendance?! And I thought I'd seen it all."

"It doesn't have to be a wage increase, or a bonus, or overtime, or anything like that. I'm just trying to brainstorm here. Maybe we can give them paid leave later. Or, we set up child care for some of the folks whose kids are now home from...?" The Teams software overrides Binks' voice as Jeff interrupts.

"Set up childcare? Are you serious? You must think we have margins like Google or Apple. Do you know the amount of liability we'll have if one of those kids gets sick, or even worse, gets one of our people sick? That's about the worst idea I've heard this century." Claggart leans into his web cam, his face distorting in a fisheye lens sort of way, his button nose becoming bulbous, his gaze, bilious, disgusted. "I cannot believe you've fallen up to the level of senior vice president. Well, I for one find this all totally unacceptable," he scowls and scolds. "Dale, I appreciate you stepping in for Binks. It's clear nothing is going to move forward without your intervention. And for everyone else on the call, let this be an example. There is zero room for error. Let's learn from Binks dropping the ball. We are at a critical juncture. Mistakes will not be tolerated. Your job as leaders is to motivate. And please, don't use this silly pandemic as an excuse. The expectations are higher. Be forewarned."

After what seems nine months of gestational silence, we launch into the rest of the meeting. The merchants give their cursory reports on our tepid sales, (correction—their cursory-anxiety-ridden-hunky-dory-with-as-little-information-as-possible-lest-any-loose-threads-make-themselves-known-to-induce-a-Claggart-interrogation reports), before the agenda moves to my world. Normally, I and members of my team would report out on the performance of the various promotions in play, the upcoming calendar, and then a profitability report on the loyalty program and the various customer segments. Time permitting, we'd give an update on innovation. Seeing how the meeting is about as constricting as an Alcatraz ascot, I figure I'll share some good news.

"Okay gang. I know we're going through a particularly rough patch, but I'd love to report on some surprisingly good reports out of Oklahoma. For the last two weeks, weirdly, in the midst of COVID curbside-only protocols, the laboratory stores have been running more than 30 percent ahead of the nationwide control…"

"…Has to be something wrong in the data pull," Claggart butts in. "Impossible. Kenji, have you validated these numbers?"

Kenji is Claggart's new financial analyst assigned to the merchandising and marketing teams. His job is a manure manwich. Claggart isn't happy unless Kenji is browbeating the departments. The departments aren't happy unless Kenji is providing supporting data for the positive performance of our initiatives.

"Yes, Jeff. Our team ran these numbers. Since the holidays, OKC has been outperforming the control stores by a few percentage points. Statistically significant, but single digit. And what's even more interesting is that since COVID and the onset of curbside service, OKC is substantially outperforming the chain. I share your skepticism, but I've validated the data pull."

"Please dig into that. It can't be right. And Nick, please report out on why the overall performance is down in the rest of the stores, not some data anomaly in Oklahoma."

I think about saying… *What if these numbers are real and there isn't a data anomaly? Don't we want to spend more time trying to understand why something is working instead of focusing on the sizzling frog that is slowly, painfully, becoming aware that the temperature in the frying pan just rose by another 20 degrees in the face of COVID, and discuss why the burner is heating up? Duh. The business model is broken. COVID makes it worse. The beatings will continue until morale improves? This is fucking insane.* But I continue on with a droning anxiety-ridden-hunky-dory-with-as-little-information-as-possible-lest-any-loose-threads-make-themselves-known-to-induce-a-Claggart-interrogation report.

Upon exiting the Teams meeting, I pick up the phone and call Helen, my assistant (as well as Gerald's and Dale's).

"Hellooo. How are you?"

"Not great," I say. "Listen, does Gerald have any time on his calendar today? I'd like thirty minutes with him."

"Doesn't sound good, but I won't pry."

"Same old shit, but it's gotta stop."

"I was just talking to Jan. I think she's going to quit. She says Jeff is intolerable."

"That's funny. I think that's what's on everybody's mind. He's running the company. And Gerald seems fine letting him."

"If anyone can get him to intervene, it's you."

"Don't count your chickens," I grumble. "This COVID thing has been the very type of crisis that makes it easy for people like Jeff to double down on command and control."

"He's open at 4:30 PM for an hour. It looks like you have a OKC team meeting at that time."

"It's okay, I'll skip the first thirty minutes and have Eli kick it off. Getting time with Gerald is more important. Book it."

Home Office
4:34 PM Haller/Meade Teams Call
April 1, 2020
303 days to POSS
CSP: $4.64

I'm running a bit late from the previous meeting, not quite used to remote working. When I log on at 4:34 PM, I see Gerald in the Microsoft Teams window, his iPhone in his left hand, his right index finger scrolling away.

"Hi Gerald," I say.

"Oh hey Nick."

"Sorry I'm late.

He stares at the camera and says nothing.

"Uhm, look, I know you're busy. And I don't want this to be kindergarten or anything, but I want to talk to you about this morning's meeting."

"Mmm hmm. What about it?"

"You know I can take care of my own problems. This isn't about me. It's about the rest of the company. If you care at all about morale, you need to rein in the inquisition that Jeff has turned these meetings into."

"That's exactly what I want him doing. Business is bad. Jeff is working his ass off and holding people accountable."

"I get that. But do you think these are easy problems to solve?"

"No."

"Then don't you think a little empathy and collaboration instead of, oh, I don't know, disdain and distrust might go a long way toward solving them?"

"It's clear we have very few people on this team that know what the hell they're doing."

"It's retail. It doesn't necessarily attract the best and the brightest, present company included. But a lot of that old guard is loyal—to an illogical level—to this company that's done nothing but let them down."

"So Mr. Empathy. What would you have me do?"

"I'm not here to tell you what to do. You're running the company—not me. I can only advise you on the ramifications of the current path. Let's take the Binks conversation."

"That guy's the biggest blowhard I've ever had to stomach. You're saying we shouldn't hold him accountable because he's loyal?"

"No. Please let me finish. Binks is a blowhard of Old Faithful proportions. He's not the one I'm talking about. It's all the earnest middle management, hardworking people who just need a little motivation, guidance, and affirmation. What happened with Binks today created demotivation, confusion and, uhm, denial. Rejection."

"How so? It showed the folks that inaction and apathy won't be tolerated."

"First, everyone, including the janitor, knows we're in this freight situation because Jeff had a Mexican standoff with UPS and lost. Some ownership of that might create a modicum of trust. To put that all on Binks is about the most chickenshit thing I've ever seen. Second, it shows the team they can't win no matter what they do. Binks should have been fired five years ago. He's myopic. A busy body. But instead of taking the sick, lame, puddin'-headed mutt into the woods and giving him a Moe Greene, you took him to the dog park and whipped him in front of all the other dogs. And those dogs are now standing there shaking, worried they're going to get whipped no matter what they do, so they do nothing. Take no risk. Make no effort."

"I see your point."

"As far as Jeff is concerned, I've eaten a lot of shit for the sake of teamwork and showing a united front. But if this continues unabated, just know that the kids are going to watch Mom and Dad fight right in the middle of the family room."

"Dog parks, *The Godfather* and now Mom and Dad? I'm confused."

"Sorry. Bad metaphor. Jeff is Dad. I'm Mom. Y'know, because he would never stomach the other way around. The kids are the rest of the team. I've held back. But, unless his mind games stop, I'm going to call him on it in front of everyone."

"Understood."

"Thanks for your time."

I pick up my toys and exit the video.

> Home Office
> 8 AM Daily COVID Exec Call
> April 21, 2020
> 288 days to POSS
> CSP: $6.96

Since the onset of the pandemic, our overworked attorneys have been sorting through town, county, state and federal mandates pertaining to which stores can operate in one of roughly four protocols: (A) Fully open, (B) Open for Delivery@Door (we make customers meet us at the door since many stores are only manned by one employee), (C) Closed to customers but open as a ship-from-store hub for e-commerce fulfillment, and (D) Fully closed. Because the situation is fluid, we've created a standing Teams call every day at 8 AM, including weekends, to assess the various puts and takes. The participants are C-level executives and managers essential to working through the challenges of operating a global retailer amidst a worldwide pandemic—the lawyer assigned to interpreting the various mandates, the head of loss prevention, and my internal PR and comms head, Terry. Ergo, the meeting has effectively become the de facto heart of the operation. Military folks seem to like it this way. Tight group of individuals. Not much room for loose lips to sink ships. I have scheduled a subsequent 9 AM call on Mondays, Wednesdays and Fridays to cascade to my core team whatever shareable new information arises, but they mostly just want to kibbitz and gossip about the state of the union.

On this morning's call, about six weeks into the pandemic, many of the territories that had required us to be fully closed or operate only in the Delivery@Door protocol, have now started to relax their mandates and allow nonessential businesses to reopen.

The notion of reopening begets a frenzy of activity. Store operations must round up and query store personnel for their willingness to return to work. My team must segment the customer file and send an email and app notification to inform affected customers, which we've decided to do along with a five-dollar come back and shop coupon. Terry must also notify local news outlets about our decision to reopen and answer any questions.

Once we get through this morning's agenda, Gerald asks his direct reports to stay on after the call concludes. You can see the faces of every other Hollywood Square light up in the curiosity that only develops when someone knows they won't be in the room where it happens. We wait about forty-five seconds for all but one of the other participants to exit. Jeff, one of the few who is always on camera, excoriates the straggler, who's had her camera and audio off all morning.

"Deon, please exit the meeting. We can't start until you go." We wait another thirty seconds. "Deon, you're muted if you're trying to say something."

In a flash we see her screen turn on, her normally done up face looking like she'd just come down from a turnt up shelter-in-place shindig, her hair tossed wildly into a baseball cap, and then blink off as she exits. Either she still hasn't figured out how to unmute or she doesn't want to deal with Claggart. If I were a betting man, I'd put it all on the latter. Regardless, more of Claggart's expensive time elapses, and his face exposes his contempt for any civilian that doesn't operate with military precision.

"Are we good?" Gerald asks.

"I can confirm only your direct reports are on the call, sir," Jeff responds.

"All right team, two broad topics. First, it looks like we're heading into a proxy fight. As you know, last year we mutually agreed on two new board additions with the activists. Then, in February, we added three new board members who bring us deep gaming industry and retail knowledge, allowing three of our more tenured directors to roll off. Now, Pestia and Hermit want their own representation on the board, not just members we mutually agree to. The board and I are opposed to that. They're investors, and not very sophisticated ones to boot. They lack the qualifications and experience to help us in our transformation efforts. Our short interest allowed them to influence last year's board seats with only a 5 percent stake. The board size is unwieldy beyond ten directors. They're going to contest a board recommendation that doesn't include them, which means we'll more than likely have a costly, time-consuming and distracting proxy fight. There's nothing most of you need to do. Jeff and our investor relations consultant are working through the details, but I thought you should know. Jeff, anything you want to add."

"Other than if we'd followed their path we'd be out of cash, as they wanted us to spend almost all of the $700 million in proceeds from the sale of the phone business on stock buybacks, and none on debt reduction. Instead, the team should know we've been measured, prudent, and incredibly aggressive in lowering our debt costs by paying down over $400 million in notes, and only buying back $200 million in shares. And, our cost reduction efforts so far look like we're on pace to have reduced SG&A by a $120 million annual rate once the measures take effect. In hindsight, we would not be able to weather this COVID downturn without making these important strides."

"Thank you, Jeff. We applaud and are grateful for your efforts. Please be mindful of the extraordinary work that Jeff will be undertaking as it relates to this potential battle," Gerald bootlicks his subordinate. "Now, the second item...ahh...in the spirit of cost containment. You all know the situation we're in. And not knowing how much longer we're going to have to operate like this, I think it's prudent to discuss taking additional cost saving measures. As a starting point, I and the board have decided for the foreseeable future to take a 50 percent cut in salary. For the EVP group, I'd like to recommend a 30 percent pay cut, and between a 10 and 30 percent pay cut for the remainder of the Support Center corporate staff. Discuss."

Naomi, head of HR, chimes in first. "So, uhm, Gerald, what were you thinking about how we communicate how long this cut will last."

"We need to be equally definitive but still have complete flexibility to remain in the cut as long as we need to. Consoles are coming out this fall and will be a huge boon to cash flow. We just have to get across this chasm. My hope is we'll be able to reinstate full salaries by the fall."

"The critical factor is store profitability," Jeff jumps in. "Regardless of how well we're doing with Delivery@Door, we're not profitable at the store level. We'll need to close many more if they can't turn their profitability around."

"Two things to consider," I weigh in. "First off, I think all of us taking a cut is a good thing to do. I'm fully supportive. Additionally, I'm wondering if we give some employees the option to work part time for a much greater pay cut than 10 percent. I bet some folks staying at home might be willing to work half time for half pay until things are back to normal."

"If employees can take off half time, they should be laid off or furloughed minimally," Jeff rebuts.

"Jeff, let's be real," I sigh. "There are numerous employees in the Support Center that are mission critical when we're operating at full strength, but not as much now, so they might need to be on call while we're in this hunker down mode. And, out of blind loyalty to the company, they're trying to make busy work out of guilt when they really don't have as much to do. Moreover, some are now dealing with kids home from school and may appreciate more flexibility. All I'm saying is to give them the option. It would mean more savings than not offering it up. If we furlough them, legally, we can't contact them for work matters, right Naomi?"

"That's right," she concurs.

"Jeff and Naomi, you two discuss and come back tomorrow with a recommendation," Gerald directs. "Any other questions?"

"Uh, yes," I say. "I didn't get a chance to get to my second point."

Jeff eyerolls, deafeningly, as Gerald responds, "And that is?"

"I'm not sure this isn't better communicated one on one, but whatever. For those of us with contracts, a reduction in pay might trigger our 'good reason' clauses, enabling someone to argue they're due full severance for such a reduction in pay. You might want to come up with some legal language that creates this event as an exception and ensures that those employees with 'good reason' clauses don't try to pull a fast one."

A lot of eyes on the call lift their gaze in the contemplation that only comes when considering new information. The next day, our general counsel issues each of us a waiver of "good reason" for the condition of a cut in pay until things return to some semblance of normal.

Home Office
8 AM Daily COVID Exec Call
Wednesday, June 17, 2020
231 days to POSS
CSP: $6.08

"Reminder to those attending the shareholder meeting, it will be in person, socially distanced and masked," Gerald appends to his concluding remarks.

Today's meeting was super short as there were no changes in mandates requiring adjustments to store opening status.

"Do we know who won the proxy fight?" I ask as everyone else on the call is clearly moving toward hanging up.

Gerald's and Jeff's eyes dart to their screens as if that's old news. None of us have been informed. The shareholder meeting is in two days.

"As previously mentioned," Jeff cuts in with knife sharp exasperation, "the board will include the two members from the Pestia-Hermit team. Two of our more tenured members will roll off in addition to the other retirements we previously announced."

"I don't recall it being mentioned. So, we lost?" I ask.

"The other slate prevailed," Jeff snips.

"Enough on that," Gerald intervenes. "One other thing. Dale, do you want to fill the team in on your news?"

"Sure, Gerald. Just FYI, yesterday was Binks Toole's last day. Please let me know if there are any matters you were working directly with him on, and I'll help navigate."

A moment of silence. Not in mourning, but in existential examination. Everyone's face but Gerald's, Jeff's and maybe Dale's says, "I wonder if I'm next."

"Okay gang. Good call. Talk to you soon."

Gerald ends the Teams video and I immediately text Dale:

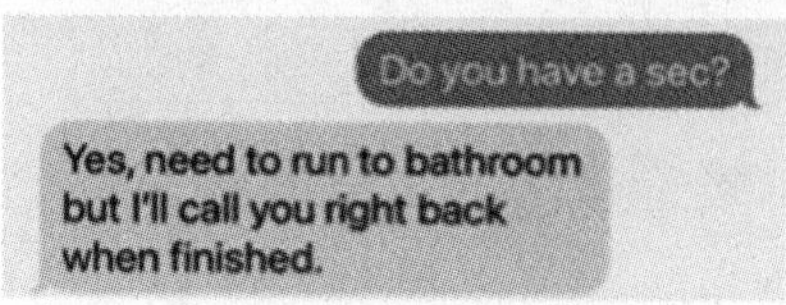

Thx

Three minutes later, my phone vibrates with Dale's incoming call.

"Hey. How are ya?" I answer. "Everything come out okay?"

"Ahh. Haha. Yeah yeah. All good. How are you?"

"Oh, as mindful as the Dalai Lama, and as happy as a pig eating a shit sandwich. Thanks for asking. And, thanks for your time. Shouldn't be too long. Listen, I know amongst our four horsemen of the apocalypse..."

"You think that's where we're heading?"

"Ha. You know it's just a manner of speech?"

"I never know with you, you snake-tongued devil."

"Hehe. Fair enough. But honestly, it was just the first group of four guys that came to mind. I could have said the Beatles, or our little barbershop quartet, or hell, even uh, let's see if I can remember them, Michelangelo, Raphael, Leonardo and uh, oh shit, uhm, D'Artagnan?

"What in the hell are you talking about?"

"The Teenage Mutant Ninja Turtles. Oh shit. Not D'Artagnan. He was the fourth Musketeer. Actually, probably a better descriptor for us four. You, Gerald and Jeff are Athos, Porthos and, uhm, what's-his-name? Arista? No Aramis. You know that was the answer that won the guy a million rupees in *Slumdog Millionaire*? Anyway, I'd like to think that I am the noble protagonist in my own mind, D'Ar-fucking-tagnan. We duel in the beginning. But, I'm hopeful by the end we're all friends."

"Back to earth, Nick. You're losing me. Why did you call?"

"Shit. I can't talk until I remember the name of the fourth Ninja Turtle."

"My God, man. How old are you?"

"Well, I always say I'm precisely the arithmetic mean of a pubescent, sap-rising, uh, let's see, severely hormonally dysfunctional fourteen-year-old and a grumpy, tired, and demented ninety-year-old. Do the math. And how old are you?"

"Fifty-two."

"See, we're the same age. Sort of. But it goes to show you that averages are evil. Your age is a single data point. Mine is a bimodal distribution."

"Holy cow. That's one busy brain."

"Tell me about it. More like addled and unstable. I'd stay as far away from it as possible."

"So, Nick, enough ADHD. What do you want?" I note just a hint of impatience in his voice. Of the main leaders in the company, he is by far the most approachable and human.

"Donatello! It's fucking Donatello!"

"Donatella Versace?"

"No, but that's funny as shit. She looks like the monstrous, botox and filler spawn of Victor Frankenstein, MD, board-certified plastic surgeon. Have you ever seen Maya Rudolph's version of Donatella Versace? It'll make you chortle."

"Nick, we've already been on five minutes. We've covered more territory than an episode of TMZ, you've tossed out at least two dollars' worth of fifty-cent words, and you still haven't told me what you're calling about."

"Sorry. All work and no play makes Nick a dull boy. And anyway, in answer to your question, Donatell-OH, not Donatell-AH, is the fourth Teenage Mutant Ninja Turtle. You know, they're all named after Italian Renaissance artists."

"Goddammit, man. The point."

"Well, I blame you. You double-clicked on Four Horsemen, you got what you deserved. Okay, all right. Anyway. Two topics. One, what the fuck happened with Binks? And two, did you know about the result of the proxy fight? And, uh, if so, any color you can share?"

"Oh my God. Binks Toole. What a piece of work. That guy is probably one of the most bizarre I've ever encountered in my career."

"I always thought he looked like the Disney version of Tigger in Winnie-the-Pooh. Google it. I dare you."

I hear Dale typing. A pause. And then, "Oh my God! He does!"

"See. Don't tell me my non sequiturs are a complete waste of time. Anyway, what the hell took you so long? You guys take great pleasure in firing people. Thought you'd leave a few for leftovers?"

"Fair. But ouch. No, Nick, you won't believe it. You know that waiver legal drafted so that we couldn't quit for good reason?"

"Yes. I, the most dutiful Musketeer, brought that up."

"Oh yeah. I forgot. Thanks a lot. I'd be happy as a clam taking my full severance."

"Yeah. I'm a dumbass. My apologies."

"Anyway, Binks, the sonofabitch, refused to sign."

"Wait, seriously? So did he quit for good reason?"

"No. Instead of attempting that, he refused to take the pay cut. Made us pay him full salary while all the rest of us signed the waiver and took the haircut."

"Man, and I thought I wasn't a team player."

"I know. Right? So anyway. That was the straw that broke the camel's back. I was planning on firing him after we got through this whole UPS/FedEx fiasco, but then he just became completely belligerent and unbearable. Good riddance."

"Yeah, I guess. But I gotta say, the way Jeff raked him over the coals a few weeks ago was a bit much. Just excoriated him. I called Gerald after that and said, 'Just take the dog out back and shoot it.'"

"Yeah, Jeff had a moment. And yes, we should have fired him then. But we needed him to get through the FedEx transition."

"You mean the exhaust from Jeff's Mexican standoff? The 'let me show you pussywillow grasshoppers how a man negotiates' fiasco? Don't worry. I'll make UPS an offer they can't refuse."

"God. Ain't that the truth. That guy's hubris has made my life a living hell these past few weeks. Smartest guy in the room."

"Ya think? I mean look, I'm probably too much of a kitty cat, but, I always tell my people to treat business partners as if they were your own employee—pay them fairly for their work. They need coaching and motivation, even, occasionally, a foot up the ass, but with most, you still need to work together in the future. No point in making ultimatums where, when your bluff is called, you're holding your dick in your hand. The male ego can be a lead apron, can't it?"

"Uhm. Yes?" Dale, like everybody, isn't following me. Hell, I can't even follow me.

"Anyway, back to Binks. Since he had a contract, I'm sure he made out okay, didn't he?"

"Just the opposite. We didn't pay him out according to his contract. We got him on gross negligence."

"What? Wow. Really? That's not like PwnShop. Haha. We're famous for paying inept, fired executives handsomely. Present company included."

"Not this vintage of PwnShop."

"I guess not. So, he got nothing?"

"Well, that's where he is right now, because he refused to accept the severance we were willing to pay him—drastically cut from the contractual obligation."

"He refused out of principle? Or he's suing?"

"Lawyered up immediately. It'll be a protracted legal battle."

"Innarestin'."

"Interesting indeed. But, my life has actually been a lot easier with him gone. Okay, uh, what was the other thing you wanted to talk about?"

"The proxy fight."

"Oh yeah. I can't believe you didn't know about that."

"Are you kidding me? The way this place just brims with free-flowing information? We work for the KGB. Gerald has canceled our last six weeklies. I presume I'm the next Binks. He's probably giving me enough rope to drum up a plausible gross negligence story on me."

"Nah. Seriously? He can't promote you to EVP less than a year ago and then fire you."

"That's like saying our stock price can't get any lower. Things can always go to zero. I mean, I don't know. Stranger things have happened. Fuckers have completely reneged on their 'holding innovation dollars sacrosanct' promise. And they don't believe the Oklahoma City numbers, which is just baffling to me. Like I'm trying to pencil whip them. And they love to bring up the hygiene of the customer database, as if that's going to solve world hunger. That ruffian Suprit has had a hard-on for me ever since I called him on trying to manipulate my loyalty guy's selection of a loyalty vendor."

"I forgot about that. That's funny. It's clear in every meeting that guy hates you. But most of the other directors seem to love you, dontcha think?"

"That's a strong word. I think they sometimes LIKE, APPRECIATE, and/or uh, VALUE the yin I bring to your Three Musketeers yang, but it ain't love. And if there is any love, it's rolling off the board with this new slate. I think everyone likes being able to check the box of doing something innovative without really committing to it. In reality, they think I have the emotional intelligence of a stray dog. I'm comic relief. Comforter. Philosopher. Lifelong twit. You know. Servant to the poor. Butler to the great. Hypocrite and smartass and inebriate."

"Huh?"

"Jesus. Do you have any cultural literacy or have you been selling tiles your whole life? I'm paraphrasing the innkeeper in *Les Miserables*. Comic relief. Duh."

"Heh heh. Unbelievable. You're such a geek."

"I know. Right? A boy among men. Brimming with cowardice. How can they fire such a lovable loser?"

"That's what I'm saying. They can't fire you. Seriously. And not because of all that crap you just spewed. We need your perspective. I know you're not in a lot of those conversations, but OKC is all any of our vendors ever bring up to Gerald. He would have a lot of 'splainin' to do if he fired the architect of that whole initiative."

"Yeah. That whole initiative that they can throw out with the bathwater thanks to this giant excuse for all austerity—SARS fucking COVID-19. Great timing on my part. Let's launch an initiative that's 100 percent reliant on making our stores an IRL community gathering place two months before the greatest worldwide pandemic since the Spanish flu. And people ask me why I'm a pessimist."

"Oh, I think things are opening back up. You don't think those stores will be up and running in the next thirty days or so?"

"Hell no. Not now that we're running under the rule of martial law. COVID gives Gerald and Jeff the ability to substitute military authority over civilian rule. Just like they like it."

"Jesus, you are one cynical bastard aren't you?"

"Yeah, I guess I sound antimilitary. I actually don't think I am. I'm sure it's my own innate guilt for not serving. My dad did. Was an officer in the Navy during the Korean War. He's the only hero I have in this modern, antihero world. But he and all of his contemporaries had character. And, he's probably the funniest person I've ever met."

"Dude. Get a shrink."

"Speaking of shrinks, did I ever tell you the story about telling the corporate psychologist that PwnShop hired to 'coach' me that I always wanted to kill my father and fuck my mother?"

"You did not."

"Did too. It took him a bit to realize that I really didn't have an Oedipal complex and I was simply messing with him."

"My God, man. I'd love to hear that full story, but I have a meeting in twelve minutes. And I still don't think we've gotten to the shareholder's meeting/proxy stuff."

"Yeah, yeah. Sorry. But one more thing on this state of a suspended writ of habeas corpus that we're now operating under. Jeff has usurped all PR under the auspices of IR and keeping a 'tight' messaging strategy."

"Yeah, that's been super effective. The publicity we're getting is just atrocious."

"Well, in Jeff's defense, with the shorts making sure every negative story gets amplified and the lifelong hatred of the consumer gaming press, it's no easy task. But, 'no comment' is typically a recipe for completely losing control of the narrative. You have to work with the reporters. Not stonewall them."

"Same could be said for UPS."

"Indeed. Anyway, between that and him now hiring my candidate for VP of strategy out from under me, I'm close to having enough justification for good reason myself."

"Wait. What?"

"Oh yeah. That ACG guy who's moving here from Atlanta? The little Judas who I took a whole Saturday to show him and his wife all the various neighborhoods in Dallas, the one who I didn't really have to put on the slate to have Jeff interview him but I did so out of courtesy, which, of course, is a courtesy I haven't been extended on any of his hires. Psychological warfare."

"So Jeff is hiring him?"

"Yep. Never said a word to me. Stetson came to me to ask my advice. Said that when he went into the interview, Jeff ambushed him to come work for him. I told the kid that he'd do real blue-sky strategy under me, and financial strategy under Jeff. But if he was a betting man, he should know that Jeff's power base in this company is infinitely more solid than mine, particularly now that COVID has more than likely put the nail in the coffin of Oklahoma."

"But didn't you just report that OKC is killing it relative to the chain?"

"Oh it is. But that's as much an indictment of his vise grip on inventories as it is a win for OKC."

"Tell me about it. He's got a vise grip on the ball sacs of me and the entire buying team. We have, believe it or not, a large open-to-buy, but he's not signing off on purchase orders. You know, to preserve cash above all else."

"Have you been out in stores recently? Shelves are completely bare. I mean, look, they're 100 percent right to clamp down on all spending with the uncertainties of the pandemic, but when we make more money with an in stock position on high turn items, shouldn't we take on some of that risk? Isn't that retail 101? I don't know much, but I do know it's super hard to sell something that ain't there."

"Agreed. But he's saying we make more money with lower inventories. In contrast, you're saying you can prove that when we run with more inventory on the balance sheet, we are making ourselves more money?"

"I can in OKC. The inventory is turning there. Sales comps have been running 45 percent up to the chain. Forty-five fucking percent! With the doors closed, only doing Delivery@Door. I pulled OKC off of the company inventory management system. It didn't work when we can only put 50 percent of the SKUs on the shelves. So, we're hand-assorting it. Shit is in stock there. That accounts for about half to 60 percent of the lift."

"Oh. Well that's not fair. It just probably means OKC has become a big ship-from-store hub for any e-commerce order in the country, since they're in stock. The system is finding inventory there and their sales lift accordingly."

"Nope. That's not it. Thought of that. Because of all the community stuff we're asking the staff to do, we had to simplify their lives. We pulled OKC off of the available stores for ship-from-store once we reopened after the remodel. Too much of a task lift for the associates otherwise."

"Interesting. So all the sales lift from having appropriate stock is going through Delivery@Door?"

"One hundred percent. And that's only 50 to 60 percent of the overall lift. The other half, Jeff's analysts agree—because you know he thinks it's fox in henhouse for my analytics guys to run any numbers—is some kind of halo effect. More traffic. I like to think it's from the goodwill and community we've created in those stores, but I'm sure that's a biased hypothesis."

"Makes sense to me."

"Think how much more business we could be doing if we could open the doors?"

"Yeah, why aren't they open? Texas is now open."

"Deaf ears. We've created a prototype in the mock store of plexiglass dividers between the gaming bays. Have instituted a plan for hourly disinfecting. But there's no way that'll get greenlighted. Just gaslighted."

"Are you pushing hard enough?"

"You're the guy with loads of big company political experience. Tell me what I'm doing wrong? I'm pushing so hard I feel like the band in the *Animal House* parade that's marching double time ass-to-elbow into a walled alley. Be real. With the stellar publicity PwnShop's already received about thinking we're essential? Not a chance in hell. With my luck, we'd reopen OKC and it would become ground zero for some massive super-spreader event. Anyway, enough doom and gloom on that. What happened with the proxy fight?"

"Well, I'm not so sure Jeff's power base is as strong as you think. I've been on a few board calls where he's starting to show his true, aggressive, can't be wrong, dogmatic colors. And there is zero rapport between him and the two Pestia-Hermit directors."

"Well, clearly. Hence the proxy fight."

"Yep. And you know why we lost, right?"

"Same reason we caved on giving them board members the first time? The long shareholders that are leasing their shares to the shorts can't vote their shares?"

"Exactly. The activists own like 6 percent of the company, but that might well be over half of the votable shares. Plus, there are many other hedge funds making noise, they're just not asking to remain on the board like Pestia. Regardless, those who aren't leasing out their shares, the noninstitutional guys, are mostly embracing the activist thesis. Too many shorted shares. Not enough voters."

"So fascinating. Man, I hate shorts," I bemoan. "It's just positively un-American in my oh-so-humble opinion. Betting on the demise of something. So morose. Coldhearted. They're like that 'Bring out yer dead' John Cleese character in *Monty Python and the Holy Grail.* Clubbing struggling companies to death to accelerate their ability to toss them on the heap of ex-companies. Do they not think we're earnestly trying to fix this thing?"

"It's capitalism. Keeps the markets efficient."

"Oh bullshit. The SEC tried to regulate it, but Wall Street makes too much money off of it. Deep-pocketed financiers have outsized influence on Congress. I hear all that efficient capital markets bullshit from my masters of the universe B-School buddies. I believe if you don't like the stock, sell it and/or don't buy it. The price will still go down. But don't stand to profit on it going out of business. That's no better than Michael Vick betting on the death of a pit bull. Positively depraved. Yeah, I know, it's capitalism, and believe me, I'm all for the invisible hand of the market and the allergies it brings, but stock shorting creates anaphylactic shock, and in this day and age of unbridled greed, the SEC is hardly an EpiPen."

"Ahh, the Nick metaphors. Never a dull moment. And a conspiracy theorist to boot."

"And lifelong allergy sufferer. Don't get me started. I guarantee you Big Pharma has a cure for allergies but it would kill the sales of all their symptom relievers, which they should really call symptom reprievers. No root cause cure in sight. Why address the root cause when we can profit like mad with temporary salves?"

"Good God, man. Where do you come up with this shit? Hey, did you hear we have a call coming up with Eiffel Murray?"

"I think I remember Jack Floyd saying he made a sizeable investment in us in 2018, but then he quickly sold his position in 2019. And I remember Gerald saying he and Jeff had a call with him a few months back, right before we opened The new OKC stores. Was apparently professing the need for us to cut costs. Same imagination as every finance guy. What's he up to now? I guess, now, he, like every other hedge fund wonk, is shorting the shit out of us?"

"I think he's long on us. He thinks we have the biggest short squeeze opportunity since Volkswagen.[3] With just a little financial discipline, he thinks we can win big. He's written a few letters to the board."

---

[3] On October 28, 2008, in the panic period of the global economic meltdown, Volkswagen shares shot up to over four times their value, as their primary owner, Porsche SE, cornered the hedge funds that were shorting their stock, forcing the funds to cover their positions and drive up the stock in geometric fashion. For a brief period of time, Volkswagen was the most valuable company in the world. Within days, as Porsche relieved some of the abnormal upward pressure on the stock by selling 5 percent of their holdings, the stock price tumbled. Within weeks, the share price was back to its original level.

"Let me guess. Spend all our cash on share buybacks. That must be where Pestia and Hermit are getting their profoundly crude and callous antidote for our illness. Did he ask for the old guard to resign from the board?"

"Yes, and he even said Gerald should surrender his board seat to someone more qualified."

"Ouch."

"Anyway, we talk to him next week."

"We, or just you Three Musketeers? Little old D'Artagnan here, won't be invited. You know, always a swashbuckling apprentice, never a knighted, emotionless mercenary. Just like I'm not allowed to speak on earnings calls. Might actually get a conversation started that won't end quickly. Of course, I guess, the character D'Artagnan became a Musketeer in the end. Not me. My pen and mouth ain't a sword."

"I have no idea what you're talking about."

"I don't either. I think I'm slipping. The call sounds like it could actually be interesting. Just saying, I guarantee you I won't be told about it, much less asked to attend, by Gerald or Jeff."

"Well, if it makes you feel any better, I probably won't either."

"At least you've been informed. Your one-on-ones with Gerald must still be happening every week."

"Yep. They are."

"Anyway, do you think this short squeeze opportunity is real? Nothing we do seems to move the stock price up. At some point, maybe they'll try innovation as a storyline, but what do I know?"

"God, you really are a cynical bastard aren't you?" Dale pauses, then continues just as I start to open my mouth. "Nope. Don't answer. I mean, look. You know and I know our short interest is well over 100 percent. Shit tons of naked shorts. With just a minor upward movement in our stock price, the shorts would have to cover their backsides, which could theoretically send the price up even higher."

"I understand a short squeeze. That's what happens every time I stick my hand down my pants."

"Ha ha ha. Good lord. TMI."

"Sorry. Can't help it. Continue."

"That's about it. With all this short interest, any good news will send the stock soaring. It's a virtuous cycle for those on the long side of the trade."

"Long side of the trade? What a crock of shit. Nobody's on the 'long' side of any trade anymore. Everybody's a share flipper. Fucking speculators. Nobody, particularly no investor in this company, could give one shit about the long-term prospects. They either think it could collapse massively, in which case the shorts clean up, or it could go up very quickly, in which case the longs, which are really just short-term share flippers, clean up. But then that would be a speculative bubble, so they'd need to get out quickly. And then we're right back where we started, but with all of our available cash invested in the now—share buybacks. I agree business exists to maximize shareholder value, but the world seems to have forgotten that the term shareholder is a compound word. The first word is share, meaning you own a piece of the company. The second word is holder, meaning, y'know, oh I don't know, a keeper. A steward. A custodian. Hagrid. The keeper of the keys. Somebody who cares about the long-term prospects and viability of the company. Who cares about employees? Who cares about investment, strategic evolution, and so on? Not somebody who just wants to make a quick buck. We should no more listen to those people than to the shorts. They're made of the same greedy stuff. We exist to maximize the value of this company over time. Not starve it of investment and buy back shares so a bunch of hedge funds can make a quick buck. That's my opinion. Oughta be yours."

"Well, look at you. The last Boy Scout."

"Hardly. I mean I was an Eagle, but I did it out of a severe inferiority complex relative to my much more impressive brothers. I'm a flake. I'm just saying, we've lost our way if we're taking advice from some heavy metal financier."

"Uhm, he did predict the housing market meltdown. Dude is really fucking smart. Don't you think we can do both? Make money in the short-term and the long-term?"

"Honest to God, I don't. Not in this situation. It's too far gone. I'm sure Murray is a smart guy. I'm just saying, he doesn't really care about the viability of this company. And he definitely doesn't care about the 30,000 people entrusting their careers to us. He's just doing math. It's clearly undervalued. He wants it to go up. Saving money in the short-term makes money in the short term, but it's not sustainable. It's clear-cutting a first-growth forest and never spending any money to reseed, much less hold off some cutting every year to keep the forest healthy. Everybody just wants to make hay while the sun is shining, not prepare the fields to endure whatever weather we face. And, I don't think any of Murray's prescriptions, Pestia-Hermit's, or even Gerald's and Jeff's austerity are doing a bit of good as it relates to share price. Every time we've announced massive cost cutting, share buybacks or debt relief, new board makeup, blah, blah, blah, it's just a minor blip in share price. We need to give investors a reason to believe. A competitive advantage that's achievable, that embraces the digital disruption and makes PwnShop the local place for the gaming community, and makes our employees the distributed salesforce and media company for an industry that desperately needs their digital wares discovered."

"I don't think that's why the price isn't going up. The reason is the short interest is just compounding. A lot of downward pressure on share price," Dale submits.

"Nah, I don't believe in silver bullets. It would take a miracle for investors to pour into this stock quickly. Ain't gonna happen. I say, we play the long game."

"Believe me. Your position is quite clear. I, for one, would like to see the stock price go up while I'm still vertical and ventilating."

"Fair enough."

PwnShop Reports Preliminary Voting Results: Four directors retire; Pestia and Hermit nominees elected.

> Bonnie and Clyde Historical Marker
> Gibsland, Bienville Parish, Louisiana
> Friday, September 4, 2020
> 152 days to POSS
> CSP: $6.40

"No, no, no. Take it in slo-mo," I yell. "Do it again," I direct.

"Shut up, Nick. You're not the boss of me." Fred Rhodus chides while his brow is furrowed, trying to figure out how to get his iPhone camera into slow motion mode.

"Dude, we're losing this beautiful light," Lucie Raines chides back. "You look more confused than my mom with that phone. How freaking old are you?"

"Fifty-two. About two months older than you, bee-atch. Just shut the fuck up and hold on a sec," Fred smirks.

Lucie and I are standing in front of the bronze marker attached at about a 60 degree angle to a formed concrete pediment, some three feet high. You, dear reader, might ask, "Why?" We might respond, "duh..." It's the thirtieth anniversary of Tour '90, the trip we took together right after college. Since true crime's really the only history a pessimistic Dallas native can find in our fair and otherwise optimistic city—boasting legendary delinquents Bonnie and Clyde, Lee Harvey Oswald, and the Highland Park high school graduate, John Hinckley, Jr.—I have always wanted to see the ambush site that ended the bank robbing spree for Parker and Barrow. In reverence to our trip from our early twenties, we thought it might be fun to take a weekend excursion and enter a bass fishing tournament in southeast Texas—the Big Bass Splash on Lake Sam Rayburn. Bienville Parish is not at all on the way, but the real purpose of the trip is to spend hours being in the moment and catching each other up on music that we've discovered that we think the others might like.

While we're still waiting on Fred, my phone vibrates. I've taken the day off. Most of us are back in the office off and on, but with all the remote working, nobody really knows who's taking time off and who's simply working from home. I look at the screen. Caller ID says Dale Spivey. I click the message balloon and select, "Can I call you back later?" I mean, c'mon. I'm busy here. Once we finish the half-assed reenactment of being machine-gunned to death, we get back in the car.

"Where do we want to go now?" Lucie asks

"Why don't we go to Shreveport?"

"Oh no. Have I told you about my honeymoon? Ansel and I were at an intimate resort in Mexico and overlapped with a couple from Shreveport. Or, Shrevesport, as he called it. Dude got really drunk one night and told me, and I'm not kidding, 'I could graze on you.'"

"Wow. Nothing more romantic than the eating habits of a bovine," Rhodus muses. I'm racing along while Lucie has the conch, meaning she's manning the music. For old time's sake, she streams the Beach Boys' "Good Vibrations." At its ending, I remark, "We should do a dashboard karaoke to this song. Could be epic.""I love that idea," Lucie muses.

"Such a good song," Rhodus adds.

"One of the best," I say. "A musical masterpiece, except for the ending."

"What, you don't like that electro-theremin? Iconic dude."

"Oh I love the electro-theremin. I don't like the way Brian Wilson punted on the ending. Repeat and fade? C'mon! As much creativity that went into that song and production, you gotta do better on an ending." Holding forth, I continue, "Clearly he was just tired and couldn't figure it out. When you play live, you must have an ending. Recorded music ruined all that. Repeat and fade is such a copout."

"Oh, so you think you have the authority to criticize one of the greatest pop productions of all time?"

"Yes I do," I preach.

"You're such a dick, Nick."

"Oh shit, that reminds me. Y'all shut up for a second, I need to call Dale back."

"Is Dale a dick?" Rhodus asks mockingly.

"Not at all. I don't know why being a dick reminded me of work."

"Oh, hey Nick," Dale says. "Reason I was calling is I just got a Google alert about an SEC filing from a guy named Garvin "Garv" Pastor. Has bought up 9 percent of the common stock over the last few weeks. The stock price has tripled in after-hours trading. Bizarre news on a dog days of summer Friday."

"Tripled. Really? We're still undervalued IMO. Stock needs to go to about twenty dollars for us to be priced right. Who is this guy?"

"Was the founder and CEO of Chompy.com."

"Innarestin'. Must have scared out some shorts."

"Either that, or they all have to cover their naked positions. Didn't you tell me one time you almost went to work for Petco? Did you ever hear of this guy?"

"I was finalist candidate for CMO when I was on the bench after my first tour of duty with PwnShop. They had purchased some small tech company and the CEO that came with that acquisition was a digital guy. I think they liked me, but I don't think they could decide if they wanted an experienced CMO or not. Plus, I think the skillset overlap between the acquiree CEO and me would have been too high. Anyway, I took the job with Tailored Brands. And as far as, what's his name?"

"Garv Pastor."

"Yeah, Garv. I don't know him from Adam, but I know a fair amount about the company, at least from the perspective of its traditional big box competitors. Chompy was giving Petco fits."

"Hmm. Seems interesting. I've put a call into Gerald to see if they're in communication with him. Super young guy. Might be good for your innovation stuff."

"May be. Could be fun. Chompy in its early days was trés new school, all about market share over profit, if memory serves. Apparently, its early investors and VCs were more than willing to invest heavily in market share. Chompy was happy to free-ship a forty-pound bag of dog food 20 percent off retail back in the day. Great deal for the consumer. I have no idea if they ever made money. The old 'lose money on every transaction but make it up in volume' bit. I thought that mentality died with Web 1.0. PetStop ended up buying Chompy because they had to take out the dumbest competitor. Tanking price integrity in the category. Was getting like the airline business right after deregulation. I'll bet this guy Garv made a bunch of money on the transaction, even though his company never made a thin dime of profit when he was running it."

"Oh, he made a bunch. I think the company sold for like $3 billion. He's thirty-five years old. Apparently, he's now just running his own investment firm. That's the entity that filed the 13D. Proud Priest Ventures."

"Proud Priest? Sounds like a metal band."

"I hear it's the etymology of his two names."

"Well, that's even weirder."

"Is what it is. Anyway, speaking of PetStop, you know one of the new board members is their CEO? C.S. Rowling."

"Oh yeah. Forgot about that. Haven't met him yet."

"He's a good guy. Smart. Levelheaded. I think he'll be a much-needed voice of reason. But I'm wondering if he knows this guy, Garv."

"I'm sure he does. Probably no love lost there. I'm guessing paying some young upstart ten figures to eliminate a race to the bottom competitor makes for a fair amount of jealousy. Especially, I'm sure, when his big box retail stock price is languishing. Garv makes the real dough. Gets to go to the beach. The PetSmart CEO only gets the consolation prize—one less worry when he goes to bed at night."

"That's the truth. And, he may have added another worry, which is how to ingest the acquisition, and maintain its momentum, without it eating into your core business."

"Heavy hangs the head. So, do you think Garv Pastor is in on Michael Murray's short squeeze thesis? Or with the Pestia-Hermit guys?

Or maybe Murray is the lead guitarist in Pastor's Proud Priest death metal band?"

"You're so weird. Maybe on Murray. Who knows what goes on between masters of the universe? But doubtful on Pestia-Hermit. Those guys are playing at activism."

"Sounds interesting nonetheless. Any notion if this guy is an activist himself? Or is he just betting big on us now that the console releases are imminent?"

"Not sure, but I can't imagine he's going to be a wallflower if he owns 9 percent of the company."

"True that. Thanks for the heads up. Juicy stuff. What are you up to today?"

"I'm actually in the office. Wanted to meet in person with some of the merchants. Was going stir crazy in the corporate apartment. I take it you're working from home?"

"Hardly. I took the day off, whatever that means anymore. Presently, I'm departing the historical marker for the ambush site of Bonnie and Clyde with my two oldest buddies. We just made a slow-mo movie of me and Lucie playing like we're getting ripped to pieces by tommy-guns. Check my Insta. It's uh, you know the adjective every video game developer deploys when launching their next AAA title: EPIC!"

"You are one weird dude."

"Thank you. I plan on staying that way."

PwnShop: Chompy's Founder Garv Pastor Finds 'What's Next'.

PwnShop Bored Room
Wednesday November 18, 2020
77 days to POSS
CSP: $12.76

"Okay, I've looked over everybody's board presentations." Gerald launches into to our preparation huddle in advance of tomorrow's first in-person board meeting since the beginning of the pandemic. "I want all of our focus to be on the progress of our Reboot initiatives. Dale, since tomorrow is the release date of the PS5, and given the speed with which we sold out of the new Xboxes last night, be prepared to field questions about our preparation for tomorrow night's launch. Jeff, you'll need to reprise your audit committee presentation for the full board—our cash position and all the fantastic progress you've made there needs to be understood and celebrated. And, I'm sure we'll spend a lot of time getting approval on the ATM."

"ATM?" I ask naively. "We're getting into teller machines?"

"Haha. No, no, no."

"Good lord. I thought this was some new harebrained diversification scheme."

"It stands for an at-the-market offering. Jeff, do you want to fill the team in on how that all works."

"Not sure it's a good idea to get everyone involved, sir. Particularly since it's not even approved," he all but chastises his boss with feigned respect. "But, in a nutshell, an ATM filing enables us to issue new shares of stock at prevailing market prices in a secondary market. We do it through a brokering bank. Basically, it's a good idea to do this in a period of rising stock price. And because of all the hard work we've done on the balance sheet and in SG&A reduction, we're trading well above our ninety-day moving average."

Right. Better balance sheet and SG&A reduction. The stock price has tripled because we have a rich, young entrepreneur who's conveying a story for the way forward. Could you please call a spade a spade?

"We must strike while the iron is hot. Basically, it's a great way for us to raise additional liquidity at by far the lowest cost of capital we've seen in quite some time. That's about it. More to come. By the way, Gerald, are you sure it requires board approval? I think we may have the right to make this decision on our own."

"We can discuss in private, Jeff. To summarize, there are many important things we'll be talking about, so if you could please keep your presentations as concise and focused on brass tacks wins as possible, I would greatly appreciate it. Also, please don't get your feelings hurt if there's not enough time to get to everything," he says, clearly targeting me. "Okay, gang. Let's wrap this up. We good?"

"Just one quick confirmation," Naomi, head of HR, queries. "Want to make sure we're still going forward with a dinner with the board tomorrow night?" Given that she's been on point to work through the challenges of social distancing, masking, work from home policies and procedures, it's clear in the way she asks she's got a bit of a nervous tic as it relates to human beings sharing common physical space, especially as winter is coming, and nobody knows whether there will be a COVID resurgence in the colder months.

"Yes." Gerald responds. "Dinner is at 7 PM at TruFire. Anybody else? Otherwise, Jeff and I need to huddle."

"I've got one item. I think I can guess the answer, but just want to make sure you read my whole presentation. I've got stuff in there about OKC's performance. You know that even though the gaming section is still closed, we're holding our own in terms of regular retail sales at the front of the store."

"Yeah, I saw that. I'd not put those slides in there. Have them in reserve if it comes up. Maybe just put them in the appendix," Gerald hedges.

"I appreciate that, Gerald," Jeff launches in, "but I would leave those slides out. As you said earlier, this meeting needs to focus heavily on the ATM, capital structure, and only in a minor way on all the progress we're making on Reboot initiatives—our significantly strengthened balance sheet, our inventory management, our strong cash position. Nothing needs to be about innovation. Tilting at windmills is not the message we need to convey. We need to show the board that we've successfully crossed the chasm created by the pandemic and the holdback in anticipation of these new consoles. And with the stock price where it is, we're well poised for a very successful at-the-market offering. We're now ready to make hay."

"Wow. I thought you didn't think metaphors were helpful? Tilting at windmills? Making hay? When did you get to be such a poet?" I wink, wondering if he can take a little good-natured ribbing.

He smirks. "Who says I hate metaphors? I love metaphors."

"Right. Okay. I'll just focus on the big win from the changes to the loyalty program and..."

"Old news," Jeff interrupts. "Please don't mention that. That launched back in February. It's in the Reboot exhibits the board gets every month. I think they know how to read."

"It's about the only thing we can point to that's actually been accretive to sales. Everything else is store closures, layoffs, vendor renegotiations, financial engineering, and so on. Nothing positive about our fundamental business."

"A dollar saved is a dollar earned. It's ironclad. I just had a meeting with the consultants about what they're going to get paid for these initiatives. I'm questioning the math with my team on loyalty. I don't think the win is nearly as big as we've been reporting."

"Is that because ACG's fees are at risk, and you don't want to stroke them a check, or is it because the initiative has my name on it, and you want to make sure anything with my name on it is sullied? Tainted? Destroyed?"

"Oh, c'mon man. Be professional. You think this is personal? It's just math."

"Just math my ass." My playful interplay quickly devolves into my own anger management problem. "It's revisionist history. We all agreed on your team measuring these initiatives. We all agreed on the scientific test/control methodology for revenue enhancements. Do you not remember the meeting a year ago when we were coming up with initiatives and you challenged all of us that we weren't thinking big enough? That everything was little toe in the water tests that weren't really moving the needle? And I said, 'Let's get our ass in the pool with the loyalty changes.' You agreed. Your team's math says it's created $63 million in incremental revenue, and that's what we're reporting. It's clearly personal. I don't know what the hell I've done to make you hate me, but it's fucking petty. Stop the bullshit and let's celebrate wins together. It's not about credit. It's about progress."

He stares me down, moves his head to his shoulder. "How are you coming on the whole data hygiene project, building a DMP, and so on. You haven't made any progress on that."

"Oh come on. We're going there? Total redirect. Why don't you answer my questions first? In fact, why don't you ever answer my questions? You know damn well where that is. Stalled because we had to announce your beloved partnership with Microsoft. And stalled because we've laid off half of our data warehouse team. I've got Acxiom lined up to help, but you don't want to spend any money on it. And you want to make it out to be a dereliction of duty on my part?"

"That's exactly what it is. You have a duty and you're dropping the ball. We've made no progress. That's the definition of dereliction of duty. Moreover, I can't fully prove the efficacy of the great strides we've made in store closures without clean customer data. Enough about that. Back to the loyalty math. How can it be possible that we've made $63 million in incremental revenue when our sales comps are down double digits? It's impossible."

"Really? Our sales would be $63 million less if we hadn't done it. It's just math, Jeff. Basic arithmetic in fact. I know. It requires doing subtraction, the elusive and oh-so-tricky mirror image of the much more straightforward procedure called addition, but I would think a CFO of your stature knows how to subtract, yes?"

"Enough you two." Gerald intervenes. "Nick, just leave your loyalty slides in there. We probably won't get to it anyway. I'm pretty certain there won't be a large amount of time for management presentations. Garv Pastor is taking on a pretty activist posture. Keep this under your hats, as is this is very material nonpublic information, but he's reached out to me and the board and wants a private hearing. Has a draft of a letter he's prepared to make public if we don't kowtow to his demands."

The call ends. I immediately back channel Dale to see if he has any color on this new potential activism.

"Hey, man. So Garv is going active?"

"Oh yeah. In a big way. Jockeying for board seats, changes, the whole bit. I think he's bought up even more stock. Apparently, he's pissed about us trying to do an ATM offering. Thinks it will wildly dilute his position."

"Oh man. Could get interesting."

"Very."

"Have you met the guy yet?"

"No, but there's a Zoom call with him tomorrow during executive session with the board. Gerald told me to be on call in case there's something he needs me for."

"Surprisingly, he didn't say the same thing to me."

"Well, I don't think it's going to be much fun. Apparently, the guy thinks we're in the dark ages with our e-tail offering. Gerald says Garv told him he thinks digital commerce is the entire opportunity."

"Meaning he's willing to actually invest in digital and not just do the minimum on the cheap?"

"I think so. Chompy spent hundreds of millions, if not billions, on e-commerce infrastructure."

"Man, that would be nice. Except for us, digital is mostly just a waste of time."

"You think so?"

"I know so. What's your biggest worry from a competition standpoint in our business? Amazon, or Sony, Microsoft, Nintendo, and Steam?"

"Definitely Sony, Microsoft, Nintendo, and Steam. Amazon is a blip."

"Exactly. When I was at Guitar Mart, Amazon was melting the iceberg. But in this industry, the platform developers have out-Amazoned

Amazon. Now, I suppose, Amazon has enough of a war chest where they might invest more heavily in this category, but right now they're a distant seventh in market share behind us, Walmart, Best Buy and the three platform guys. If e-commerce were the way forward, Amazon would be one or two in video game market share, just like they are with most tangible goods. All the money's in the software, and the software can be distributed through the ether. Game over unless you've got a viable gaming platform."

"Well, as you said, it's gonna get interesting."

"Power to the players. Never a dull moment at PwnShop."

"Never. Talk soon."

"And oh yeah. Please let me know if you get any more intel. I'm actually kinda excited for the first time in a long time. We might finally have an activist that wants to play the long game."

"We'll see."

PwnShop CBI
(Center for Big Ideas)
Friday November 20, 2020
75 days to POSS
CSP: $12.00

Yesterday's afternoon kickoff session for the board meeting was straightforward and drama free. Just the facts and a little bit of back and forth with Dale on the console launches. Last night's dinner was sterile, except for the fact that none of us were socially distanced, and Jeff couldn't get close enough to Suprit Shetty. There were a lot of whispering side conversations, but neither Dale nor I got bupkis about how the board call went with Garv.

We're holding the meeting in the CBI. The space allows Naomi's facilities team to arrange eight-foot rectangular folding tables in a large 'U' so that there's at least three or four feet between seats. They've also papered the windows so no would-be voyeurs can catch a peek.

The agenda for the morning was Jeff going through the Reboot initiatives, including loyalty, for which he said the $63 million is directional and we're evaluating that number more closely. I kept my fucking mouth shut.

Sitting next to him is Suprit. He looks worse for wear. His rich brown skin seems more yellow, with a glow of sweat around his pock-marked forehead. Last night after dinner, I got up and left as quickly as I could, along with the female directors and the two fish out of water contentious activist investors from Pestia-Hermit. As we were saying our awkward goodbyes, I noticed Jeff pulling in even closer to Suprit, and pouring more red wine. My house is fifty minutes from Trophy Club, unlike the mercenary Three Musketeers who all live in corporate apartments within a 7 iron of the office. It looked like they were settling in for a bit more conversation. This morning, it looks like he might have had more than conversation.

"Hey look, team, I know we're going until 1 PM this afternoon, but I am really not feeling well," Suprit interjects as Jeff winds up his Reboot presentation. "I think I'm going to head back to the hotel and call in for the remainder. Probably better to err on the side of caution."

"Oh, man. I'm sorry to hear that," Jeff says. "I hope you feel better."

"Thanks, man. But listen, uh, before I go, Nick, I saw we brushed over the loyalty initiative. That's all well and good, but I'm wondering how you're coming on the data hygiene project. I haven't heard an update on that, and I can't think of anything more important than that to help turn this company around," he says with his politely tuneful yet accusatory Indian accent, 'haven't' coming out more like 'he-went'.

What a preordained planted fucking question. The guy looks like shit, needs to leave the meeting and wants to double down on fucking data hygiene? What a motherfucking conspiracy. Data hygiene? Do you motherfuckers play chess? This is zugzwang at its finest. Not a creative bone in either of your soulless bodies. You're compelled to move pieces around the board that have no bearing on affecting the outcome of the game. Vanity checks. Are you hoping time runs out and this thing is a draw? We're fiddling on the deck while the ship is sinking.

I pull my brain out of its free falling fugue, pull back my shoulders and eat shit. "We've had another delay, and the completion date has been pushed to January."

"Care to elaborate?" Suprit inquires with glee.

"Uhm, not really. It's complicated."

"That's your answer? That's what you want this board to walk away with relative to one of the company's most important initiatives? It's complicated?"

"Yep. It's complicated."

"Gerald, I don't want to tell you how to manage your team, but I'd suggest you make this a top priority. This is unacceptable."

"Understood, Suprit. I hope you feel better," Gerald nips it in the bud.

Car
Friday, November 20, 2020
75 days to POSS
CSP: $11.00

I'm lost in thought as I drive home. I can't think of any music that fits the mood, so road noise is my meditation playlist. After I couldn't contain my inner adolescent with Suprit, he left and the meeting lasted another thirty minutes before Gerald excused everyone for an executive session, but asked Jeff and Dale to wait in the hallway. I went back to the office and actually made momentum on pushing the data hygiene project forward with Acxiom. All the while, my self-talk can't get over the fact that it's useless busy work that won't make a difference in the long run. And then, the dad in my head says, "Son, there's honor in making your bed."

When I departed, I noticed that neither Dale nor Jeff were in their offices so I dialed up Dale, assuming he either won't answer or went home. But it would be very unlike these guys not to lock their doors before leaving.

"Hey man," he answers breathily, like he's walking.

"Are you free for a sec?"

"Sure thing. I'm just heading back to my office."

"Are you serious? From the board meeting? It's almost six o'clock. What the hell have y'all been doing?"

"Well, I'm not sure of everything as I sat out in the waiting area for about an hour and a half. I'm pretty sure all that conversation focused on the ATM."

"Oh, I know the feeling of sitting in that waiting room. Have read the book. And seen the movie."

"So I've heard. Funny. Anyway, it's clear the call with Garv Pastor was super contentious. Gerald called me in after most of the board members had left or were packing up. We talked briefly with them. Mostly cordial. But then Gerald, Jeff and I sat in there the rest of the afternoon strategizing. It seems Garv is going public with a letter that is super critical of the board, but this whole ATM thing is what's really got him in a wad."

"Why, because he thinks it's dilutive to his position?"

"Exactly."

"But doesn't the shelf filing just give us the optionality to sell shares in a secondary market at the then at-the-market price? It doesn't necessarily mean we'll float the shares, does it?"

"No, exactly. It just gives us the option to. Clearly if the stock price is low, it wouldn't be worth it. Moreover, we couldn't sell. I think the filing will include a price below which we won't sell. And the higher it gets, the less dilutive it is to shareholders who were in the stock back when the price was in the single digits," Dale instructs. "I'm not sure if there's a limit on the time frame, but it's just a way for us to pad the dwindling nest egg in an advantageous, low-cost way."

"So did the board approve the ATM?"

"Yes, but barely. I think there were three opposed and one abstention."

"Wow. I don't ever remember any board vote that has been split. Ever. They're always unanimous. I wonder if Garv got to some of them."

"I don't know. But what's more, I think it's clear by the way the conversation went that Jeff is damaged goods with much of the board. I think Suprit voted for the ATM, and was pretty vocal about it from what I could understand. It sounds like it limped through, I'm sure with a bunch of ultimatum language from Jeff."

"Man, I wish I could have been in the room where it happened."

"I know, right? Hey, I just got to my office. Let me close the door and call you back."

"Sure."

The call kicks off from the CarPlay app on the dashboard monitor. Back to the thrumming road.

I wonder what the hell this means for me? For all of us really? On the one hand, I love that Garv has the potential to truly shake things up. I just hope he has the best interest of the company in mind. Maybe he really will take it private. That's the only way to fix this thing. Only under the cloak of privacy can we make the investments that need to be made without the Eye of Sauron from all the institutional investors, potential activists, and analysts questioning our every move. On the other hand, and more than likely, he's simply playing a trade. Probably listened to Murray about the short squeeze opportunity and is just going to flip. But if he's going to flip, why would he be all up in the board's grill? Nah, clearly, he's trying to buy himself a job. Wants to be CEO again. This could get fun. Out with the stodgy. In with the innovative.

Dale's contact info appears on the CarPlay screen.

"Well, if it wasn't already, it's getting thicker," he whispers.

"How so?"

"Gerald and Jeff just walked by looking severely at odds. Jeff scowled at me like he wanted to kill Gerald."

"I wonder what that's all about? I thought those two were thick as thieves."

"I'm pretty sure it's about the way Jeff has made everything into an ultimatum. I think Jeff thinks we have more latitude in some of these decisions, and Gerald is following the letter of the law and involving the board. Jeff obviously prefers to inform that we've made a decision rather than seek consultation. Basically, wants to tell the board to pound sand."

"Duh. Ask for forgiveness rather than permission. I've never learned that. Too much of a Boy Scout. Some of the board has got to see through his Eddie Haskell routine. He's so saccharine sweet with them. It's clear he doesn't agree with anything they say. I would hope most of them are more astute judges of personality. And what's more, management can't make a decision to sell an additional $100 million worth of stock without board approval, can we?"

"No, of course not. I think he's had to get past having the board vote on it. I think he burned some bridges the past two days. First, he presumed it was his decision to make. And second, once it was clear the board was voting, it sounds like he told them they were obtuse if they didn't vote for it."

"It's surprising to me that a guy that smart, can't self-evaluate and attenuate his ego."

"The big egos never can."

"True that. So, anyway, what the hell did you talk about for four hours? Couldn't have all been the ATM, particularly if that vote is already in the books."

"There's a lot I can't get into, but most of what we talked about was how much information we should or should not share with Garv. He's asking for tons of stuff that would make him an insider."

"Isn't he already an insider?"

"Not until he beneficially owns more than 10 percent of the company. Seems like he's hovering just below that amount so that he can sell when he wants to. That was a lot of the conversation with the board that I was involved in. He's asking for investment plans in technology, heavily questioning Jeff's deal with Microsoft, wants to know contractual freight rates, all kinds of stuff. We can't share any of it as it would violate SEC insider information rules. I don't think anybody wants to wear an orange jumpsuit."

"Definitely sounds like Garv wants to run the company. Do you think he wants to take it private?"

"Can't tell."

"Well, if he doesn't, the problem with being an insider is he can't sell when he wants, right? He has to wait until the window is open after earnings are reported, right?"

"Right."

"It's a delicate dance. I guess he's going to have to figure if he's going to shit or get off the pot."

"Yep."

"Damn, never a dull moment at PwnShop."

"Nope."

Home Office
Wednesday, November 25, 2020
69 days to POSS heh heh
CSP: $13.48

"Hey Gerald. How are you? Feeling any better?"

I'm on my Teams video call one-on-one with Gerald, the first one he hasn't canceled for the last five weeks. The meeting is normally scheduled for Tuesday afternoons, but Gerald has been out sick, and so he pushed it until today. I'm anticipating the reason he's been insistent on having this one is, once again, my disrespectful behavior in the board meeting.

"Man, this is an intense illness. You know I have COVID, right?"

"Wow. I had no idea."

"We tried to keep a tight wrap on it. No need to alarm everyone."

"I'm so sorry. You're still fighting it?"

"Yes, but it's not been nearly as intense since yesterday. My doctor was able to get me on an IV drip of steroids and Remdesivir."

"Isn't that what they used on Trump back in October?"

"I think so."

"How do you think you got it?"

"Suprit. He apparently wasn't feeling well the moment he got here. He didn't tell anyone until the board meeting."

"I just thought he was hungover. He looked like shit."

"He did. And felt like shit apparently. Jeff and I had a meeting with him Wednesday, Jeff went to dinner with him that night, then we all had the board meeting with him and then the dinner that night."

"I'm surprised Jeff didn't get it too."

"Oh he did. But you know Jeff. Kept his full meeting schedule. Just did it all virtually. He said he feels like crap, but I think my case was a bit worse. I think he's at about 85 percent strength now."

"Well, I guess I avoided it. Lord knows I avoided being anywhere close to Suprit. He and Jeff despise me."

"I haven't noticed," he chuckles. "No, but seriously, you're a grown man. I don't want to tell you how to act, but you know your aloof little 'it's complicated' didn't score you any points with the board, and definitely put the nail in the coffin between you and Suprit. Don't you think you're being hypersensitive?"

"Probably. I have a hyperactive autoimmune response to bullies."

"Oh, don't go all soft on me. They're not bullies. They're tough-minded business people."

"If you say so."

"Look, I'm sorry we haven't had a one-on-one recently. I'm just trying to gauge your temperature on the state of the union."

"My temperature? As it relates to this company and this situation?"

"Yes."

"Probably as high as yours is from COVID. I must say, this recent activism with Garv Pastor, and this is probably an unpopular opinion with you and the board, has me excited that someone actually wants to engage in a fundamental transformation."

"You know he's all about e-commerce, don't you?"

"Yeah, I read the letter. And you know I'm a huge believer in e-commerce, don't you? That's what I was hired to build out at Guitar Mart. I just don't think it's the answer in this category. I think if memory serves from reading the letter, Garv does mention prioritizing profitable locations and markets. And he sees an opportunity in esports. Sorry, but I think I might have a kindred spirit here."

"I wouldn't count your chickens. Sounds to me like he wants to compete with Amazon."

"Well we already do, right?"

"I think he wants to take on Amazon head-on in all categories. Become a global e-commerce generalist."

"Wow. And you think rolling out the Oklahoma stores is expensive? They're dirt cheap relative to building out that kind of infrastructure. Walmart is finally at least moderately competitive, and they've spent tens of billions, if not hundreds of billions on building out their e-commerce infrastructure. Where the hell is he going to get the capital? Clearly, he doesn't want the company doing it with an at-the-market offering."

"Haha. Yep. That's been made abundantly clear."

"Anyway, you asked how I'm doing. Look, I know none of us could have predicted the pandemic, but I feel like it's being used as an excuse to kneecap me on all of my initiatives."

"Again, I think you're being overly sensitive. And no I don't think you have a kindred spirit. You've been critical of the number of stores we've already closed. He thinks we're not even close to having closed enough. He thinks minimally, we should shut down half of the remaining."

"Well, is that just because he has an idea of running a different type of store? I'd be all for it. It's like creating a hub and spoke system, with mega community stores like the bigger one in OKC, but on steroids. We just have to lay out a plan. I mean yeah, closing stores without a revenue replacement strategy is shooting ourselves in the foot. The stores and our lovable associates are all we have. E-commerce is a fool's errand. I've said it a million times. Amazon ain't winning in this category either."

"Agree with you on some stores. You must remember, he's not an insider. We can't, nor do we want to share with him the unit economics of our stores. If he knew them, I think he'd be whistling a slightly different tune. Regardless, you have to believe that in the face of the e-commerce revolution a decade ago, this is the new normal. There's not a lot of appetite to invest in stores, and now with a pandemic, you'd have to be a fool to double down on in-person community."

"Well, I could make an equally compelling argument that it's not a new normal. Human beings are social animals. Social distancing is not how we're wired."

"Or, maybe that's where we're evolving?"

"Or maybe, there's so much goddamned pent-up demand from cabin fever, that once the world opens back up, community gatherings are going to be more important than ever."

"Well, we can't invest on conjecture. We can only invest in proven facts."

"Really? We can't even agree on the facts. Even when it's Jeff's team that's creating them. I just don't understand why Oklahoma gets nothing more than lip service."

I stare at a silent, vacant face on the screen. He says nothing.

"And," I continue, "do you really think cleaning up our customer data is the key to unlocking the strategic counteroffensive to digital disruption?"

Again. More stone-cold silence.

Unable to win the staring contest, I start blabbering again. "Feels to me like a big ass science project. Tedious busy work. It needs to be done, but it's not mission critical."

"Do you not think that the long arc of retail is moving to e-commerce over bricks and mortar?"

"Yes. I do think that's where the dispensary of goods industry is moving. But video games are different. Modern gaming is built around community. I think we need to get out of the mindset that we're just a retailer. We're a discovery center, a competitive arena. Potentially even an experiential media center. The distributed sales force for the industry. Moving all our business online when our customers can simply download games.... Ain't. Gonna. Work."

"Well, it will for the short term, particularly with the launch of these consoles. Sales are finally taking off again."

"Sales are, but as you know, these consoles are empty calories. Five percent gross margins or whatever. It barely covers our handling cost."

"Well, we just need to do a better job of getting the customer to add on."

"Couldn't agree more. But don't you think that's more easily done with the assist of the store associates we're investing in. Our average basket at the store is 40 percent higher than our average basket online."

"And that's why we need to focus all our efforts on digital. To make digital more profitable than the stores."

"Look, it's not either/or. The stores matter. I know y'all are so excited about closing stores that are marginally profitable, and it sounds like Garv is ten times more excited. But I think we're missing the market share and buying power implications of that decision. We're shrinking our footprint, which means we're shrinking our buying power with our vendors, which means we won't be as competitive, which means we'll continue to lose customers. Customers will have to drive farther, which exposes them to more convenient competitors. If you're small box and you don't have any more locations than big boxes, what's your competitive advantage? Walmart over time could be more convenient than us. I mean, I think our austerity in the hindsight of the pandemic, is really lucky. Thank God we did it. Kudos to you and Jeff for pushing it. But saving our way to growth is not a strategy. We have to invest somewhere. I've mostly eaten crow because it has enabled us to weather one hell of a storm. But now that the consoles are launching, I just don't understand why I'm still being told to pound sand on innovation initiatives."

"I don't think I've ever told you to pound sand?"

"No, but your and particularly Jeff's dismissal of anything I bring up that's a positive as it relates to OKC and innovation is dismissed. I couldn't even get y'all to greenlight a rollout of *D&D after Dark* to all stores. That's a no brainer. A three-month payback."

More silence. I take the hint and stare back at him vacantly.

Then I blink. "Gerald, do you remember in your first few months when you presented me with my promotion?"

"Uhm, yes. I think so."

"Do you remember I told you that I wasn't interested unless it was clear to me two things were true. First, that we wouldn't play the short game. That we would tell the Street that this was a massive strategic transformation, and that for the foreseeable future, we were not giving guidance, and that they should measure us on progress toward that transformation, and on free cash flow, not earning performance relative to expectations? And second, that we would always devote a portion of the budget to innovation. R&D dollars that we would hold sacrosanct, because they were an investment in our future?"

"Yes, I remember something like that. I'm not sure those were the exact words and I'm not sure it was a promise."

"Well, you got up in your first town hall, importantly before Jeff ever got here, and said almost verbatim what I just said. Maybe not a promise, but I'm sure I can show you a videotape of it."

"Okay. So what's your point?"

"My point is neither of those things are true any longer. We're giving guidance every quarter, running around like mad shaking the can to try to hit expectations, and even when we do meet expectations, the stock price tanks. Moreover, as you know, all innovation dollars have been cut from the budget."

"That's not true. We've cut guidance."

"Only because we're in the middle of the pandemic and all bets are off in terms of our ability to forecast this business."

"Point taken. And for innovation, as you know, we're happy to invest in any innovation that is proven to make us money."

"Such a catch-22. You can't prove it without spending the money to put it in market first. That's like saying 'prove to me this tree-covered field can grow wheat.' And I say, 'there's another field over there that used to be covered with trees and now it sells wheat. I think we can do the same, but I need a little start-up capital to clear the trees, prepare the soil, buy the seeds, plant the seeds, fertilize the soil, and water the crops before I can prove to you that I can sell wheat.' There has to be some level of commitment to start-up capital. And, in the scheme of things, all I was asking for was 1.5 percent of EBITDA. And, now, on top of it, the open headcount I have to assist with innovation strategy, Jeff has hired the guy out from under me and you say that's a better fit. No, you haven't told me to pound sand. But you're happy for me to build castles out of sand that you can quickly wash away."

"Well, look. And please don't take this the wrong way. Your employment here is at-will. It's your choice to work here."

"Hmm. What's the right way to take that?"

I'm at least going to stick it out see if this Garv Pastor character is really going to get involved. If he takes it private, I might get a little more leash to put some structural steel in my sandcastles.

We change the subject and move on to other mundane matters like preparations for Black Friday before ending the call awkwardly.

Garv Pastor, a cofounder of pet supplies ecommerce company Chompy.com, has acquired a near 10 percent stake in the video games retailer and is holding talks with the board and several directors.

Home
Thursday, November 26, 2020
68 days to POSS
CSP: $13.48

I head out of my office into the kitchen to check in on Maura and discuss the day.

"How are you?" I ask.

"I'm good. Just been eating bonbons all day. Cooking dinner like a good little housewifey," she says with saccharine disdain. "And how are you?"

"Not sure. It feels like Stephen Gossamer all over again."

"How so? You're getting fired again?"

"Not sure. Gerald told me that my employment is at-will, and if I'm not happy, I can quit. Anyway, I called my employment attorney this afternoon."

"What? Really? Here we go again?"

"Maybe. I hate it too. But after the last go-round at this godforsaken company, I just want to understand my contract, the 'good reason' clause, and what leverage I might have if shit gets ugly. Who knows with this activist. He now owns almost 10 percent of the company."

"Well then, I guess it is smart to talk to your lawyer. What did he say?"

"He said I'd be a fool to quit, that I'd be much better off being asked to leave. He said if I go to them with a 'good reason' case, I'll get something less than the contractual amount, since I'd be the one initiating the negotiation. It's possible but improbable I could make a case for 'good reason,' the case would be specious, and it would give off an appearance of being selfish and greedy, particularly in the face of the pandemic. I definitely agree with his last point."

"Well, don't quit or get fired without having another job."

"Not planning on it. Though Dale shared with me some precedent that doesn't give me a ton of comfort. Do you remember meeting Binks Toole, former head of supply chain and the ROC? Bald guy. Looks like Tigger?"

"Don't think so."

"He was one of the guys who, unlike me, got hypnotized by the hypnotist that Lance hired for the 2018 Christmas party. You know, when I got kicked off stage immediately because the hypnotist knew I would call his bluff."

"Oh yeah. That was the least bad PwnShop holiday party. Awful, but not nearly as painful as the other ones."

"Well, we've never had a party with this new regime."

"Thank God."

"Yeah, right?"

"Anyway, I think I vaguely remember this guy."

"Well, they fired him earlier this year. He had a contract. Refused to take the COVID pay cut."

"Wow. That's daring, if not a little selfish."

"Yep, and stupid. They fired him for gross negligence and didn't pay his severance."

"Was he negligent?"

"Debatable. But usually at this level, at his over fifty age, a protected class, with nine years at the company—nobody wants to get into the legal hairsplitting about what is gross negligence versus just no longer a fit, and they usually get paid. Not this crowd."

"I guess you were smart to call your attorney."

"Hopefully it was a $350 insurance premium on which I hope I never make a claim."

Track 12: Money For Nothing

"You know, there's a philosopher who says, 'As you live your life, it appears to be anarchy and chaos, and random events, non-related events, smashing into each other and causing this situation or that situation, and then, this happens, and it's overwhelming, and it just looks like what in the world is going on. And later, when you look back at it, it looks like a finely crafted novel. But at the time, it don't.'"

—JOE WALSH

All fifty-two-year-olds, except me, have grown up. It's my tragicomic flaw. Shakespearean and Mel Brooksian in proportion. Oh, it's not that I didn't go through puberty. I did. It was way late. The arrested physical development played a role, but I don't think it's the lynchpin. It's not that I don't exhibit signs of emotional maturity. I think I'm reasonably humble, available, vulnerable, decisive, and responsible. The nick on me is I don't have a filter. In my being, the mental barrier between the basal ganglia and the tongue is nonexistent. It's a physiological deficiency.

It's widely known that the amygdala of Alex Honnold,[1] the famed rock climber who was the first man to free solo El Capitan, simply

[1] Alex Honnold is the first ever American rock climber to have his last name enter the English language as a verb, "to honnold." Honnolding occurs when one stands on a precariously narrow ledge with no ropes to arrest your fall. With your back against the wall and your arms spread out in swan dive fashion, you stare into the abyss without an ounce of fear. Brain scans of Honnold have identified that his amygdala, the central portion of the brain that governs fear response, doesn't fire in situations that arouse fear in 99.9 percent of the population.

doesn't fire. He doesn't experience fear like the rest of us. Unlike him, my amygdala fires like a scatter gun. I'm afraid of my own shadow. But both of us "honnold"—stand in thin air, on rickety, rocky perches, and stare into the abyss. Alex faces his fear and mocks it. I turn my face to the vortex and belch and vomit TMI all over it.

I don't know why I snub adulting. I guess I'm a Toys "R" Us kid.[2] Apropos, as Toys "R" Us is the poster child for private equity leveraging a specialty retailer all the way to bankruptcy. Peter Private Equity pinched a peck of pennies. How many pennies did Peter Private Equity pinch? Not quite enough to make sure he could service the interest payments on the prodigious debt, but more than enough to never invest in people, process or products. And so, Geoffrey the Giraffe fell off the bricks and mortar wall and broke his crown. Or something like that.

In physics, the amount of effort required to lift a load is in inverse proportion to the length of the lever arm. For financing businesses, it's an absurd metaphor, and trust me, I know a bit about hollow metaphors. Every investor wants extraordinary returns on invested capital. The problem, however, is that most businesses can provide only ordinary returns. That's where other people's money comes in. By borrowing someone else's money, the equity investor can own a large stake of something without putting up most of the cash. The more insatiable one's greed, the more they borrow. It's basically what created the mortgage crisis that led to the big short that made Eiffel Murray a household name. Why pay $1 million for a house when I can own it using only $10,000 of my own? I can let someone else lend me $990,000. When the price doubles in five years, my $10,000 down is now worth $1.01 million. One percent of the time, it works 100 percent of the time.

---

[2] Ever-present on children's television shows in the 1980s, the jingle "I don't wanna grow up, I'm a Toys 'R' Us kid" was cowritten by James Patterson. Yes, one of the the most prodigious and richest authors of all time, Patterson, had worked his way up to a creative director at the J. Walter Thompson advertising agency when he wrote the tune. His co-writer, Linda Kaplan Thaler, went on to write the jingle for...wait for it...Kodak. Yes, the film company that was blindsided by digital photography. I guess she had a thing for companies that are too obstinate to transform. Anyhoo, at least one crappy marketing guy went on to be a successful author. Present company excluded.

Shorting equities is another way to achieve extraordinary returns with other people's money. One doesn't actually own the shares. They simply borrow them from somebody else, sell the thing they don't actually own, buy it back when the price goes way down, return the shares and pocket the difference.

The problem with both scenarios, of course, is the length of the lever arm. When it gets too long and things don't go as planned (you lose your job and can't pay the mortgage, for instance, or some internet entrepreneur invests big in the stock you're shorting and you have no cash left to cover your short position) because you were a greedy sumbitch, you let your lever arm extend to a point that its inherent rigidity can no longer support the load. It snaps and you find yourself naked, exposed, cussing Newton, his goddamn gravity, and the long arm of his third law of motion. Who says longer is better?

PwnShop Offices
Vineland, TX
December 14, 2020
51 days to POSS
CSP: $17.36

The executive team is proofreading the press release associated with third quarter 10Q SEC filing, and I'm questioning the word choice about our performance.

"Sustained progress? More like a bloodstained dog mess. Our sales are down more than 30 percent, and most of it is because we're shuttering stores like they're made of straw."

"For the last time, Nick, we're de-densifying stores, not shuttering them. It's crucially important that we use the right syntax," Claggart crows.

"I think you mean diction," I say, lingering lugubriously on the first syllable.

"I've had it with your lip. It's entirely unprofessional," Jeff jabs. "Last I checked, the stock price has tripled."

"Not because of anything we're doing. Everybody is lathered that there's another activist who seems to want to invest in a transformation. If by professional you mean heartless, inhuman, and rigid, yes, I pride myself on being just the opposite. I call it having a soul. I mean, can't we call a spade a spade? The iceberg is melting and we're selling shaved ice, because it's a great idea to accelerate the depletion of our one asset—the stores."

"Not productive, Nick," Gerald intervenes. "Do you have anything constructive to say about the release? Otherwise, let's call it a wrap."

"Nope. Constructive is something that left this company's vocabulary three console cycles ago. Hope is not a plan. Diversification is surrender. And relying on the console releases to fix our problem is like walking 1000 miles barefoot on broken glass for a nickel's worth of business. Do we not think anyone is doing the math that we make a penny or two on the dollar from a new console? Sales go up but our margin rate is tanking? This is a farce. Let's gather round the drain and celebrate the cool sucking sound of the disappearing whirlpool. On what planet does shrinking sales mean progress? Our audience is becoming more selective?[3] At this rate, we're in danger of no longer being number one in market share. Walmart will take that spot. Then, will anyone in the industry take us seriously?"

"We all know where you stand. And I think you know you need to watch your tongue." Gerald scolds me like the child that I am.

Fuck this place.

"Let's move on to the next topic," Gerald continues. "Since we're going ahead with the ATM—tomorrow's Black Friday press release will give it a mention—I think we've poked the Garv Pastor bear. For those of us that voted for the ATM, he wants our heads on a stake, and yet again, if he goes any more active, we're in for another potential proxy

---

[3] One of my favorite lines from *This is Spinal Tap*.

fight for board makeup. He's super disappointed that the ATM passed. I just heard from our fair chairwoman that he sent her a text expressing his displeasure with the board's decision."

"It goes without saying," Jeff adds, "that he has no idea what he's talking about. All our shelf filing does is give us the option to sell additional stock on the open market. That's why they call it a shelf filing. It's an opportunity that sits on the shelf until it makes sense to take advantage of it. We don't necessarily need the cash. And to think it's dilutionary is just selfish on his part, and patently not factual. The higher the price goes, the less dilutive it is. This is the lowest cost of capital fundraising we'll ever find. We would be foolish to not take advantage of the rising share price. Plus, half of the crap he's spewing for raising capital is impossible in a public company. He's a one trick pony. Has only operated under the cloak of privacy. He's got a lot to learn about public disclosures, governance, SEC compliance, and quarterly reporting."

We all nod in a rare moment of consensus.

Home
Dallas, Texas
January 4, 2020
30 days to POSS
CSP: $22.00

"What's up, Dale," I answer my phone.

"Did you see the latest?" he asks.

"No. What?"

"Garv just disclosed that he's now over 10 percent ownership. Up to 12.9 percent in fact. Saw it on my Google feed."

"Does that mean he's going to kick ass and take names?"

"First he has to become an insider. So I assume, he's definitely going active. Might even want to run the company."

"The plot thickens," I say. "I don't know why these guys insist on becoming insiders. I thought they were traders. Do they not realize that the moment they either own more than 10 percent or take a seat on the board, they can't sell their fund's position at the most opportune times?"

"Crazy, right? Greatly limits their flexibility."

"Do you think he'll clean house?"

"They always do. But I'm more than happy to wave my contract and take the severance," Dale bursts.

"If only it were that easy. I heard the guy is pissed about our contracts."

"He is. But they're legally binding. If he wants us gone, he's going to have to pay us."

"Do you think he'll invest in a transformation?"

"No idea. He's going to have to figure out how to raise capital."

"I wonder if he plans on taking it private?"

"He owns 13 percent. Pretty straightforward from here."

"I guess so," I nod.

"You're not thinking about sticking around, are you?" Dale prods.

"Are you kidding me? Gerald tells me I've lost favor with everyone on the board after blowing off Suprit. Pretty sure the bloom is off whatever rose I once had. And Jeff would love nothing more than to see me spontaneously combust. I'm not anticipating a glowing recommendation."

"The way Garv is acting, that may give you *more* of a shot. I don't think he respects anybody on that board, least of all Jeff. If Jeff says you're damaged goods, they may think you know something."

"Who knows? If this thing goes private and there's a defined strategy, I'd probably be game. But if it's just more cost cutting, I'll take my toys and go home."

"You'd actually consider staying? The stock price is over twenty bucks. You know all of our shit vests upon departing without cause or with 'good reason.' Dude, I ain't going to work for some thirty-five-year-old inexperienced know-it-all."

"I like to think of myself as a wise child. I may be twenty years his senior, but I bet I'm still more of an adolescent. But yeah, it might be foolish to stick around. We're already close, finally, to being appropriately, if not overly, valued."

"True that."

PwnShop Offices
Vineland, Texas
January 18, 2021
16 days to POSS heh heh
CSP: $20.96

"Happy Monday!" Helen greets me in her always-sunny-and-75 disposition.

"Aren't they all?"

"Gerald wants to see you first thing."

I turn to look at his closed door. "Should I interrupt?"

"He's on the phone with Suprit. Won't leave poor Gerald alone."

"I'm sure he's got some hot sports opinions about this Garv Pastor stuff."

She looks down at her phone. "Oh, he's off. I think it's safe."

I knock while cracking the door open. Gerald is staring at his iPhone. Hundred dollars says it's stock quotes. "Helen says you wanted to see me before the day got moving."

"Yes," he says. "Uhm, sorry." He looks up. "Come on in."

"Door closed?"

"Yes, please. Did you see the stock price? It's back up around twenty dollars," he says as I sit at his conference table. "We haven't seen this kind of run-up since Pastor first announced his position."

"We've become a momentum stock," I agree, somewhat haughtily. "Trading on rumors and innuendo. Totally speculative."

"I'll take it," Gerald rejoins in kind. "Listen, I want to apologize."

"For what?"

"Sporadic communication."

"I don't feel left out any more than I already have. Sucks to be the marketing and innovation guy in a worldwide, hunker down pandemic running a fundamentally disrupted company."

"Yeah, poor timing for you."

"Comes with the territory."

"Well, you need to be aware of what's coming down today."

"Shoot."

"The board and I have been negotiating with Pastor on a go forward board makeup. Four members including the chairwoman and your good buddy Suprit will be stepping down, though they'll be around until the annual meeting."

"Let me guess. Garv wanted them off because they voted for the ATM. They made sure they weren't going to leave until their stock grants vest."

"No comment. But you seem to be more in the loop than I thought."

"None of this is surprising. The writing was on the wall as of the November board meeting."

"I guess you're right. Please keep it under your hat. It will become public at market close today. Anyway, Jeff and I have been doing a lot of back and forth with him and his former Chompy CMO and CFO. I don't think Jeff is scoring any points with these guys."

"Oh. Oh. May I guess again? The golden rule?"

"Really? Do unto others…"

"…until you're done," I interrupt.

Gerald cracks a rare, brief smile.

"No, the other golden rule," I continue. "Y'know. Whoever has the gold makes the rules. And rule following, particularly when enacted by a thirty-five-year-old internet tycoon, doesn't jive with the ego of a former navy pilot who gets a nervous tic if he can't be the smartest guy in the room."

"Taking the fifth on that one too. But now that he's an insider, they want an update on all the stuff you were working on."

"Why the past tense? Is there something else you need to tell me?"

"Oh no. Nothing like that. Though that kind of thing might not be far off. I just meant the pandemic has put an indefinite hold on plans to double down on the store experience."

"So we're not at least going forward with new fixtures and video screens?"

"With some stores. But most of that is being funded by the vendors. These guys have no desire to invest until they have the complete picture."

"Okay, do you need me to give Garv a presentation?"

"It will probably be his former CMO, Quint Haddad. I think you two might hit it off."

"Meaning he's a smartass with no filter?"

"Ha. No. Meaning he talks like a marketing guy."

"What does that mean? You think he's a charlatan?"

"Not necessarily. You marketing types just have a vernacular all your own."

"Hmm. Not sure how to take that."

"Doesn't matter. I'll be introducing you two over email. Spend whatever time with him he needs, and get back to me with any observations or intelligence."

"Sounds like spook shit."

"Whatever. See you at the meeting. Be forewarned, it will probably be cut short since Jeff and I need to finalize the release with Garv's folks and the board."

"Good luck."

"As you were. And thanks."

Grady nudges me as we're walking out of the Bored Room after the Monday business meeting. "Hey, Nick. Have a sec?"

"Sure thing. My office or yours?"

"Yours."

The obligatory, après-meeting queue at the restroom forms. While most still wear masks, social distancing has become synonymous with close gossiping. We walk past the murmurs. As informed, Gerald cut the meeting short, since he, Jeff, and Dale have another video conference with Garv, his posse, and various members of the board. The urinal talk is rife with turbidity, uric rumors, and asparagus-smelling opinions.

Grady, the biggest gossip of them all, closes my office door behind him. We sit at the corner of the conference table.

"Do you know what I have been up to for the last week?"

"Don't bury the lead."

"Dale has us working on complete category reviews."

"And let me guess. You think they're for Garv Pastor?"

"I think something's coming down today."

"What was your first clue, Sherlock? The fact that Jeff's beloved two-hour Monday business review meeting didn't last more than twenty minutes?"

"Did you see how grumpy he was?"

"Jeff's always grumpy. Heavy hangs the biggest melon in the room."

"But still," Grady probes earnestly. "Don't you think something's coming down today?"

"I know something's coming down today," I say, tantalizing. Like Peter Lorre's portrayal of Joel Cairo in *The Maltese Falcon*, I was thinking one thing and saying something else.

"Willing to share?"

"Come on, Grady. You'll know in like two hours. I love watching you try to draw out information in a 'I'll show you a little leg if you'll show your world to me' sort of way."

"It's what I do best."

"I'll say."

"Do you want information or misinformation?"

"Real facts please," he retorts.

"Damn, I was hoping to tell you that Garv wants to make you CEO."

"A black gay man as CEO? Ha. Seriously, what's going on?"

"He is Jewish. And Canadian. Probably related to the original freedom riders. Maybe wants to make real headlines."

"You are such a cracker."

"Well, my dad's name is Stonewall Jackson. Anyway, you're no better. You're just a squirrel trying to crack a nut."

"Oh stawp. Just tell me what's going down or I'll get you canceled as a southern white racist. You did go to school in Charlottesville didn't you?"

"Oh, Varys, what a sly blackmailer you've become."

"You said black."

"Busted. Look, it's not that big of a deal, yet."

"What's not that big of a deal?"

"The news coming out today."

"So if it's not that big of a deal, why won't you tell me?" Grady can't help himself.

"Because, as a C-level officer of this company, I have a duty of confidentiality."

"Oh puh-leaze. You're more like a juvenile delinquent than a C-level officer."

"Shh. Don't unmask me as a fraud. Don't you know my imposter syndrome is two sandwiches short of a picnic?"

"Oh. My. Gawd. You really are a redneck."

"Whaddya mean? You don't like picnics?

"And fried chicken? And watermelon? You are so politically incorrect."

"Is that the same thing as apolitically correct?"

"I have no idea. Just tell me what's going on."

"What do you think is going on?"

"Garv is going to become CEO and all you guys are going to be out, leaving me holding the bag and breaking in the seventh CEO in less than three years."

I pause on that one. "Seven? I only count five."

"Claude, Tom Testa as interim, Harvey Handler for a hot minute, Tom Testa again, Lance Park, Gerald, and now Garv Pastor," Grady says while tallying his fingers with each name.

"Oh, I wasn't counting Tom. He was chairman. Super interim."

"But the official CEO twice."

"Fair point. All I'll say is this. And it's the same thing I said to my daughter when she was six and I couldn't bring myself to have 'the talk' after she gave me the cutest, most cockamamie little girl explanation for how babies are made. I said, 'You're exactly right.'"

Home Office
Dallas, Texas
January 20, 2021
14 days to POSS
CSP: $32.40

"That's all super interesting. The problem is, we're not planning on addressing anything in the stores for at least two years. What are you going to do for the next two years?" queries Quint.

I've been on the Teams video conference for the last two and a half hours with Quint Haddad, who may be the brains behind Pastor's elaborate activist scheme. I've presented my assessment of the problem, the initial solution, the bastardized solution as seen in Oklahoma, the realities of the pandemic when it comes to doubling down on the stores, and the hope of being the distributed sales force, new game discovery center, and Pop Warner league of esports.

"If we really want to live up to the potential of being the in-person media environment for the industry, there's tons of work to do as it relates to building an efficient CDP,[4] and I think that would mesh well with your and Garv's desire to invest heavily in e-commerce. We put a band-aid on the loyalty program last year that's been somewhat helpful, but it's still in dire need of a redesign to reflect the massive shift in the

[4] Customer Data Platform. Yet another acronym in the world of technical marketing alphabet soup. They're endless. CDP, DMP, OLAP, CMS, CPC, CRO, CRM, SEO, SMM, API, LTV, NPS, and BI, just to name a few. And no, the last one isn't a sexual orientation. It stands for Business Intelligence and is almost as much of an oxymoron as Military Intelligence. The military gave us FUBAR, SNAFU, AWOL, ASAP, WTF, SWAG, BZ, BFE, and KISS.

way gamers consume gaming. And we need to rotate in a team that's more equipped to work on those things."

"Clearly, your team isn't digitally savvy."

"My team has been heavily decimated by vigorous cost cutting. As a marketing guy, I'm about spending money to make even more money. Gerald and Jeff believe a dollar saved is a dollar earned. If I'm being honest, we wouldn't have made it through the pandemic had we not been so austere. And they were under even heavier pressure from activists and other investors who were looking for a short squeeze to cut even more. You'll not find any area of this company that isn't in dire need of investment."

"I'm convinced the only way forward is to basically compete with Amazon," Quint doubles down on the initial investment thesis he recited chapter and verse earlier on the call.

"Suicide," I rebut.

"Why do you keep saying that? Are you really this much of a Luddite?"

"I am NOT a Luddite. Technology is everything. That said, the only logical place to make a massive investment in technology is in the stores."

"Dude. You seem like a smart guy. Brick and mortar is dead."

"Traditional retail? Couldn't agree more. But I'm talking about thinking about us as a gathering place for gamers. That would categorize us more as an entertainment center like Topgolf than a dispensary of goods like CVS. And compete head on with Amazon? That will require billions of dollars of investment. We have no expertise in general merchandise. We need to stick to the knitting, but reimagine what our role is in the industry—a place of community and discovery that will open up new services revenue streams like pay-to-play gaming, local esports leagues and battlegrounds, and an immersive video-led environment that becomes a major source of advertising revenue."

"Dream on. We live in a post-pandemic world. People are cocooning. We have to shift this business to bring them the goods where they are."

"The goods are digital. Don't you get that? The thing that presently drives traffic to our stores and to our website is new video game releases.

You can now download those directly to your console. Sony, Microsoft and Nintendo have out-Amazoned Amazon in terms of friction-free convenience. That's why Amazon is still seventh in market share."

"Come on. They're more like fourth."

"Not in console gaming in the States. We're first. Walmart is second. Best Buy is third. Then Sony. Then Microsoft. Then Target. Then Amazon. And then Nintendo. Amazon's mousetrap isn't trapping console or PC gamers. And Steam is bigger too, though it's technically not the same category, even though it's an ultra viable substitute."

"Well, we did it with Chompy and we can do it here."

"Only if you take it private. You need to invest a shit ton of capital to build that kind of infrastructure, and we don't have a low cost of capital way to raise money. And, I heard you guys were none too pleased that Jeff floated the idea of an ATM shelf filing. Seems like a logical way to raise money if there's momentum in the stock price. Where are you going to get the capital to invest if not through the open market?"

"That's not something you need to worry about."

"I'm not an ass-kisser. Far from it. But, I'm super happy there's finally somebody here who thinks there's something worth investing in. We are 100 percent aligned that we have to re-break the leg.[5] We can't limp our way into bankruptcy. Early reads are the digital download penetration on these new consoles is well over 70 percent. As you know, we make no money selling consoles. We have to find a new method to drive customer engagement. I just disagree with what that method should be, as I've made abundantly clear. So, I'm kinda puzzled. Where do we go from here?"

"Not sure. You've definitely given me something to think about. But we have lots to figure out. One of the things giving us conniptions is the contracts of some of you folks. We have a completely different philosophy on compensation, far more reliant on stock performance than base salary."

---

[5] I had related my broken ski accident metaphor earlier on the call.

"I've heard. That's one I need to think about as well. I wouldn't have come back here if it was 100 percent betting on the come. The situation is too volatile. The contract is a solid bird in the hand. My main thing will be the ability to sell shares when the window opens in March. I've done two tours of duty and have never been able to take any chips off the table. Now that the stock price is almost 4X my grant prices, I feel I need to de-risk my position a bit."

"We're not very tolerant of management selling when the future is so unclear. Just like we're not very tolerant of the company selling shares on the open market and diluting existing shareholders. We need to put forward a posture of confidence and show the market we're betting on ourselves."

"I'd love to bet on myself. I'm just not so sure I want to bet on the rest of you." I wink. "Just kidding. Mostly. Just not yet bought into the plan. Need to understand more."

"Fair enough. I appreciate the time. I must say, you're quite different than your peers."

"Understatement of the year. Problem is, different, more often than not, is misunderstood."

"True. Oh, one other thing. We're bringing in a new SVP of customer care. Don't know if Gerald mentioned it. She'll probably start beginning of March."

"He mentioned there might be some new hires, but not someone on my team. I presume she'll report to me?"

"No. She'll report to the CEO."

"Hmm. Interesting."

"Look, I gotta run. Late for another call. Talk soon."

His face disappears, replaced by my own reflecting in the blank screen.

They're hiring an SVP of customer care that doesn't report to the chief customer officer, but to the CEO. He didn't say reporting to Gerald. Is Gerald out? I wonder if Garv has already made a move? There's no way he's going to sit back and be a passive investor. Regardless, sounds like a material reduction in scope that could trigger a 'good reason' resignation.

It's 4:04 PM Central time. 5:04 PM Eastern. Market's closed. I check my phone to see the closing price of GME.

$31.40? This makes no fucking sense. That's more than a 50 percent increase from yesterday. I pull up a *Bloomberg* article that says we're experiencing a short squeeze. *Finally*. I call Dale who answers immediately.

"Holy shit, did you see the stock price?" he asks.

"Exactly why I'm calling. What the fuck?"

"This is the short squeeze Eiffel Murray was talking about."

"That motherfucker. He's killing it again. The big short, and now the big squeeze?"

"Yep, the rich get richer."

"Smart dude."

"Pain in the ass. You should have been on the call with him."

"I wonder if he's sold out? He was in at like four bucks and now he's looking at about an eight-bagger."

"Guy's got balls. I wouldn't be surprised if he's still holding on for technical reasons. The volume is through the roof."

"If I weren't a named officer, I'd be selling. Sucks to be an insider."

"Seriously."

"When does the blackout window lift? Late March?"

"Don't think I haven't looked. March 23 is when we file the 10K and annual report. Trading window should open the next day."

"I bet we're back below fifteen by then. Regardless, I don't think this new regime is going to let us sell."

"They can't keep us from selling."

"I don't know the law, but I had a long call with Quint Haddad this morning…"

"He seems more rational than Garv," Dale interjects.

"I've never met Garv, but Quint does seem to be the Todd Wagner to Garv's more public Mark Cuban."

"Agreed."

"But, he was clearly pissed off about our contracts and was mighty derogatory about officers taking chips off the table."

"They can't do that."

"I think our selling forms have to be approved by the board, which it appears they now control. I'm assuming they'll try to prevent it. Anyway, I bet these guys are pissed they're insiders this afternoon. Fools can't sell. Have to wait like the rest of us. I've never understood why activists want more than 10 percent and/or board seats. They can influence from afar. It's clear Murray did."

"Same with Pestia-Hermit."

"I know. And they've been sitting on this for almost two years. I bet their investors are demanding they sell."

"I know I would be."

"But they can't sell, right? Even though they're less than 10 percent, because of their board seats, they're insiders, right? And the funds they manage are subject to the same insider rules, right?"

"That's how I understand it."

"So do you think the price increase is from all the shorts covering their position? Or is something else going on?"

"Both. The volume was through the roof. *Bloomberg* hints at day traders jumping in in droves," Dale says as I hear him clicking on his laptop.

"Well, I love it that these shorts are taking it in the shorts."

"Punny. Me too. The plot thickens."

"Or not. Mark my words, neither you nor I will ever profit from this silly runup."

"Marked. And mark my words, you're a damn pessimist."

"Expect the worst. Anything better is a happy surprise."

PwnShop Surges Most Ever in Short Squeeze after Pastor's Move.

PwnShop Headquarters
Vineland, Texas
February 1, 2021
2 days to POSS
CSP: $77.80

Grady pokes his head into my office.

"Can you believe this?" he asks.

"Believe what?" I say, peering around my computer monitor.

"Are you not watching the stock price?"

"I mean, occasionally, but I'm actually trying to get this presentation sorted. What's it doing?"

"It's up to around $150."

"Seriously?"

"Seriously. There's a guy on my team who showed me the message board on Reddit—WallStreetBets—where all these retail investors are holding hands to stick it to the hedge funds. It's as irreverent as the subreddit for PwnShop managers that want to stick it to the management 'man.'"

"Yeah, that thing is a smorgasbord of sarcastic intel."

"On this WallStreetBets PwnShop thread, a guy who works for me says his neighbor has been following all of this stuff since August and has made a killing. Trades on a free app called Robinhood."

"I've heard of that. Free trades. From your phone. And I thought day trading during the dot-com boom was a fad," I say, shaking my head.

"Anyway, he says they're all following this guy Bawling Bitty. Apparently, he was posting as early as late summer last year about how undervalued he thought it was. Now all these people, they call themselves 'apes'—they've developed a bizarre language—are bonding together to hold—or HODL as they say—indefinitely. They call it 'diamond hands.' Our guy's neighbor says he plans on holding on to his position until the stock hits $1000 bucks."

"Isn't that stock manipulation?"

"Who knows? What's funny is all of their Reddit posts end with the phrase 'This is not investment advice.'"

"Yeah right. Genius. He should sell right now. Of course you can't say anything."

"No, I can't. It's unbelievable. Said he bought one hundred shares at fifteen dollars. If this price holds throughout the remainder of the day, he'll have turned $1500 into $15,000."

"'Murica. Gotta love it."

"Yep. And as insiders, we'll never see a thin dime from it. This thing is going to crash hard."

"No doubt. I just hope those day traders have the wisdom to sell and don't get caught naked. I wonder how all these hedge funds that are shorting us are dealing with this?"

PwnShop jumps amid retail frenzy, shares double at one point in wild trading.

PwnShop Headquarters
Vineland, Texas
February 2, 2021
Eve of Peak of Short Squeeze
CSP: $148.96

PwnShop jumps another 90 percent above $140, but short sellers aren't backing down.

Home
Vineland, Texas
February 3, 2021
Peak of Short Squeeze
CSP: $348.52

"Do you know how insane this is?" I ask Maura as I slump in the fashionable-yet-non-functional chair in our family room, my tech neck at a cantilevered pitch, my blue-light protected readers staring vacuously, mesmerized by a 3" x 6" piece of alloy and glowing glass toast. Maura has a matching chair. We face each other every morning in the wee hours after I've finished the obligatory morning COVID conference huddle, after one of the dogs has licked her awake as they can't stand it when I'm up and she isn't, and we sip our coffee until she's coherent.

"Shhh! Not ready to talk yet. Need coffee."

"Sorry." I grab my coffee, sip, and scroll on. Short sellers are holding their ground and doubling down on our fair company. These Redditors are forcing the "smart money" to continue covering their positions, squeezing them like a distributed hive mind anaconda.

"Okay. What? COVID, a school shooting, more capitol stormers or more civil unrest?" She can't wait. The mere question forces her busy brain to get in gear.

"The stock hit $150 bucks yesterday and closed just down from that at like $148. It hit almost $160 day before yesterday but got pounded and closed just under eighty dollars. But yesterday, it held its ground. I can't bear to look at my portfolio. Water, water everywhere but not a drop to drink."

"What do you mean?"

"We're in a blackout period until our earnings release in late March. This is hilarious to watch and think what might have been."

"Don't even look at it. It's not real. It's all paper. Will crash in a day or two. It's like the dot-com bust all over again." She sips her coffee concoction audibly.

"Seriously. Do you remember, oh what's his name from business school? The guy who was a pharmaceutical salesman who did that B2B startup that was merely an online catalog for chemicals? Chemalog or something?"

"Oh yeah. Phil Berry."

"Yes. At one point during the dot-com boom I heard his company was worth something like $800 million, and as founder and CEO, he borrowed money based on his paper stock to buy a Gulfstream?"

"Didn't know about that."

"Yep. Had to declare bankruptcy a year later as he was sitting on a jet he couldn't pay for because his company's valuation went almost all the way to zero. That's what this is like."

"That's what I mean. It's a mirage. A sheen of water on an ebb tide."

"I know. But don't you think it's kind of fun to think about? I mean, at today's price, my stock, if vested and I could actually sell it, is worth like $40 million dollars."

"What?"

"Yes. You heard me. Insanity."

"I don't want to hear about it. Get it out of your mind. What's your day like today? You going into the office?"

"No. Nobody ever shows up but on Mondays, and that's only a select few. It's so awkward there. All masked and socially distanced. Anyway, the day's not too bad. Morning is pretty full but frees up some this afternoon. I have a call at nine I need to prepare for, and then have to do a Teams call for Unidos."

"What's Unidos?"

"It's our employee resource group for those of Latino descent. I'm the executive sponsor."

"Your lily-white heinie is executive sponsor? Is this some kind of joke?"

"Well, Claude Prendas, who was born and raised in Costa Rica, used to be the sponsor. After he died, there wasn't a sponsor, so Jack Floyd asked me to do it when I came back in 2018. They're a great group. I speak my broken Spanish with them at every conference. I think they like me, but yes, it's a bit of a farce. Whatcha gonna do?"

"Put someone of Latino descent on your executive team," she eyerolls.

"A fair point. Down with the patriarchy!"

"If it looks like a duck and smells like a duck…"

"…¡Mata al pato!"

"Whatever that means. Je parle français."

"It means kill the duck. And anyway, there ain't no Francophile employee resource groups, so you're more worthless than I, Maura Antoinette."

"Oh wow. You're right."

"I know I'm right?"

"Not about your employee group. About the stock price. My text box is full of people asking what we're going to do with all that money? I've already gotten like twenty texts this morning."

"Not money. Paper. A mirage. You already said it. I can't sell any of it."

"Still. Here's one from Susan Thornton. I haven't talked to her since, like, college."

"Since, like, college? And you were an English major? Is it since some past event that resembled college or is it, actually, since college?"

"Oh, shut up. Susan always thought she was better than everyone. She's congratulating us. So weird to be hearing from some of these people."

"Yeah, I'm getting a ton of that. Congratulations for what? Watching your stock price go up ridiculously for factors completely out of your control?"

"I guess. People are fascinated with money, aren't they?"

"Despite all the Founding Fathers' high-minded insistence on freedom of religion, you know we're a theocracy?"

"Whaddya mean? With the fundamentalist right? Yeah, probably."

"No, not that. Money is our god. Regardless. It will be fun to talk about while it lasted. Anyway, I'm curious to see where we open at. Market opens in five minutes, when my call starts."

"Open at? Ending a sentence in a preposition? And you went to Harvard? Oh shit. Here's a text from Gunter that says it went up like crazy in after-hours trading."

"Your stepbrother?"

"He's not my stepbrother. He's the son of my dad's second wife. But yes, that Gunter."

"This is certifiably insane. How often do you talk to him?"

"Like never."

"Never or something resembling never."

"You're insufferable."

"The, uhm, visual dictionary has your face illustrated next to the word insufferable. But yes, this is nuts. It's a bubble. Bubbles burst. Doesn't do any good to think about it." I get up, put my mug in the sink and walk out back to my COVID lair—the room above the garage. My band and I rehearse there as well. My bandmates call it "Upstairs at Ser Nick's," in homage to *Game of Thrones* and the seminal synth-pop album of our youth, Yaz's *Upstairs at Eric's*.

I dial into my call, greet the team, and Jim, the head of digital, pipes in, "Dude, what are you going to do with all that dough?"

"Jim don't talk like that. You know I can't sell until the earnings call in March. Nor can you for that matter."

"Why can't I sell? I'm not a named executive officer. I just bought 10,000 shares in December on top of my grants."

"Because you're an insider. And we're all in a blackout period. Plus, don't you know the SEC will be all over your ass if you buy and sell within a six-month period?"

"What the hell for? I don't hold any MNPI.[6] That's bullshit."

"Because. It's untoward. But, I will say you're right about MNPI. We only know what everybody else knows, this stock is way overvalued. It's not nonpublic. It's material PUBLIC information. This thing is trading at a multiple that defies any sense of logic."

"So I really can't sell?"

"Do you like picking up highway litter in an orange jumpsuit?"

"Now is the time to sell."

"But we're in a blackout period. No employee can sell until the earnings call."

---

[6] Another obfuscating abbreviation that business people use to make others feel stupid. It stands for Material NonPublic Information, data or news that insiders might have that could affect stock price if made public. It's against the law to buy or sell securities when in possession of material nonpublic information.

"When is that?"

"March 23."

"That's like two months away. No way this thing will be this high in two months."

[A period of time that resembles two months away or actually two months away?]

"Definitely not. It's the myth of Tantalus. Maddening."

"Holy shit!" Jim blurts out even louder. "Did you see where we opened? Three-hundred and seventy-nine fucking dollars! It more than doubled overnight."

"Now, now, folks. Let's not get carried away. None of this is real. Let me tell you a cautionary tale from the dot-com bubble." I relate the story Maura and I just discussed over coffee about borrowing money against paper stock to buy a Gulfstream.

When I finish, I bring the meeting to order, and make Jim, the ranter, report out on his projects first. While he's talking, I'm surreptitiously looking at my Morgan Stanley app, beneath the view of the webcam, to see that it's blossomed to well over nine figures, even though the price has already dropped to around $350.

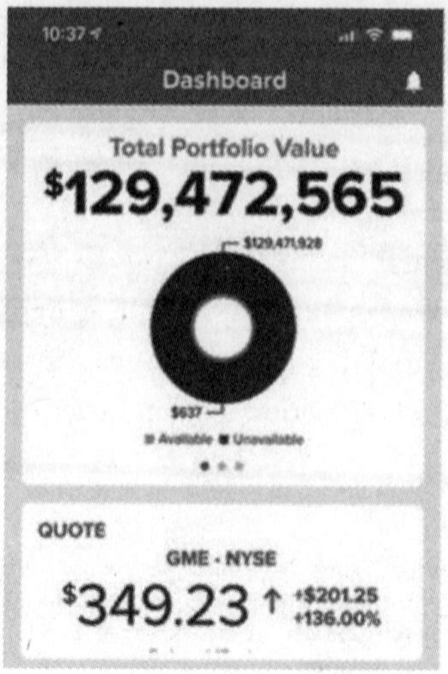

Not real. Not real. Not real.

PwnShop jumps more than 130 percent even as hedge funds cover short bets, scrutiny of rally intensifies.

Home
Dallas, Texas
February 4, 2021
One day after POSS

I enter the house after my evening commute from Vineland. I went to the office today. All the fuss from yesterday made me realize I needed to be around people that were experiencing the same thing I was.

"How was the day?" Maura asks.

"You didn't see?"

"You told me and I told myself not to look, that it wasn't real."

"Good plan. Yesterday, after hours, Elon Musk of all people tweeted 'PwnStonk'. The price roared in after-hours trading. Today, Robinhood has shut down the ability to buy the stock. You could only sell it. Stock price tumbled almost 50 percent. It's back down under $200. And while I do think the whole thing is a dangerous bubble, I think for the sake of those retail traders it's bullshit that they only shut down the ability to buy. That just gives an advantage to those that want to short us. They should have shut down all trading if they couldn't afford the float."

"It was fun while it lasted."

"It's still at $200, an insane valuation. We were trading around $40 bucks last week."

"And there it shall head."

"Probably so."

> Netherland Park
> Dallas, Texas
> February 5, 2021
> 2 days after POSS
> CSP: $194.60

I do a military boot camp every Monday, Wednesday, and Friday when I'm not traveling. It's a good group of guys. The instructor, Mac, is a former Army Ranger. Unlike the academy-educated military officers that I work with, Mac was an NCO—an enlisted man who was promoted to sergeant during his tenure. He earned his stripes. The hard way. He's an energetic, optimistic, driven guy, who has made his way in the world trading on his eye-catching, ebony physique. From his humble childhood in South Georgia to being an endzone flag carrier for the Dallas Cowboys, he lives and breathes fitness. At fifty-four years old, he regularly wins regional bodybuilding competitions, always in senior categories, and sometimes against jacked-up tools half his age.

He puts up with my sorry ass, even though I'm late to the 6:30 AM workout more than half the time. I go, I'm sure, foremostly out of some mental dysfunction surrounding my guilt of not measuring up to my father who served, and secondarily to inwardly prove to myself that I could outrun and outlift the pasty, flaccid, lumpy bodies possessed by the retired military officers I call colleagues. They have dad bods. I like to think I have a father figure.

During COVID, our merry platoon of age deniers and fat phobics had to find a park that was out of the leering eyes of law enforcement, as congregations of this size were banned by social distancing ordinances. We found Netherland Park, tucked away in a quiet neighborhood with its eastern border formed by the twelve-foot high wall that serves as a sound and collision barricade from the cars whizzing by on the Dallas North Tollway. As such, it's not the most bucolic of settings, and stays firmly under the radar screen of most patrolling constables. We typically work out on the tennis courts, which are badly in need of resurfacing and whose nets have been removed to discourage using them.

Today, I'm tardy, per usual. The group has just finished their warmup (usually consisting of high intensity calisthenics such as three sets each of twenty-five jumping jacks, star jumps, side oblique bounces, squat lunges, bicycles and pushups), which means they're prostrate on their exercise mats, breathing hard and performing the instructor-led five-minute sequence of stretching. As they see me saunter up with my disheveled bedhead in my smoky rose colored Dead & Co. hoodie (from the 2019 show Rhodus and I saw at the Hampton Coliseum in Virginia), they begin to stand and clap a beat in marching tempo.

"What the hell did I do?" I ask no one. "I'm late as always. Why the walkup music?"

"PwnShop, dipshit," one of them says. "I hope you dumped that shit wholesale."

The others start to chant, "Sell. Sell. Sell. Sell..." in precise rhythm with their steady clapping beat.

"Get back on your mats," I command. "You know I can't sell shit, right?"

"Surely there's something you can do. Buy some covered derivatives or something?"

"Not if I want to stay out of prison. It is what it is. As an NEO, I can't trade..."

"What's an NEO?" one asks.

"Named Executive Officer. One of the dudes in a public company that has to make public any trades we might make in the stock. So, I can't trade at all, much less sell, at least until the blackout window lifts," I lecture.

"When is that?"

"End of March."

"Oh never mind," another one says. "Let's get back to stretching. Haller's going to watch, helplessly, as his wealth craters back down to zero."

"Boo," another one says. "I'd be selling that shit yesterday."

"And you'd be joining me in Huntsville."

"I'd take the risk, you pussy. There's gotta be a way to collar this thing?"

"Whatever," I eyeroll. "Didn't you guys read that Elizabeth Warren is all over the SEC for not clamping down on market manipulation. The scrutiny on this is going to be overwhelming. Plus, Robinhood shut down the ability to sell on their app—that's the day trading app all these Redditors are using. The stock dropped 50 percent yesterday. It's over."

"Man, what a skull fuck," another one says.

"Indeed." The turn of phrase triggers a thought I can't contain. "Some folks trust to reason. Others trust to might. I don't trust to nothing. Cuz shit never turns out right," I say, paraphrasing the lyrics to "Playing in the Band" off Skull Fuck, the nickname of the Dead's live compilation album that first introduced the song.

"You're one weird dude, Haller."

Home Office
Dallas, Texas
February 7, 2021
4 days after POSS
CSP: $325.00

Wondering what all these Reddit cats are saying today, I open the Reddit app with its eerily happy alien face. This whole thing is alien to my ass.

/r/wallstreetbets /u/[deleted]
1/31/2021, 10:52:29 AM

Somebody read this please and tell me if its possible!!!!

PwnShop and AMC should form some sort of partnership... I created a whole long post about why but it was removed.. but

TL:DR–"Right now, the way people hang out with their buddies is on a headset in the comfort of their own homes. Do they want to do that on a regular basis in real life? That's the question. If they do, there's going to be a place for us, a place for the **big arenas**, all those things."–Nick Haller–Chief Customer Officer

Who has space for the big Arenas? Movie theaters.

In a perfect world they do a stock offering.. only let retail investors buy (not sure if that is possible) but we buy up the shares at YOLO prices and hold forever..

We will be forever motivated customers as we are also stakeholders.

The definition of power to the players... idk tho i ate paint chips for breakfast

> Haller Home Office
> Dallas, Texas
> February 9, 2021
> 6 days after POSS
> CSP: $91.00

"Has anyone thought of how we might capitalize on the PR miracle we're witnessing?" Suprit interjects on the board call about the first draft of the 10Q, the annual report we plan on releasing at the end of March.

Suprit may be a lame duck, but he's honking like a goose. And, since my status with Suprit, in particular, is troubled, I wait for my colleagues to take the lead.

Crickets.

The stock bubble is finally starting to burst. The day of boot camp, it ran back up to over $300. It closed on Monday at $225. It dropped like a rock today, and closed at a mere $90. Armed with that knowledge and the fact that my inquisitor, Suprit, along with the three other colleagues who voted for the ATM, is rolling off the board at the annual meeting in June per Garv Pastor's power play, I figure what the hell.

"Well, Suprit. My team has thought about it."

I see Gerald's 2D eyes dart up from his downward gaze contained within his Hollywood Square on the Teams call.

"And what was your conclusion?" Suprit drips with presumed contempt.

"Well, sir," I sniffle as my throat is quite sore and my head is starting to ache. "For the first time in forever, PwnShop is in the zeitgeist. Our consumer love prior to this LOASS..."

"LOASS?" Suprit mocks.

"Lord of all short squeezes. It's what the Redditors are calling this meme stock craze."

"Oh. I thought that was you butchering the word 'loas.'"

"Well, that works too. But, no sir, I was referring to the short squeeze."

"Enough buzzwords. Go on."

"Since we're truly in the zeitgeist, I asked my team to come up with some ideas on how we could harness this surge in popularity. Y'know, make the most out of it."

"And what are some of those ideas?"

"Well, sir, they're simply napkin sketches at this point. I don't want to burn any cycles or spend any budget against this unless the group thinks it's a good idea."

"Nick, you sound under the weather. Have you tested for COVID?" Gerald asks, after fumbling with his mute button, with the concern of someone who has had the dreaded virus.

"Not yet. I'm pretty sure it's just some kind of a head cold, but thanks for asking."

"Can't be too careful. Those are the early symptoms. It can sneak up on you. You should get tested. Anyway, back to the topic at hand. This whole notion of capitalizing on the stock phenomenon seems very imprudent. You do know that the SEC is in contact with our general counsel? I might be subpoenaed, as there will be a Senate investigation. I hope to hell you haven't put anything out there," Gerald implores.

"No sir. My social teams and PR are under strict orders not to engage until we formulate a strategy. Of course, you're probably shocked to know, I think we're fools not to engage."

"Not shocked at all. But I do appreciate you holding off. Discretion is the better part of valor. I think we remain silent, but since Suprit has posed the question, let's hear what you've come up with."

"We have a range of ideas going from low cost and quick-turn products and collectibles that could generate sales around the buzz. Then, we have some social media missives I think you'll find clever that we believe could go viral. And finally, we have an idea for a Super Bowl spot."

"A Super Bowl spot?" Suprit queries. "The Super Bowl is in five days. No way you can make anything happen by then, unless you already have inventory. And I thought you said during my orientation that PwnShop doesn't buy in the upfronts. I seem to remember you griping about the marketing spend as a percentage of sales."

"That's one of my favorite soap boxes. But no, I misspoke. We don't plan on buying our own spot. I'm talking about creating a spoof of Robinhood's spot and tweeting it out directly upon the completion of theirs airing. Requires very little production and we can make it happen."

"Funny how you can make this happen but you still have made no progress on the customer data file."

"Not true. Would you like an update on that?"

"Not yet. First the ideas." He takes a slurpy sip from his YETI tumbler. "Robinhood, you say, is doing a Super Bowl spot?" Suprit asks incredulously. "How do you know that?"

"Our agency was able to dig it up through a very close relationship with their CBS sales rep. We have a bootleg copy. It's fairly low budget but has a catchy backing track and shows fast cuts of regular people in all walks of life with the tagline, 'We're all investors.' Our plan is to license exactly the same backing track, cut together people from all walks of life playing video games cut to the same pacing as the Robinhood spot, and have the voice-over mimic their spot with the tagline 'We're all gamers.'" I take a breath.

Multiple faces in the Hollywood Squares are smiling and a few seem to giggle as the notion catches on. Silent giggling, as Jeff has a perennial boner to be the proctor that scolds any call participants who forget to mute.

"I think we'll win Twitter," I continue. "Our fans will retweet the spot. The Redditors are miffed with Robinhood right now."

"Somewhat clever. But I think you'll get sued for spoofing their spot." Suprit deadpans.

"As long as we pay the music publisher for use of the bed, there's nothing Robinhood can do. It falls under satire laws."

"Risky. What are some of the other ideas?"

"As mentioned, we think there's a big opportunity to sell T-shirts and other merchandise. For example, we believe a T-shirt, officially licensed by us as a collectible, with the word 'PwnStonk' done up in black and red in the same Impact font as our logo would sell nicely."

"Yawn," Suprit groans.

"Maybe. We can put the mockup up for free, and not print any until we have orders. Kind of like Kickstarter. Anyway, that's not my favorite. My favorite idea is to put up a pair of red athletic shorts with our logo on the bottom of the right leg. We merchandise them simply as 'PwnShop Shorts.'"

More eerie Hollywood Square heads bobbing in silent laughter. If a joke creates head movement on a muted video conference and no one can hear the laughter, is it funny?

"And then, we have a killer social media idea."

"What is it?" Suprit moans.

"The board is aware that Elon Musk has entered the conversation, right? He's the one that tweeted 'PwnStonk.'" Hollywood Squares heads nod. "And you're aware of some of the lingo the WallStreetBets crowd has been using, like Apes, Diamond Hands, and To The Moon?" More head bobbing. "The idea is to put out a post calling out Elon, to put him on the spot. Whether he answers is immaterial. The point is to get the audience calling him out, creating memes on top of ours."

"And how do you plan to put Elon Musk on the spot?"

"Give him a challenge. Tell him we will issue him a stock certificate with a single share of 'PwnStonk' stock," I say, making air quotes into the webcam. "The challenge will be, 'Hey Elon, we believe you're an Ape with Diamond Hands. We'd like to give you a share of PwnShop Stonk to put on the next SpaceX rocket and take it To the Moon!'"

Smiles all around, but for Suprit, Gerald and Jeff, who puts his "paper" hand to his forehead.

"You do know that's stock manipulation," Jeff warns. "We can't do anything to falsely promote the stock."

"It's clearly a joke," I beg. "It's a single share of stock. We're calling out one of the richest guys in the world to physically carry it with him to the moon. It's intentionally absurd. That's funny, right? We'll get more PR from this one Tweet than we've seen in ten years combined."

"Too risky." Gerald admonishes. "I'm not going to allow anything that creates additional scrutiny."

"Well. Again, I figured as much. We'll stand down and sit on our, uh, you know, diamond hands."

"Thank you, Nick. And don't be so self-defeating. Don't get me wrong. Those are clever ideas. I just think we need to take the high ground here."

"Understood."

"That said, why don't you at least cut together what you're talking about for the Robinhood parody."

"Yes sir. Will do."

> **My daughter's bedroom**
> **Dallas, Texas**
> **February 26, 2021**
> **23 days after POSS**
> **CSP: $41.60**

I shower for the first time in four days—we've been without power until today. Snowmageddon is finally relinquishing its icy grip on the South

Central United States. To add insult to injury, I've been down with COVID for the past two weeks. What started out like the flu, has now entered both lungs. The symptoms I felt on the board call a few weeks ago have turned into double pneumonia and I'm taking breathing treatments of Albuterol and Pulmicort every three hours. I dial Gerald.

"Hey Nick. How are you feeling?"

"Well today is the first day, honestly, that I've been able to even sit up for a phone call. Damn ERCOT and the blackouts didn't help either. Did they get you?"

"I'm actually in South Carolina at our vacation home. Have been here the past week. But yes, I've been reading about the management of the Texas grid. What a fiasco."

"Indeed. I bet you're glad you've managed to avoid said fiasco."

"Yes, I guess so. But have been quite busy with other fiascos nonetheless." He quickly deflects. "Anyway, tell me about your bout with COVID."

"It's been a doozy. Right after we had that board call a few weeks ago, I went way south. My internist wouldn't see me. Said I needed to go to the hospital. Such BS. I figured the hospital would be certain death. So, my wife found some guy who came by the house. Tested positive immediately. The first week was like a bad flu. Fever ebbed and flowed between 103 and 99. Maura also knows a guy who runs a clinic. Ex-military doctor. Super unorthodox. I went by to see him. He heard something in my lungs. Had chest Xrays and got the stellar news that I have double pneumonia. He put me on a regimen of heavy steroids, zinc and some medicine from the Vietnam war used to treat malaria. Called Iverpectin or some such. Said he'd had good success with it and had only one patient who'd died on him. Stellar science, right?"

"Jeez. It's Ivermectin I think. I saw a report that said the FDA hasn't approved it for COVID treatment. It's used to treat parasites."

"Well, I'm not dead yet." I pause to cough up half a lung, and then continue. "Once the initial round of steroids wore off, I really went south again. On Maura's birthday (for which I had dinner reservations at

Georgie—I sent her alone with my buddy Fred Rhodus and his wife) two nights ago, I woke up in a cold sweat at around 3 AM. My fever spiked and sweat had soaked my T-shirt, my sheets and the underside of my comforter. I got up to go dry off and began to shiver uncontrollably. The house was down to 44 degrees. I'm pretty sure most doctors wouldn't prescribe living in an igloo to someone with double pneumonia. Anyway, I can assure you Nietzsche was wrong."

"How so?"

"What doesn't kill me is definitely making me weaker."

"I'm sorry to hear that. Sounds like you have quite the case. I'm surprised they didn't get you on Remdesivir."

"By the time I tested positive, my doc said that I had been symptomatic too long for it to be effective. Plus, he said it was in short supply and should only be reserved for severe cases."

"Just by the sound of your voice, yours seems pretty severe to me. They gave it to me immediately and it seemed to work well."

"Well, how old are you?"

"Not much older than you, I don't believe. I'm fifty-eight. How old are you?"

"I'll be fifty-three in June. But based on this damn illness, ninety doesn't seem far off. A vaccine can't come soon enough."

"Sounds like we're close on that. Well, I'm sorry you've had such a bad case. You feel okay to talk?"

"Yes. I'll be fine. What's up?"

"First off, I want to make sure you understand why we didn't allow you to run that parody spot on Twitter."

"Water under the bridge. I knew none of that stuff would ever see the light of day. I think it was a mistake, that we had an opportunity to be cool again, but I get it. Lots at stake."

"In another lifetime you'll have a job where you actually get to be creative."

"Based on this case of COVID, that might come sooner than you think."

"Well, I hope not. Onward. The second item is the bigger of the two. I'm sure you'll be disappointed to know that we're moving on from Jeff Claggart. He's announcing his resignation, and his last day will be March 23."

"That's the earnings day, right?"

"Yes. I'll do the call on my own, but want him there if any technical financial questions come up."

"Can I ask why he's leaving?"

"You can ask but I won't answer."

"You mean I'm not the only one who's noticed his unbearable smartest-guy-in-the-room antics."

"I'll take the fifth."

"Well, I actually am disappointed. Probably the devil you know, or Stockholm syndrome." I giggle at my dark humor. Gerald doesn't. "The guy is good at heart. We all have flaws. I have no filter. He has no heart. That said, I don't think we'd have made it to the console releases had he not led the cost cutting in such dramatic fashion. Hindsight's twenty-twenty. As much as it pains me, it's almost like you guys knew the pandemic was coming. We're in much better financial shape that just about any other specialty retailer. Anyway, I'm done grieving. Does this mean you're next?"

"We'll see. For now, Garv wants me to stick around."

"I don't get it. The guy's thirty-five years old. Dale and I surmised that he definitely was going to make a play to become CEO. But the more time passes, the less it looks like that's what's happening. Why would he want to become an insider if he doesn't want to run it?"

"Why is not a question that ever warrants an answer. It's rhetorical, right?"

"I guess so. Who, what, where and when not so much. But why and how are definitely rhetorical. As in, 'how do you solve a problem like Maria?'"

"Huh? Maria. Who is she?"

"*The Sound of Music*. Y'know. Julie Andrews."

"Oh that Maria. You're a pop culture vending machine."

"Sorry. Can't help it. But back to this rhetorical question. He's going to leave you in the seat?"

"I don't think so. Confidentially, we've had conversations. While I believe in and have run rather large e-commerce businesses, I'm a bricks and mortar retailer. I'm sure at some point he'll want to bring in a digital native. Someone from Amazon or similar. For now, I'm holding down the fort."

"Are you interviewing all these new hires?"

"Not a single one."

"Don't they all report to you? None are reporting to me, right?"

"That's the other thing I want to talk to you about."

"I'm out?"

"If you want to be."

"What do you mean, if I want to be?"

"He's hired a chief customer care officer. By the time earnings come, he's going to announce a CTO and a chief growth officer. All of these will have responsibilities that overlap with yours. I think you have a viable case for 'good reason.'"

I play dumb. No point in mentioning I've already had two conversations with my employment attorney about initiating the clause. "How would that work?"

"As far as I can tell, I'm still CEO. If you resign for 'good reason' under the circumstances, I would sign off on it."

"And what's the alternative?"

"Not sure there is one. It's a whole new cast of characters. You had that call with Quint. What did he say?"

"He said it would be two years before they even contemplated any of the location-based innovation stuff. Plus, it sounded like they'd force me to negate my contract."

"Look, I'm not telling you what to do, but I think what I'm offering is one hell of a bird in the hand. You do know all the stock grants you've received will forward vest in such a circumstance. Plus, you get two years of severance. This place is going to be in high-speed chaos, and between you and me, I'm not sure any new leadership will be so generous. They'd probably negotiate something less than the full meal deal."

"It's certainly something to think about. When do you need to know?"

"No deadline, but the clock is ticking."

My daughter's bedroom
Dallas, Texas
March 11, 2021
36 days after POSS
CSP: $133.36

"Can I get you anything?" Maura asks without the normal edge in her voice.

"Nah."

"Feeling better?"

"I feel okay for about an hour after my breathing treatments, but then everything tightens up again. And one of those drugs makes me wired, so I'm having a really hard time sleeping."

"Poor thing. I wish there was something I could do."

"I'm better than I was a week ago. It's just hard to see progress day by day."

"Just text me if you need anything." She pauses before closing the door. I see it open a little wider again in my peripheral vision. "So have you decided?"

"Decided what?" I respond, confused.

"If you're going to resign. You've been sitting on that for over a week."

"I've had COVID and double pneumonia, and four days of it in a house with no heat in a once-in-every-three-decades Texas ice storm. You can't make this shit up. It's not like I'm on my A game."

"Well, you've been in Eliza's bedroom for two weeks. Haven't you at least been thinking?"

"I've been contemplating my mortality."

"Of course you have. My little hypochondriac."

"What part of COVID and double pneumonia is psychosomatic?"

"None. I'm just saying, you love to focus on the macabre."

"Just saying. Just saying."

"I'm just saying, don't you think Gerald wants an answer? If you wait too long, he'll be gone, and you won't get as good a deal."

"You're right. But why can't you give me enough space to let it be my idea? Now I just feel like I'm doing it because you're pestering me to do it."

"I don't care what you do. Seems to me you're procrastinating, and don't you think you just might be using this illness as an excuse?" She cops a bit of a baby voice.

"It's not an easy decision."

"Why not?"

"Because, I feel like if I go, nobody will stand up for the stores and the associates. They are the asset. This thirty-five-year-old has no history of turning a profit. He only has a history of flipping a company at a much higher valuation. And trying to convince public company investors that you're playing the long game, losing money to gain market share like mad in the short-term to make it up in the long-term, like he did with Chompy, won't work. They don't have the patience. He has to take it private. But with the stock price so high, there's no way he can afford that. I bet he's thinking Claggart's at-the-market shelf offering ain't looking like such a bad idea after all."

"So you're saying you'd rather fight it out with some dot-com ne'er-do-well..."

"I'd say he did pretty well. He's a friggin' billionaire."

"Yes, but you just said it. He doesn't know how to turn a profit. And," she pauses, "he doesn't even think the thing you were working on was worthwhile."

"True."

"So why would you stick around?"

"Because my work isn't finished. People are counting on me."

"Heroism? In corporate America? When did that ever work? You have this notion of loyalty to the company. No company is ever loyal to their employees, so why would you be loyal to them? You'll just stick around and become jaded and bitter. Anyway, don't you think they'd nullify your contract if you stay? Having that insurance policy, you told me, was the only way you'd go back."

"That's true, but what will I do if I quit? Get another head of marketing job at yet another disrupted bricks and mortar retailer? Might as well stick with the devil you know..."

"I thought you wanted to teach? And your store idea might have been a good idea before this pandemic, but do you really think anyone is going to invest in gathering places anytime in the next ten years?"

"You sound like Gerald and Jeff. And, we can't afford this lifestyle on a professor's salary."

"But if you quit, won't you be able to sell your stock? It's worth a fair amount right now."

"Yeah, it did bounce back pretty well upon those Redittors hearing Claggart got ousted, didn't it? I'm sure it would do the same if I announced."

"My favorite pessimist. Anyway, I'm just saying, I love your idealism, but don't be blinded by it."

"Fair enough."

She closes the door. I get out my laptop, sit on the side chair in my daughter's bedroom, put on the nebulizer, and start the thrice daily breathing treatment regimen. As the vapors waft through my nose, down my trachea, and into my fluid-filled bronchioles, I have an idea.

What if I don't resign yet? What if I submit the form to sell my vested shares on March 24? If they don't approve, I guess I have my answer.

I fill out the internal form, basically a preview of the Form 4 I'd have to file with the SEC within two days of selling that our internal counsel uses to keep records of intended trades, and send it to our general counsel. And wait.

PwnShop Offices
Vineland, Texas
March 17, 2021
42 days after POSS
CSP: $266.00

The execs are all together in the offices for the first time in a while. We've been going through the first draft of the earnings script with our investor relations consultants. As we walk out of the Bored Room, Dale grabs me.

"Have a sec?"

"Yep." I step into his office just two doors down from the conference room.

"Did you fill out the sell form?" he asks.

"Sure did. You?"

"Yes. Are they approving yours?"

"Nope. Approving yours?" I ask.

"Nope."

"It's bullshit, don't you think?" I ask, rhetorically.

"It's not only bullshit, I don't know that they can prevent it. I'm calling an attorney."

"I'm told they can mandate that NEOs not be allowed to sell at any time, even if it's in an open window after the earnings release?" I say, remembering the conversation I had with Quint Haddad and subsequently with our general counsel upon submitting the intent-to-sell form internally. "But interestingly, they've approved the forms of some of my employees who intend to sell."

"Same here. It's insane."

"Since they're not named executives, I guess they figure it will fly under the radar. They just don't want the appearance of any senior execs dumping shares," I add.

"We're not dumping shares. We're just taking some profits, taking some chips off the table. We have that right. It's utter bullshit. We don't possess any MNPI. It's completely public that this thing is trading well above any normal multiple on projected earnings."

"Well, I guess they've made the decision for me."

"What decision?"

"Can you keep it between you and me?" I ask.

He nods. "Don't you mean between you and I?"

"Nope, you ignoramus. Objective case."

Dale rolls his eyes. I continue.

"Gerald said he'd allow me to resign for 'good reason.'"

"Oh yeah. He said the same to me. But that's since been rescinded. Garv wants me to stick around and consult until he gets his team in place. Somebody's got to be in charge of the merchandise."

"Have you thought about pressing the issue?"

"No. I've just asked for a big ass stay bonus for my time."

"Your time? This stock could tank any day. The longer you wait, the higher the likelihood it plummets to pennies."

"I know. Is what it is. But that's why I'm so pissed off they're not letting us take any chips off the table."

"Never a dull moment at PwnShop."

"Never."

I exit Dale's office and stop by Helen's desk. "Is Gerald on the phone?"

She looks at her phone's speed dial lights. "Nope."

I stick my head in Gerald's door. "You have a sec?"

"Yes, glad you stopped by. I have a few things for you, too."

"Okay. Door closed?"

"Yes please."

I move to my obligatory seat at his conference table. He comes and sits across from me.

"You look like a shadow of yourself."

"I lost seventeen pounds. It's not a diet I recommend."

"Crazy. You feeling any better?"

"Finally tested negative on Saturday. Slowly but surely getting my strength back."

"Such a strange illness. How it affects everybody differently."

"I know, right? Looks like the vaccine will be available shortly, however."

"I already got it. Convinced my doctor to classify me as high risk. I didn't want to mess around."

"Oh, I thought you might be an anti-vaxxer."

"I've had every vaccine my doctors have recommended. Hasn't killed me yet."

"Fair enough. So what do you have for me?" I decide to ask first, in case any new information factors into my decision.

"Garv and company are bringing on another C-level individual. A chief growth officer, whatever that means."

"Sounds like a made-up title to woo somebody from a more stable company."

"You may be right. Anyway, it sounds like he's going to be in charge of a lot of the responsibilities in your area."

"I thought I was in charge of a lot of the responsibilities in my area?"

He shrugs.

"So does this mean I'm out?" I continue.

"Do you wanna be out?"

"Based on the fact that you guys aren't letting me sell any stock, that seems like the rational decision. But, I'm not sure it's really what I want."

"They're not letting me sell anything either. We're all in the same boat. You have the luxury of leaving sooner than later. I think you'd be a fool not to take it."

"So what would it look like?"

"Like I said. Full severance. Resign for 'good reason'—they're materially reducing your scope. This chief growth officer is the most egregious example of that."

"And timing?"

"I initially thought your last day would be the twenty-third, but I think we need to wait one more week. Last day would be the thirty-first. We'd announce through an *8K* on Monday the twenty-first."

"Why's that?"

"Ours is to not ask why.... That's the offer."

"And am I free to sell on the thirty-first?"

"You'll no longer be an insider as of the thirty-first. That said, if you're in possession of MNPI, you should probably wait thirty days."

"Oh I get it. You don't want me selling off on the same day Claggart's selling. Is that it?"

He stares at me and blinks once.

Home Office
Dallas, Texas
April 8, 2021
64 days after POSS
CSP: $192.44

"I've decided how I want to do this." I'm on the phone with the broker assigned to PwnShop senior executives at Morgan Stanley.

"Okay. How?" she queries.

"Once you have confirmation from the company that all of the grants have vested and are free and clear, I'd like to sell 10 percent of my holdings every day, dollar cost averaging it, for seven straight days. Then, I want to put a limit order in for $250 for the remaining 30 percent."

"You really think it will go that high again?"

"Do you want me to use thought or feeling? Logic or imagination? This whole event has been a lesson in the futility of control and common sense. Chaos theory rules."

"That's true. But, you realize these things can go to zero as easily as they can come close to their fifty-two week high."

"Well aware. I'm a pessimist at heart. I'm sure that's what will happen."

Maura's Family Beach House
Virginia Beach, Virginia
June 14, 2021
131 days after POSS
CSP: $280.00

I've decided to surprise Maura and the kids with my famous pico de gallo. I leave the beach and enter the house. Grabbing my phone, I see I have only a single voicemail.

Man, funny how few calls you get when you're unemployed.

It's my broker. I call her back.

"Hello," she says.

"Hey it's Nick Haller."

"I'm just calling to let you know that the stock hit $250 right after noon today. We've sold the remainder of your holdings."

"Seriously. Where'd it close?"

"$280."

"Damn, so I left thirty dollars on the table?"

"I think you did just fine, sir."

"I guess so. Wow. I can't believe it's gone back up that high."

"Believe me. None of this is believable."

SIDE D

After the Sold Rush

PERSONNEL

The Band		
GamerTag	Instrument	Title
Nick Haller	Ride Cymbal	Resigned Chief Customer Officer
Fred Rhodus	Didgeridoo	Best Friend
Grady Bledsoe	TR-808	VP, Video Game Merchandising

Track 13: Here We Go

"Moving ahead, so life won't pass me by."

—JIM CROCE

Mia's Tex Mex
Dallas, Texas
September 28, 2021
237 days after POSS
CSP: $190.96

Life is backwards. It is the great paradox. The seed of our essential nature spreads, slaking our thirst for knowledge, and jading our humble innocence. It becomes the bacterial germ that infects us all from within. We inevitably become a septic caricature of ourselves. Things are too good to upset, yet so awful we can never leave well enough alone. We strive for perfection, becoming overridden with imperfection somewhere along the way.

So it is with this human. And celebrities. And companies.

"So, how are you doing?" Rhodus asks.

Having known each other since dirt, it's not hard to tell when we've moved from the good-natured, juvenile grab-ass to the brief moments of maturity that we avoid like death, taxes and Kierkegaard.

I blow a sigh. "Guilt-ridden."

"You shoulda been a Jew. Or at least a Catholic."

"No, you had me at Jew. I so appreciate the Old Testament God that smites me when I fuck up. All this shit about grace, forgiveness, immaculate pregnancies and everlasting life makes my head hurt."

"Funny. So why are you guilt-ridden, Nick?"

"Oh, let me count the ways. Because I don't deserve this. Because I was merely a witness. An accidental jurist. Because I'm one big imposter. I committed no crime, but I sure didn't right any wrongs. I finally understand why people kill themselves when they win the lottery. I always thought I would do something meaningful. That I would put in the time and make something lasting. With my wits, my hands and my sweat. And if it was good enough, only then would I be rewarded. And it wouldn't be just an extrinsic reward, it would ease my burdens from within. But the way this thing went down, I get no nor deserve any satisfaction. The thing I was working on ended up on the cutting room floor. I failed our employees. I was supposed to be the Moses that took the unwashed out of the desert and into the promised land. Instead, I'm more like the rich kid in *The Kite Runner* that stood in the alley, watched, and did nothing while the better boy gets ass-raped. And then, in a vulgar dose of anti-karma-matter, I get rich via some bizarre, chaotic market hysteria master manipulated by some dude named Bawling Bitty or DeepThroatedValue or StonkSchlong69. I received an outsize reward for the immaculate fruit of my misdirected labor. It's like winning a tennis match by shanking the ball off the frame only to have it dribble on the other side of the net. I'm a mishit winner. It makes no sense. It gives you about as much faith in humanity as Jeff Bezos taking a dick pic."

"Well, that's a lot to unpack there, Sigmund."

"Unpack? Really? Most overused self-help word of all time. And you're calling me Sigmund? Unpack this," I say while cranking my middle finger to full mast. "You been reading *Psychology Today*? Been talking to some earnest youth ministers? Practicing mindfulness?"

"Yes, I have." He sniggers. He says it a second time while drawing out the yes, leaning forward, and steepling ten fingertips together in a mockful pose of intellectualism. "*Yes*, I have." Then he leans back from the table, a busy array of Mexican tarot cards covered in clear resin topped with a humble basket of chips and a bowl of salsa above reproach. He continues, "But no, seriously, that's a pretty pessimistic way to view all of this, dontcha think?"

"Uhm, duh. I'm a pessimist. And, I think too much, so yes, I think."

"No, I'm serious. Do you really think everyone else who hit it big didn't have outsized luck?"

"I don't believe in luck. I guess you do. Fucking Presbyterians. Dontcha know Brittney Spears is an anagram of Presbyterians? Predestination and all that preprogrammed pop culture."

"Haha. I did not know that," he says in his best imitation of Dana Carvey imitating Johnny Carson.

"So. Let me get this straight. You're saying this is my fate? That God had this plan for me all along? C'mon. I'm a Whiskeypalian. I believe in freewill and probability and outcome. This was an extremely low-probability outcome. Like a stray speck on the far right of the dust cloud in a scatter plot diagram. An outlier. Despite what Malcolm Gladwell says, you can't engineer edge case outliers. They're simply statistical anomalies. Same thing as Warren Beatty getting pulled from his bike wreck too soon by some overeager angel. Asinine. Beatty's angel was Buck Henry. Mine was BawlingFuckingBitty. It happened, and I'm dealing with it."

"Rich man's problem."

"Tell me about it. I'm not looking for pity. I'm looking for enlightenment. A way to make sense of it all."

"Well, I think you said it yourself. It's a freak accident. It's just that the outcome was positive. It makes about as much sense as being swept off a beach by a rogue wave. It happens. But it's rare. And, if you're about probabilities, how do you feel about all those people that were shorting your stock? Wasn't that one of the reasons you went back to work there? That you thought it was artificially undervalued because of all the short interest? Do you think it was a freak accident for them or a stupid bet to make?"

"Shorting stocks is positively un-American. They got what they deserved. And if the SEC had any sense, they would have outlawed it long ago, and none of this would have happened."

"So, isn't the inverse true? If they got what they deserved, why didn't you get what you deserved? You were a trader. You just were on the other side of the bet."

"No, no, no," I say, spitting a piece of the salsa ambrosia of the Tex-Mex gods across the table. "That's just it. That's what's wrong with corporate America. I wasn't a trader. I comfort myself with the notion that I was an innovator and a populist. Probably lying to myself, but whatever. Employees matter. Everybody else was playing a trade. Nobody gives one shit about building something. The whole system benefits the parasites. The financiers. The bankers. The fund managers. The agents. The lawyers. The consultants. The so-called activists. The leeches, critics, and vipers, oh I don't know, waiting at the gates of dusk to prey on the value creators."

"Oooh. Nice. I see what you did there. Pulling out the first Syd Barrett Pink Floyd album.

"Yeah, that was good, wasn't it? Or not. Anyway, back to my madness. What about the poor stiff who makes a buck from industry?"

"Oh, so now you're saying you're a Marxist? Why don't you give it all to the government then?"

"Believe me. Uncle Sam made out pretty damn well. All mine was ordinary income. No tax loss carryforwards here. No itemized deductions. Nope, he took almost 50 percent. And no, I'm not a Marxist. Like Winston Churchill, I think capitalism sucks, but there's no better system. I believe in a meritocracy. Capitalism thinks it's a meritocracy, but it's not. It rewards transactions, not meaning and consequence. And oh yeah. My favorite anagram. United States of America—deem it as an utter fiasco. Better than Presbyterians as goddam Brittney Spears. Oops I did it again."

"Haven't heard that USA one. So unpatriotic," he slathers on the irony. "Focus please. Do you not think the work you were doing had meaning and consequence?"

"It's on the wareroom floor. Garv Pastor is so young, I don't think he even knows what a store is. He was born after the great store dinosaurs grazed the land. I think the work we were doing had meaning for a brief moment, and then the cost cutters came along with the logic that a dollar saved is always a dollar earned even if that dollar is being spent to attempt to find a future. And then COVID reared its head—talk about a rogue wave—and then I let it get the best of me, became jaded, and simply gave up. It was too lucrative not to. It's a bunch of sound and fury amounting to no meaning. No consequence. Just a big-ass pile of money."

"Better than a big-ass pile of shit." He smiles as if he's said something clever.

"True."

"You're going to drive yourself crazy with this notion of worthiness."

"And what was your first clue?"

"I'm serious. You were out there prospecting. You bought the donkey, the pickaxe, and, I don't know, the pan."

"The pan?"

"Shut up and work with me here. I'm thinking out loud. You know, panning for gold."

"Oh. Gotcha."

I wait while he snarfs down some more of the best chips and salsa this side of the Sierra Madre. He gulps, washes it down with a dripping swig of Negra Modelo, and continues.

"Anyway, you fucker, you were prospecting. You went into the mountains. And you weren't just a regular Joe. You worked your ass off. You got into Harvard Business School. You worked your way into becoming a C-level officer at a Fortune 500 company. It's not like you're a schmo. And from that perch, which by the way most people couldn't get to that perch, you didn't find the small vein of gold on the lease you purchased, but you tripped on the mother lode on the way down, when you were dejected and gave up. It happened. Deal with it."

"Fair enough. Falling up. Thanks for helping me work through this. And now that I'm thinking about it, and listening to you, it reminds me of when I won the blue ribbon for my egg-dropping device at the Texas high school physics Olympics in '86."

"You won the blue ribbon for what? Good god, man. You really are a tool at heart. A bucking dork."

"Nerds rule. Anyway, I busted my ass to build the best damn mouse-trap driven car geekdom has ever seen. That car, my pride and joy, the fruit of my mental and handiwork labor, got fourth fucking place. But I won the blue ribbon for the thing I slapped together in a desperate two minutes because we didn't have an entry. I seem to remember it was made out of a toilet paper tube and a piece of panty hose. It's absurdist poetry. It's like songwriters. The thing that they're least proud of ends up being their biggest hit. Cheeseburgers rule. I was rewarded for a fluke. The thing that I put the effort into didn't even make the podium. It got me bupkis."

We both pause for a bit to duel over access to the salsa bowl. The waiter arrives. Fred orders the brisket tacos on flour tortillas. My normal go-to is chicken enchiladas, but it's Tuesday, the only day they offer Mama Mia's Chile Relleno, which I get with the beef filling.

"Hey, did I tell you about the T-shirts I just got?"

"No, how old are you? Is that what you're doing, blowing your winnings on T-shirts?"

"Fuck off. It'd take a LOT of T-shirts to go through these winnings."

"Oh, so now you're one of those rich dudes who thinks you're better than everybody else?"

"You know I'm not worthy. That's what we're here working through. I DEFINITELY know I'm not worthy. And as far as wasting money on a few T-shirts, it's like I tell Maura when she's losing it when I'm not listening to her babble because I'm so focused on checkmating some dude in Poland on the Chess.com app, 'at least it's not cocaine and hookers.'"

I scoop a generous portion of the tomato and dried guajillo concoction onto a particularly greasy chip, and then start talking with my mouth full.

"Anyway," nom nom nom, "in her honor," nom sllch nom, "I did design a custom one on Printful for Maura. Gave it to her yesterday. It says. NICK'S SHORT SQUEEZE."

"Hahaha." He takes a sip of beer. "Did she like it as much as that stupid Brooks & Dunn chachka you once gave her in a Tiffany box?"

"That was a failed prank. She actually got the humor in this one."

"That's funny. Really funny. What's the other one?"

"The band gave it to me. It's just one of those shirts with block letters. It says, MORE MONEY THAN TALENT."

"Hehe. Have you worn it?"

"Yep. At the Barley House gig two weeks ago. Do you know what I said to the, uhm, and I use this term hyperbolically, the crowd?"

"Can't wait. What'd you say?"

"Well, I told them that the band—the folks they see up on stage with me—gave it to me. And then, I said, 'It's loads of talent, right? Ergo, it must be shit tons of money.'"

"Haha. That's the first confident thing I've ever heard you say in your whole life. Did they laugh?"

"Oh yeah. But I'm pretty sure it's because, based on my lack of talent and the fact that I'm fifty-three years old playing in a bar band, I must be broke."

"And he's back. There's the Nick we know and love."

After lunch, when the bill comes, I grab it.

"I got this. Thanks for the therapy."

"You damn right you've got this. And every other lunch from here on out. Repeat and fade. And by the way, you think you're so cool now being able to buy my lunch?"

"First, as we discussed in Louisiana about Good Vibrations, I'm certain repeat and fade is a copout. Let me get this straight. I'm a dick if I don't buy every time now? And, I'm a dick if I do? Dickifidon't, dickifido. Let the skull fuck continue."

"You're the smartest dumbass I know."

Track 14: Watching the Wheels

"I faded away for a while out of necessity."

—PHOEBE SNOW

Dunston's Steakhouse
Dallas, Texas
October 11, 2021
250 days after POSS
CSP: $172.36

"Oh Grady, I can't believe I got your metrosexual ass out of the burbs and into this dirty old place."

"Metrosexual? That's for wannabes," he declares. "And yes, this place is dirty. Ratchet in fact."

"Oh, this is REMODELED. You shoulda been here before. Much better. Much dirtier. Less parking. The same burnt on the edges and raw in the middle steaks, and the last great salad bar that somehow made it through COVID. This ain't no metrosexual True Food or Flower Child. And, to defend my carefully measured diction, you gotta admit you do dress more like a put together metrosexual than a preening queen. You look like a member of Vampire Weekend in that V-neck sweater."

"Um, I guess I'll take that as a compliment. Anyway, who is Vampire Weekend?"

"White boy music. Actually, supertalented. For millennials."

"Oh good. Don't want no part."

"Enough of all that."

"So, Nick Haller. Long time. How have you been?" He draws out the been, as if he's calling for someone named Ben.

"Pretty good, I guess. I just married off my daughter on Saturday."

"I saw Maura's post on Instagram. It looked like a beautiful wedding."

"It was."

"But you do know I'm pissed Micah and I weren't invited. Were you too ashamed to admit you have a gay, black friend?"

"Oh come on. Really? I'd have loved for you to have been there. But we promised Eliza it was her wedding. Not ours. As such, we didn't invite any of our friends who weren't a part of Eliza's life. There were guys in my wedding who weren't invited. You've never met her, right?"

"Never. Is that my fault or yours? It sounds like you planned that answer."

"Not planned. Well maybe. But those are the facts. I'm sorry if you're offended. Are you really upset?"

"No. It's just the cross I bear." He sighs dramatically. "I bet it was an uh-mazing event. The pictures were beautiful. Eliza looked gorgeous and her new husband seems hunky."

"She did. Not sure I'd call him hunky, but he's a great guy. We're so lucky to have her marrying someone we adore. The ceremony was lovely, and it was one helluva reception thanks to your wedding band."

"Oh, you ended up hiring the David Whiteman Band?"

"Dude, after seeing them put it all out there for you and Micah, I knew they were the ones. I'm old school. And since I footed the bill for the whole thing, it's the one thing I insisted on—mutual agreement on the band. You know I have a visceral reaction to anyone who doesn't perform live music in real time. If it's choreographed, and it's a franchise, like the Spazmatics, and you simply hit play on a computer, I'm out. Whiteman's crew could flat play. Plus, I love the irony of his last name. The entire party danced for three solid hours. A celebration of humanity. Not bad for a bunch of white folks being shown the way by a black man named Whiteman."

"Well, you would know, Mr. Musician."

"Puh-lease. In my dreams. But I do know enough to know what's good. And as a bass player, you know I love old school funk. They played Cymande's 'Brothers on the Slide.' They played some Graham Central Station. They played 'Express Yourself.' They even played the 'Theme from Shaft' and the 'Sanford and Son Theme.' I mean, who else does that?"

"Nobody. I'm glad we could teach you white folks about good music."

"Much appreciated. So, who do you hear from? From the old gang?"

"Not many. You know there's virtually nobody left."

"I know. And those who are still there say it's more fucked up than ever."

"Yeah, I don't get it. Strategy is everything, and once again, there is no strategy."

"I think I've heard you say that before."

"Well, it's true. I heard they finally hired someone from Belk, because they're starting to realize that, uh, oh I don't know, the stores and the store associates are the only point of difference. But it's too little too late. And this whole NFT marketplace? What a waste of time. I know I'm old school, but I guarantee you even digital natives ain't gonna put much stock in digital tokens. And even if they do, in gaming, the publishers will control the IP, so that's where any value would reside. And now, did you see they're doing a deal to become a crypto marketplace. They've signed on to be the exclusive partner with some firm named FTX. WTF?"

"Yep. I feel ya. It's crazy."

"And the biggest irony. You remember how pissed off Garv Pastor was at Jeff Claggart and Gerald and the board members who voted for the ATM? Did you hear he ended up issuing his own at-the-market stock sale, and instead of the $100 million we were going to offer, he sold over $1 billion? They're now sitting on a nest egg of well over $1 billion in cash. The stock is now the core business."

"Too bad they don't have an idea for how to spend it. Speaking of Claggart, did you hear what happened to him?"

"I heard he went to some outdoors e-tail company as CFO and then resigned after like six weeks."

"Resigned? I heard the CEO gave him an ultimatum. Apparently, he came in, treated everyone like shit, and acted like he was CEO."

"Sounds familiar."

"Doesn't it? Yep, he pulled his tried and true power play stunt. The story I heard was the CEO, who's a woman..."

"...Oh?! I'd love to be a fly on the wall with Jeff working for a woman."

"Right? Anyway, she pulled him aside after some episode where he had ridden the staff hard, and she said something like, 'I'm going to tell you this only once and you decide. Number one, you can't treat people the way you're treating them.'" Grady talks with his hands. And he's bending down his index finger on his left hand with the index finger on his right hand. "'They're your teammates. Their opinions are valid, and you need to work collaboratively. And number two,'" he bends down his first two fingers on his left hand, "'I'm the CEO. You're not. If you can change accordingly, I'll give you the benefit of the doubt. If you can't, please resign.'"

"Let me guess, he didn't like being boxed into that corner?"

"Nope." He lets his index finger go on his left hand, leaving only an extended middle finger. "I heard he quit right there on the spot."

"I wonder if that's true. That's a shame if so," I say, without any irony in my voice. But, because of my normal sarcasm, Grady takes it the wrong way.

"Yes, such a shame," he emotes. "Couldn't happen to a nicer guy."

"I'm serious. I don't wish the guy any ill will. He's one of the smartest people I've ever worked with. He just has a hard time looking in the mirror."

"Wow. You've been on the bench too long. He was insufferable."

"Well, with perspective, and the hindsight of the pandemic, that company wouldn't have survived without his broad shoulders leading the charge on heavy austerity. You gotta admit. The guy worked tirelessly, which is a lot more than we can say about 90 percent of these millennial and Gen-Z great resigners."

"Listen to you. He was a first-class a-hole."

"And that's probably what it took to get the job done."

"Sounds like you've been thinking about him a lot."

"Only for medicinal purposes. My personality doesn't mesh well with…"

"…Bullies?"

"Yeah, bullies. But I was going to say people who are so confident they can't imagine they have any flaws. I would be a horrible politician. I imagine flaws I don't even have. Politicians think they're perfect.

"Not to mention, Nick, if you were a politician, you'd be canceled in ten minutes."

"Surprised you haven't canceled me."

"Oh, I know you. You just have a nick or two."

"That's why I love you, Grady. You're so forgiving." I smile. He beams like a third-grader who just earned a sticker. I continue, "So, what have you been up to?"

"After the exit, I looked at Micah and said, 'Boy, we can now live life like a bunch of rich white dudes. I am now the man!'"

"Too funny. That's fantastic. So, how'd you live life like an old white guy? Did you go join up with the Proud Boys and storm the Capitol? I mean, y'all are some proud boys. Or men. Of pride."

He chuckles while rolling his eyes and shaking his head.

"Sit back and cuddle to the dulcet tones of Tucker Carlson and Sean Hannity? Just curious how two gay black guys live like the Man?"

"We took a cruise in the Greek Islands."

"Whoa. I've heard they're gorgeous. Was it fun?"

"The best. Like a second honeymoon. And we did Gay Pride week last year in Aspen. I think we're going to do it again."

"Sorry to be puzzled. You and Micah ski?"

"What'choo talkin' 'bout, Willis?" He cops his best Gary Coleman, then turns into Mr. T. "I pity the fool who think Black men can't ski."

"Can white men jump?"

We both smile and shake our heads at our mutual absurdity.

"And what have you been up to since?" I break the silence.

"I'm back in the game. Run merchandise for Michaels."

"From games to arts and crafts?"

"Yep. Good ol' specialty retail."

"Is it everything you want it to be? As FUBAR as PwnShop?"

"Nothing's that fucked up."

"Well, I've always said that every company is fucked up. It's just a matter of degrees. But it's like outrunning a bear. You need only be the second slowest. You need to only be slightly less fucked than your competition. Barnes & Noble outran Borders. Best Buy outran Circuit City."

"True that. So, what are you up to?"

"I've gone on the board of some nonprofits—the Dallas Theater Center and a homeless shelter. And of course, they're as messed up as for-profits but it's even harder to have an objective conversation, because you can't focus on profit as the goal. But mainly, they just want my money. I'm sure the only reason they asked me is they read *The Dallas Morning News* article about our exits. So, I give it freely out of guilt. And, uh let's see, I'm guest lecturing occasionally at UVA about career decision-making, chaos theory really, and at the Brierley Institute for Customer Engagement at SMU about customer engagement, experience and relationship management. I've thought about doing that more full time, but I gotta say, I have a strong aversion—I've recently learned now that I have F-you money—to anyone telling me where I need to be and when. I'm really diving into chess. Playing my bass with more intent. Trying to figure out the interconnectedness of it all. I guess you could say I'm also just part of the Great Resignation."

"Yeah, right. First world Great Resignation."

"Now that I'm out, I at least understand why the young people feel the way they do. Maybe I'm the first real experiment in what will happen to people if AI operates the world and we all get basic universal income.

Will we do something productive and meaningful or just pursue pure hedonism? Being the captain of your own clock is emancipation of the first order."

"Oh, so now you're saying your lily-white, Harvard-educated ass, was previously bound to indentured servitude?"

"Yep." I smirk. "Thirty years a slave."

"Oh Lawd. Puh-lease."

"And oh, did I tell you I'm writing a book?"

"No, really? I guess that's cool. Or maybe super lame. Nothing more cliché than a retired white guy writing a book. Let me guess, a cookbook? No wait, a self-help book, like the Seven Deadly Marketing Sins?"

"No, nothing like that. It's about PwnShop."

"So, you're the next Michael Lewis? That's fantastic."

"I wish. He actually does a bunch of research and is thoughtful. This is more of a memoir. A coming-of-age story of a boy who sorta becomes a man at the age of fifty-three. The protagonist realizes he was never really cut out for business, that he's an artist, and a lame one at that, at heart. It's my way of dealing with my shit. I think the lesson for all of us is that ego is our downfall. It gets in the way. We all fight too hard to impose our worldview onto others. Our record's former grooves have eroded into deeply entrenched ruts, but we think it's the only album worth listening to. We need to unlearn everything. Get out of our ruts and back into a groove. Free our mind so our dumbass will follow. Admit that none of us can be certain. Nobody has all the answers. You can't dominate markets anymore than you can dominate the tides. You have to take what comes to you, receive it as a constant, and chart your course with the acceptance of that reality. Until we let go, risk failure, and embrace new possibilities, we'll never be free. To grow up, we need to return to youth. Of course, we'll never get all the way back, because along the way, we've allowed our ego to take the reins. Our innocence is gone. But, we have to let go to try to get it back. Anyway, I'm doing it as fiction."

"Well, that sounds simply awful. Who the hell wants to read that?"

"Not really sure. But now that I've started, I know I'll never forgive myself if I don't finish."

"So, are you going to self-publish?"

"Never. That seems like self-importance of the first order. If nobody wants to publish it, I'll just send it to friends who care and know I did it. My kids can read it and understand how cuckoo dad really is. No, I have an agent, actually. She said it goes against her better sense to take me on. Says nobody is publishing fiction from new white male authors."

"With good reason."

"Hey, come on. You don't think I have anything to offer?"

"I don't think white males have anything to offer."

"Oh, now you're just stereotyping. You're eating lunch with me."

"Stereotypes exist for a reason. Isn't that what you folks always say?"

"C'mon. You know I don't say that."

"You've just been well-trained. I know you think that."

"We all do."

"Yes, we do. Anyway, I'm just messing with you. Don't get all riled up. You're so easy."

"Ain't that the truth?"

"Look, I think it's great you're doing that. You gonna let me read it?"

"Once I'm finished. Definitely. I want your unvarnished opinion."

"You'll get my opinion. But it may be clear lacquered like my pedicured toes."

"Perfect."

"So, am I in the book?"

"Yes. I'm calling you Grady?"

"Grady? Grady? Really?" he says, incredulity dripping from his voice.

"You look like Grady in *Sanford and Son* with that beard. It's gone from salt and pepper to pure white, mi amigo. Just sayin'."

"Hahaha. You are one cracker, aren't you? All old black people look like Grady? And you say you don't stereotype?"

"Okay, you look like Uncle Ben."

"You are awful.

"No seriously. I'm just kidding."

"Are you?"

"Yes! I'm just messin'."

"I know. Gotcha. I wouldn't like you any other way."

We finish lunch talking about this and that.

Upon walking out to our respective cars, Grady asks me, "What are you going to do this afternoon?"

"I guess I'll go shovel some words."

I get in the car, and reflect on it all.

I guess I'll go shovel some words.

I guess I'll go shovel some words.

I guess I'll go shovel some words.

I guess I'll go shovel some words.

I guess I'll go shovel some words.

Acknowledgments

Thank you Steve Becker. Over coffee one morning in late 2021 you told me I needed to go back to work because there's nothing lamer than an aging, educated white guy who thinks he can write a book. After that proclamation, you reluctantly agreed to read the first draft of the first chapter and proceeded to introduce me to my literary agent, Maura Phelan.

Thank you Maura. Your patience, persistence and positivity are infectious. To guide a paranoid, self-defeating, babe in the woods from a figment of a notion of an idea to a published first novel is no small task with anyone. With me, it's like wrangling an octopus into a pair of pantyhose. The wife in the novel has therefore been named after you.

Thank you John T. Hamlin for being the only family member to read the entire first draft of the manuscript. Your feedback was meaningful.

Gratitude abounds for all the friends who read various drafts along the way and gave me encouragement: Gary Hertz for "protecting the idiots", Danny O'Neill for the Bezos inspiration, Catherine Rhodes, Scott Jones, Dan Brody, Courtney Cohen, Joey Mooring, Ken Luce, Talmadge Boston, Anthony Chukumba, Wellford Tabor, Rob Baker, and especially, the mythical Jens Herridge.

I love you Lucy Wrubel and Greg Rhodes and I'm sorry Tour '90 ended up in the edited ether. Thank you for all the encouragement. You're two of my oldest and bestiest. Signed, your "favorite pessimist" and "the smartest dumbass" you know.

Thank you, Jennie Reeves. Glad you journeyed into your own benighted, literary tunnel recently and helped me see light at the end of mine. Your wisdom exceeds your beauty. Which says a lot, as you're the hottest octogenarian I know. *Once in the Blue Moon* should be required reading for anyone who has a family. ;)

To the old executive teams: George, Jim, Chris, Lisa, Dan, Dan, Dhriti, Paul, Rob, Mike, Tony, Jason, Mark, Bob, Eric, Greg, John, Eric, Gene, Soren, Lucy, Wes, Dennis, Steve, Tim, Mike, et. al. Fundamental disruption is no easy challenge with no one right answer. You were extraordinary people. Thank you for putting up with this black sheep colleague in such extraordinary times.

To my teams along the journey, amongst them Evan, Zach, Jim, Joey, Elizabeth, Tiffany, Jason, Darren, Eric, Kevin, Darren, Dustin, Antonella, Jeff, et. al. You worked your asses off. If only this leader could have kept your dreams off the cutting room floor.

To Holly. The best.

To all the store personnel. Your expertise and the physical locations were the only real assets.

Thank you to Mark, Britton, Stephen, and all the fine folks at McGarrah Jessee for making creativity matter.

Thirty thousand thank yous to one cool cat of an editor, Jacob Hoye, who made cutting that many words as pain-free, fun, and imperturbable as it possibly could be. You're a mensch. I owe you tickets to a Cake show.

Major love for Anthony, Caitlin, Barbara and all the fine folks at Post Hill/Permuted Press.

Thank you mom. Sorry for all the four-letter words. Luckily, you're not the target audience.

Thank you to my dad, the late great Jefferson Davis Hamlin. I just hope a modicum of your humor, humility and hutzpah oozes out of these pages.

Thank you brothers Jeff and John for toughening me up, spinning me in clothes dryers, and hanging me on the door knob by my underwear.

You're both much smarter, wiser, and more mature than I'll ever hope to be.

Thank you Liza. You're the only good Hamlin.

Thank you Henry. Dream big!

Thank you Sarah, my short squeeze. At 5′2″, you're the biggest person I know. Don't get any taller. Please. Hopefully bringing this to fruition doesn't make you think I've wasted the last three years of my life being utterly unproductive. Thanks for the "yeah, buts" and not doting. You are a force. I love you until the end of time or the end of bricks-and-mortar retail, whichever comes last.

About the Author

Devoting the first nine years of his career to the music business in Nashville with Arista Records and Sony Music Publishing, Frank "MF" Hamlin completed his MBA at Harvard University in 1997. From there, he progressed through prominent senior marketing and operating roles in retail and e-commerce. He served as chief marketing officer at Guitar Center, EVP and chief marketing officer of Tailored Brands (parent of Men's Wearhouse and Jos. A Bank), and EVP and chief customer officer of GameStop. Frank Hamlin has served on the boards of several public and private corporations and is now focused on his recent appointments to the Board of Trustees for the College of Arts & Sciences at his beloved undergraduate alma mater, the University of Virginia, and as trustee and marketing committee chair for the Dallas Theater Center.

All proceeds from *Skinny Dipping at Low Tide* will support the Causeways Program, founded by the author at the University of Virginia, to inspire and guide future student leaders in fostering constructive engagement, resolving conflicts, and driving positive change.